The Custody of Children

A BEHAVIORAL ASSESSMENT MODEL

The Custody of Children

A BEHAVIORAL ASSESSMENT MODEL

Richard A. Marafiote

Behavior Therapy Institute of Colorado
Denver, Colorado

Plenum Press • New York and London

Library of Congress Cataloging in Publication Data

Marafiote, Richard A.
  The custody of children.

  Includes bibliographical references and index.
  1. Custody of children—United States. 2. Children of divorced parents—United
States—Psychology. 3. Separation (Psychology) 4. Parent and child—United States. I.
Title.
HQ834.M27   1985   306.8'74   85-12217
ISBN 0-306-41874-6

© 1985 Plenum Press, New York
A Division of Plenum Publishing Corporation
233 Spring Street, New York, N.Y. 10013

Printed in the United States of America

To my parents, Josephine and Patsy, and my brothers, Frank and Pat, for their continuing love, support, and encouragement.

Preface

Separation and divorce have become an inevitable factor in American society. Even those of us who have not experienced these events directly have been touched by them through association with parents, friends, neighbors, or co-workers. Frequently, we have observed these individuals express a variety of negative emotions, including insecurity, anxiety, depression, fear, and anger. If children are involved, their parents' decisions and often dysfunctional maneuvers in this matter will most likely have a profound affect on them. One such decision will be with whom they will live. Although the great majority of children will live with their mothers following a divorce, this arrangement is no longer accepted as inevitable. Changes such as an ever-increasing number of mothers with full-time out of home employment and research supporting the significance and competence of fathers in child rearing have led many observers to challenge the assumption of maternal superiority. These changes, as well as those related to the law and child custody, for example the increased acceptability of a joint custody arrangement, have complicated the process of deciding where a child should live after his or her parents' divorce. Consequently, others are frequently called upon to assist in the decision making and render an opinion concerning custody and visitation. By and large these individuals will be members of the mental health profession. Who else is better equipped to render an opinion in this matter? Mental health professionals of all persuasions and levels of education, including psychologists, psychiatrists, social workers, and counselors are continuing to enter the child custody arena. Each is performing evaluations and making recommendations as to the future living arrangements of children. As one might expect in such a new area, there are few accepted guidelines across or within professions. There are no tests and procedures developed specifically for use in child custody determinations. There is little if any research which directly addresses the important questions pertaining to custody evaluations. Furthermore, few theoretically consistent models for performing these evaluations have been delineated. Consequently, it appears that most mental health professionals proceed in whatever manner is most comfortable. As expected, they use procedures and techniques with which they have had previous training and experience, although it is highly unlikely that these means and methods will have been constructed or evaluated for the particular task at hand. They are altered to fit the custody situation in whatever manner suits the individual practitioner. An even more questionable practice finds the assessor rejecting all established instruments and relying exclusively on intuition and clinical judgment, either his or her own or the collective opinion of a team of colleagues.

In this volume, I have proposed a model of assessment for determining the optimal postdivorce living arrangements for children. As I suggested above, few have systematically addressed the problem of *what* to assess to determine these living arrangements. Similarly, when this question has been addressed, rarely, if ever, has it been explicated within a logically consistent theoretical framework. The specified means and methods for data gathering have not been critically evaluated, nor has the rationale used to recommend various areas of assessment been supported by scientific evidence. This volume is intended to be a first step in this direction.

I have selected a behaviorally based system of assessment in contrast to the more traditional trait-oriented system because it appears to be clear that recent theorizing and research findings in the field of personality have indicated that the usual methods of assessment are ill-suited to answer the kinds of questions raised during the course of a custody dispute. I believe a behavioral assessment model will be more practical in this regard. Given the novelty of this approach in determining the postdivorce living arrangements of children, many questions remain unanswered. However, because of a dearth of current writing and theorizing about assessment and child custody, I believe this work represents a necessary beginning.

A desired outcome for those who read this volume will be the questioning of current practice, an increase in the use of objective methods of data collection, the control of the myriad of variables which threaten the reliability and validity of assessment devices, and the incorporation of the results of scientific data from relevant fields of investigation into the assessment process. In contrast, there would be a reduction in the current overwhelming reliance on informal, unstructured, and subjective methods of assessment, as well as the relinquishing of certain cherished but as yet unsubstantiated assumptions and presumptions. Furthermore, it is hoped that before very long much of the material in this book will be outdated. Research not yet available or even conceived will answer many of the questions raised herein, lead to new ones, and ultimately change the structures and methods employed in deciding the optimal postdivorce living arrangements for children.

I have divided this volume into three major sections: background issues, areas of assessment, and assessment strategies. In the first section, important questions related to the espousal and development of the behavioral assessment model are discussed. The chapters relate the history of child custody determinations, describe some of the current approaches to performing these evaluations, and review research relevant to the study of personality, the person–situation controversy, and the appropriateness of using many traditional trait-oriented assessment methods. The final chapter in this section provides a comparison between behavioral and traditional assessment and suggests that a behavioral model of evaluation would be a more helpful alternative. In the second section, the five major areas of the proposed behavioral model are discussed in an effort to answer questions related to what is assessed and why. In each case, I have attempted to present a rationale which is theoretically consistent, related to issues raised earlier in this book, and directly or indirectly supported by research. The final section takes a detailed look at two behavioral assessment strategies that would play a significant role in gathering assessment data, the behavioral interview and structured behavioral observations. Once again, each is presented with supporting research, its application to the child custody assessments, and suggestions for increasing reliability and validity. A final chapter discusses the importance of remaining data-based in all aspects of the assessment process, from deciding which factors are important in *this* assessment context and therefore in need of evaluation to selecting our means and methods of assessment.

The primary audience for which this book is intended is mental health professionals currently involved in performing child custody evaluations or those who are planning to do so. Although this book is not (and was never intended to be) a manual for completing custody evaluations, the material presented should stimulate mental health professionals to reevaluate their framework for completing custody assessments, as well as the means and methods they use in obtaining data, and ultimately lead to logically consistent and empirically based alterations.

One comment on the terminology I have used: Given the wide variety of custody arrangements currently available, including sole custody, joint physical custody, and joint legal custody, and the many permutations of each in terms of visitation schedules and/or time in residence with each parent, I have opted to replace the word custody with living arrangements wherever possible. This preference reflects my position that divorce merely alters the living arrangements of parents and children, whereas their relationships continue. The assessor assists in deciding which of the many alternative living arrangements lends the greatest probability for future adjustment for this child at this time. Further, my avoidance of this legal term is an avoidance of all negative implications which it carries (e.g., children as chattel; winner–loser, etc.). Obviously, there are times when use of the word is either unavoidable and/or entirely appropriate given the context and point being advanced.

There are many people who have helped in the preparation of this manuscript. First I would like to express my deepest gratitude to Fred Todd who has been my teacher, supervisor, colleague, and friend and has been involved in one way or another in every phase of this project. I am also indebted to Carl Kuhlman and Roberta Ray who served on my doctoral committee, critically read and evaluated earlier drafts of this manuscript, and kept me from straying from a position of objectivity and professionalism. Others who have reviewed and commented on various portions of this work include Tom Giles, Andy Czopeck, Diana Richett, and Tom Grisso. Their counsel was most instructive and encouraging. I would also like to thank my wife, Beth. She spent many hours typing and retyping this manuscript as well as supporting and encouraging me through many frustrating times. Finally, I would like to thank Eliot Werner and Chris Kates at Plenum for their help in preparing this volume and Lynn N., who, through her struggle to regain the custody of her three-year-old son, unknowingly provided the impetus for this work.

Contents

Part III: Behavioral Assessment Strategies: How to Assess

PART I

BACKGROUND ISSUES

Child Custody Determination

AN HISTORICAL PERSPECTIVE

The incidence of divorce has exhibited an upward trend for several years. According to the U.S. Bureau of Census (1977), the divorce rate doubled from 2.3 per 1,000 people in 1963 to 4.8 per 1,000 in 1975. The number of divorces rose from 0.4 million in 1960 to 1.1 million in 1976 (Glick, 1979). These figures are enormous compared with the estimated number of divorces in 1867 of 10,000 or 0.3 per 1,000 (Derdeyn, 1976).

Hundreds of thousands of children each year become innocent victims of what appears to be the gradual dismantling of the traditional family unit. At one time it was said that children, for better or worse, kept marriages together. Those days have past. Each year since 1960, close to 60% of divorcing couples had one or more children under the age of 18 (Glick, 1979). In 1960, 0.5 million children were involved in divorce; in 1973, this figure rose to 1.1 million and remained there yearly through 1976 (Glick, 1979). The average number of children per divorce in the 1950s was less than one (Maddox, 1975); in 1976, the average number was 1.81 (Glick, 1979).

Inevitably, each divorce involving children raises the question of with whom the children will live. Who will retain or be awarded custody? Considering the turmoil that often accompanies separation and divorce, it is not surprising that some parents are unable rationally or maturely to agree on future living arrangements for their children, especially arrangements which are agreeable to both of them *and* optimal for the children. Although accurate figures are unavailable, estimates of the number of couples agreeing to the postdivorce living arrangements of their children without judicial involvement range from

83% (Fulton, 1979) to 95% (Foote, Levy, & Sander, 1976). Therefore, most parents make this decision without the court.

When agreement cannot be reached, the divorcing parents turn to the courts to petition for the child. In so doing, each parent hopes to be chosen as the most appropriate custodian. As we will find later, this poses no small task for the trial court judges involved. The decisions they must render are awesome, affecting the lives of both parents and children. These judges typically have little upon which to base their far-reaching decisions other than unsubstantiated assumptions and pre-sumptions, inconsistent case law, vague and indefinite statutes and cri-teria, and personal biases (Charnas, 1981; Group for the Advancement of Psychiatry, 1981; Miller, 1979).

CHILD CUSTODY AND THE LAW

Children as Chattel

The historical development of child custody as a determination to be made by the judicial system, is inextricably linked to the concept of children as paternal chattel. The first recorded statute defining the parent–child relationship in this manner was the Code of Hammurabi written in 2150 B.C. (Fraser, 1976). Under the code children owed their parents (particularly their father) a duty of respect for which they were entitled to minimum care and treatment. If a child was not accepted by the father at birth, he or she could be killed or if allowed to live would be deprived of status as a family member. Even if a child was accepted, his father could use him to pay a debt owed to another, cut off both his hands if they were used to strike his father, or remove both his eyes and tongue as punishment for violating the duty of respect to his parents (Fraser, 1976). The child was simply an object that could be sold or ex-changed freely under the code.

Under Roman law, many of the same practices continued (Radin, 1927). The concept of *paterfamilias* allowed the father to reign sovereign and enjoy absolute power over his family. This included the decision of whether they should live or die. Exposure and infanticide were freely practiced under this law, and it was not uncommon for a father to muti-late, abandon, or sell his children (although by A.D. 374, the killing of infants was considered murder; DeMause, 1974). They and their belong-ings were legally his.

The seemingly limitless power given the father was lifelong unless he died or emancipated the child; for a son, this began the cycle anew, as he then became *paterfamilias*. Considered property herself, the mother was not recognized as having any rights over her children (Comments, 1936).

After the fall of the Roman Empire, the code of the Visigothic Kingdom provided children with what appeared to be a brief glimmer of hope (Fraser, 1976). In contrast to earlier codes, the Visigothic code emphasized the duties of the parent and not his powers. This idea was ahead of its time, preceding the doctrine of reciprocity ("Reciprocity," 1928) and the concept of the state as "guarantor of trust" to parents (Fraser, 1976). These concepts emphasized that parents, rather than having absolute power over their children, were entrusted their custody in return for their performance of certain parental duties and responsibilities.

This code stipulated, for example, that abortion and infanticide were punishable by blinding or execution; that the sale, donation, or pledging of a child in return for a debt was strictly forbidden; and that by statute children could inherit a share of the family property upon the death of one or both parents. In return, the children were expected to honor their parents, and parents were allowed to inflict "reasonable" punishment in raising them. Disinheritance (as punishment for disobedience or striking a parent) was the limit of their disciplinary power. Fraser (1976) referred to these regulations as "surprisingly enlightened and humane."

In feudal England, during the period of early common law, the idea of children as paternal chattel was retained, although the harsh and cruel treatment of children characteristic of the Code of Hammurabi and Roman law, was no longer being practiced. DeMause (1974) explained that "children were at the bottom rung of the social ladder, a rung below senile old men, foolish women and doddering drunks" (p. 229). Children and wives were subordinate to the father–husband. "They were merely things to be used as a father saw fit. Whether he obtained obedience by love and affection rather than through pain and fear by frequently administering beatings mattered little; legally he had the right" (p. 246).

Paternal Superiority

In feudal England rights were associated with land ownership that could only be vested through male succession. Consequently, men held

all power over and proprietary interest in their children. This was particularly important during the feudal period because fathers could hire
their children out as apprentices and later acquire income generated by
the children's skill and labor. Logically, then, when the issue of custody
arose, the paternal figure maintained absolute right to the custody (i.e.,
ownership) of his children. Who else was financially able to care for and
support a child? Since only males could own and manage property, the
award of custody to anyone else was untenable.

Case law at the time firmly established the father's unquestionable
right to the custody of his children.[1] In the case of *Rex* v. *DeManneville*,[2]
in which a father took his legitimate child from the breast of its mother,
the court condoned his action on the grounds that a father had a superior right to the custody of his minor children, regardless of the children's welfare. In a similar case,[3] the court refused to interfere when the
mother of a 6-year-old requested custody after the father had removed
the child from the home of a third party where it had been previously
placed. This decision was handed down despite the fact that the mother
had originally left the child's father due to his "cruelty and brutality"
and his "cohabitating with another woman." The father's exclusive
right to custody could not be challenged under early common law despite his poverty, failure to provide better living conditions for the child,
and even the degradation of his own life (Sayre, 1942).

The legitimacy of the child was essential in the decision to award
custody to the father instead of the mother. In several early cases,[4] an
illegitimate child's natural mother was given custody, and the father
had no such right. The significance of the child's legitimacy was undoubtedly linked to land ownership, which was familial. An illegitimate
child did not legally belong to the father, was not entitled to a share of
the land through inheritance, and was consequently not obligated in
any way to the father.

The United States also maintained the assumption that the father
was more competent financially to care for his children than was the

---

[1]*Ex parte* Andrew, L. R. 8 Q.B. 153 (1873); *ex parte* Skinner, 27 Rev. R. 710, 713 (C.P. 1824);
Rex v. *DeManneville*, 102 Eng. Rep. 1054, 1055 (K.B. 1804); *Rex* v. *Greenhill*, 111 Eng. Rep.
922 (K.B. 1836).
[2]*Supra* note 1.
[3]*Ex parte* Skinner, *Supra* note 1.
[4]*Ex parte* Skinner, 27 Rev. R. 710, 713 (C.P. 1824); *Glanaman* v. *Ledbetter*, 130 N.E. 230 (1921);
Pitzenberger v. *Schnack*, 245 N.W. 713 (1932); *Rex* v. *Greenhill*, 111 Eng. Rep. 922 (K.B. 1836)
citing from *Rex* v. *Soper*, 5 T.R. 278, and *Rex* v. *Hopkins*, 7 East 579.

mother and that he was entitled to the services they would provide.[5] One typical case[6] explains that a husband, in relation to his wife, was "wanting in respectful and kind attention to her, and has often used harsh profane and vituperative expressions to her, and to others concerning her, but he has been guilty of no such misconduct as would justify the wife in a separation." The judge continued:

> The only difficulty, if any, in the present case, in regard to the right of the father to retain the child, arises from the child being of tender age, and during its sustenance, in part from the breasts of the mother. But upon the evidence, I think these circumstances form no obstacle to the father's right.

The Development of Parental Equality

Mothers consistently lost custody decisions except in cases in which husbands died or the child was illegitimate. The court's decision making in this matter remained inflexible and tied to property interests until Talfourd's Act was passed in 1839.[7] With this act, the British Parliament gave the chancellor the right to determine the custody of a child under the age of 7 years. This law permitted such a child to be placed in the custody of either the father or the mother. This statute was the first in a series of acts which treated both parents equally in the determination of custody. Slowly, with the advent of industrialization and the burgeoning interest in child development and women's rights, the imbalance in favor of the father began to be questioned.

In 1873, with the Custody of Infants Act,[8] parental equality in the determination of custody was extended to include children up to 16 years of age. The Guardianship of Infants Act (1886)[9] raised this age to 21, and finally in 1925 another statute[10] proclaimed:

> The court . . . shall not take into consideration whether from any other point of view the claim of the father, or any right at common law possessed by the father, in respect of such custody, upbringing, administration or application is superior to that of the mother, or the claim of the mother is superior to that of the father. (p. 1163)

The gradual shaping of parental equality in custody disputes

[5]People ex rel. Nickerson, 19 Wend. 16 (1837); State v. Richardson, 40 N.H. 272 (NH 1860); U.S. v. Green, 26 Fed. Cas 30 (RI 1824).
[6]People v. Humphries, 24 Barb. 521 (N.Y. 1857) quoted by Derdeyn, 1976, p. 1370.
[7]Talfourd's Act, 2 & 3 Vict. c. 54 (1839).
[8]Custody of Infants Act, 36 & 37 Vict. c. 12 (1873).
[9]Guardianship of Infants Act, 49 & 50 Vict. c. 27 (1886).
[10]Guardian of Infants Act, 15 & 16 Geo. c. 45 (1925).

through statutory enactments is still very much a part of modern judicial decision, and recently this idea was reaffirmed by both the Guardianship of Minors Act (1971)[11] and case law.[12] During this same time, courts and various lawmakers were becoming cognizant of the rights and needs of children as individuals rather than as property of their parents. Thus, custody decisions were to be made with the child's needs foremost. Later, however, we will see how certain presumptions and assumptions appeared to have significantly undermined the concept of parental equality.

Parens Patriae

Historically, the important decision of who would be given custody of children was given to the chancellor, who intervened under the doctrine of *parens patriae* (Fraser, 1976). This term literally means "father of his country" (Fraser, 1976), and the doctrine developed because of England's concern with the transfer of land. The concept of *guardianship* preceded that of *parens patriae* and was meant to assist those children who had land or would be inheriting land. The guardian was supposed to look after the child's land as well as its profits. However, the guardianship most often benefited the guardian and not the child (Fraser, 1976). Consequently, a minor child, through his mother, could take his guardian to court and have a trustee appointed to watch over his land profits. In the case of the *Duke of Beaufort* v. *Berty*,[13] it was ruled that the court could intervene on behalf of the child if a guardian was not acting in accord with the best interests of the child. This intervention, however, was initiated only when there was property and guardianship involved (Fraser, 1976). For example, in *ex parte Skinner*,[14] although the court recognized its jurisdiction, in representing the king as *parens patriae*, to "control the right of the father to the possession of his child, and appoint a proper person to watch over its morals, and see that it receive proper instruction and education" (p. 713), the court chose not to interfere. Later, in the 1828 case of *Wellesley* v. *Wellesley*,[15] an author explained that "the English court firmly cemented the relationship of

---

[11]Guardianship of Minors Act (Imp.) 1971, c. 3 cited by A. Bradbrook (1971).
[12]See, for example, *Moyer* v. *Moyer*, 233 P2d 711 (1951); *Scott* v. *Furrow*, 104 A2d 114 (1954); *Smith* v. *Smith*, 212 S.W.2d 10 (1948).
[13]24 Eng. Rep. 579 (Ch. 1721).
[14]*Supra,* note 1.
[15]4 Eng. Rep. 1078 (H.L. 1828).

the child to parent and the State." The "parent's right," it noted, "emanated from the crown (the State)" (Fraser, 1976, p. 322).

As the doctrine of *parens patriae* further developed, a precedent was established of intervening in the guardian–child relationship when it best served the child's interests. In fact, an 1847 decision[16] made the actual transition and ruled that the state could intervene even when there was no property involved. Hence, the doctrine of *parens patriae*, as we know it today began. The state was the "guarantor of trust" in the parent–child relationship. In speaking of early America's adherence to this principle, Bremner (1970) explains:

> Although the father is entitled to the custody of the infant children, inasmuch as they are their natural protectors, for maintenance and education . . ., the courts of justice may in their sound discretion, and when the morals, or safety, or interests of the children strongly require it, withdraw the infants from the custody of the father . . . and place the care and custody of them elsewhere. (p. 364)

In contrast with the previous status of children's rights, the doctrine of *parens patriae* was a major step forward. A third party, the state, would watch over those responsible for the care of children, and would intervene when necessary for the child's welfare. During this same time, however, the father's *prima facie* right to the custody of his children was firmly established. In what circumstances, then, can the court now decide that the welfare of the child is being jeopardized and consequently remove him from his natural parents? Such a decision would have to be made in the face of a long history of case law and legal statutes that emphasized the absolute right of the father and later of both parents to the custody of their minor children. Lord Echer explained in *Queen* v. *Gyngall*,[17] that the court would have to exercise *parens patriae* "with great care" and show, by the conduct of the parent, that its application is "clearly right for the welfare of that child in some very serious and important respect" (p. 242). Only then should the parents' rights be superseded and suspended.

Parental Preference Rule

Historically, a child's biological parents had a superior, natural right to their custody against all third parties (Kram & Frank, 1982). This right

---

[16]*In re* Spence, 41 Eng. Rep. 937 (Ch. 1847).
[17]2 Q.B. Div. 232 (1893).

appears to be a direct descendant of the concept of chattel and parental ownership. After reviewing important legal decisions in the 1950s and 1960s, Kram and Frank (1982) noted:

> References to the right of a biological parent to its child's custody as "funda-mental" under "natural law" and "beyond the reach of any court" as "essen-tial to the orderly pursuit of happiness by free men" raise the parental-right doctrine to the level of an axiom equal to the "self-evident" truths and "inal-ienable rights" reminiscent of the Declaration of Independence. The biologi-cal parent–child relationship is nothing less than enshrined. (p. 95)

Children were frequently returned to their natural parents after residing for years with other relatives or in foster homes. In the fre-quently cited 1963 case, *Raymond v. Cotner*,[18] the father of an 11-year-old girl, whom she had never seen, filed a habeas corpus suit to obtain her custody from her maternal grandparents. The child's mother had died when the child was 15 months old, and the grandparents subsequently had raised her. Even though the girl wished to remain with her grand-parents, the Supreme Court of Nebraska upheld the trial court's deci-sion to award custody to the father. The majority decision read:

> Courts may not properly deprive parent of custody of minor child as against more distant relatives or unrelated parties unless it is affirmatively shown that such a parent is unfit to perform duties imposed by the relationship, or has forfeited that right. (p. 895)

This decision, and others, reflected the presumption that children belonged with their natural parents and that courts were obligated to award custody to the parents unless they were shown to be unfit. For example, a 1971[19] decision read:

> Thus, the issue is not . . . whether one choice of custody or another is better for the child, or . . . {which} would raise the child better. . . . Nor is the is-sue whether natural parents or adoptive parents make "better" parents, whatever that may mean. The power of the State . . . is much narrower. Child and parent are entitled to be together unless compelling reason stemming from dire circumstances or gross misconduct forbid it in the para-mount interest of the child, or there is abandonment or surrender by the par-ent. (p. 198)

Although the parental preference rule gained prominence in the 1950s and 1960s, it began to be challenged subsequently, especially as it came face-to-face with the best interests doctrine. Current case law ac-knowledges that parents no longer have an absolute unconditional right

---

[18]120, N.W.2d 892 (1963).

[19]*Spence Chapin Adoption Serv.* v. *Polk*, 29 N.Y.2d 196, 324 N.Y.S.2d 937 (1971).

to the custody of their children,[20] although the parental preference rule does weigh heavily in cases of parent versus nonparent.[21]

The Unfit Parent

The one factor that has been cited consistently in court decisions as powerful enough to overthrow the natural rights of parents is unfitness.[22] This appears to have applied even during the time when fathers were supposed to have had an absolute natural right to the custody of their children. In 1817, the poet Shelley was the first man reported to lose the custody of his child for what were referred to as "vicious and immoral atheistic beliefs."[23] In a subsequent case,[24] both parents were addressed as follows:

> The right of parent to possession of child is absolute, except in cases of misconduct or desertion, or abandonment of the parental rights by the parent. The Court cannot interfere with the rights of the parent. . . . The Court cannot surely take the child away from the parent merely because the child will be socially or physically, or even morally or religiously, better off, in the absences of misconduct by the parent. (p. 236)

Logically, it would appear that the crux of the matter lies in the definition of *fitness*. Unfortunately, such a definition is difficult to locate, being multifaceted, inconsistent, and understandably broad (Kram & Frank, 1982). A review of case law on this subject leaves one frustrated, with most explanations being couched in terms of unfitness rather than fitness. Fitness seems to be understood as the absence of unfitness. Definitions of unfitness are often offered as a part of the majority opinion in cases in which it has been an important consideration. Because of the importance such a definition has for overcoming the parental preference rule, a few of those definitions are presented here.

One Kansas decision[25] states:

> As applied to relation of parents to their child, the word "unfit" usually although not necessarily imports something of moral delinquency; parents who treat their children with cruelty or inhumanity, or keep child [sic] in vicious or disreputable surroundings are unfit. (p. 196)

---

[20]See, for example, *Odell* v. *Lutz*, 177 P2d 628 (1947); *Shumway* v. *Farley*, 203 P2d 507 (1949).
[21]See for example, *Claffey* v. *Claffey*, 64 A2d 540 (1949); *Turner* v. *Pannick*, 540 P2d 1051 (1975).
[22]*Corpus Juris Secundum*, 67A, at 233.
[23]*Shelley* v. *Westbrooke*, 37 Eng. Rep. 850 (Ch. 1817).
[24]*Queen* v. *Gyngall*, supra note 17.
[25]Application of Vallimont, 321 P2d 190 (1958).

A New York opinion[26] explains:

> An unfit parent includes one who is a drunkard, an incompetent, a notoriously immoral person, who is cruel or unkind towards his child and one whose conduct evinces indifference and irresponsibility. (p. 739)

Unfortunately, definitions such as these leave ample room for ambiguity and biased interpretations. There are no specific criteria for determining whether someone evinces moral delinquency and it is unclear what is meant by *incompetent, indifference,* and *irresponsibility.* And how does one differentiate between someone who is a "notoriously immoral person" and one who is only slightly immoral? These definitions are ambiguous, abstract, and certainly confusing. Possibly a more fruitful approach for uncovering the definition of unfitness would be to turn to the cases themselves. In what circumstances have parents been denied custody of their children?

Early case law demonstrates that parents were denied custody of their children as a result of their personal misconduct and not necessarily with respect to their role as parents or the effect of their behavior on the parent–child relationship. As such, the determination of unfitness had (or may still have) more to do with the punishment of a guilty spouse than the consideration of what is best for the child (Hirsch, 1978; Kram & Frank, 1982). Frequently, children were awarded to the innocent party in a divorce suit.[27] This punitive attitude is reflected in Bishop's 1873 text on the law of marriage and divorce:

> One who has conducted either well or ill in a particular domestic relation, will conduct the same in another; and so, as a general practice, the courts give the custody to the innocent party; because, with such party, the children will be more likely to be cared for properly. (p. 1197)

It was automatically assumed that if a parent behaved in a manner construed as wrong by current societal standards, then he or she did not deserve to have the custody of children. For example, immoral conduct, especially adultery, has been considered in custody disputes for some time. This became particularly evident after mothers attained equality in obtaining custody. In fact, it appears that adultery has historically been more significant to the courts when it involved mothers. In one early case,[28] the custody of a 3-year-old girl was awarded to her father. The

---

[26]Application of Cleaves, N.Y.S.2d 736 (1958).
[27]See for example, *Caldwell* v. *Caldwell,* 119 N.W. 599 (1909); *Owens* v. *Owens,* 31 S.E. 72 (1898); *Van Buren* v. *Van Buren,* 198 N.W. 584 (1924).
[28]*Helden* v. *Helden,* 7 Wis, 256 (Wis. 1858) quoted by Derdeyn (1976), p. 1372.

court stated, "A woman who has been guilty of adultery is unfit to have the care and education of children, and more especially female children." In contrast, many courts did not consider adultery sufficient in determining the unfitness of fathers (Foster & Freed, 1964). A 1903 case[29] concerning a father who frequented houses of prostitution is representative. The opinion explained that "we are unwilling to hold that his habits and temperament are so different from those of a large class of men that he should for that reason be picked out and branded as an unfit person to have charge of his own children." (p. 682). The double standard message here is clear—a man is not unfit when he commits adultery simply because so many men supposedly behave similarly. For a woman, adultery makes her unfit. Walker (1967) explained that this variance occurs because a mother violates the "basic notion of motherhood" when she behaves in such a manner.

In the 1960s the courts varied in their attitude toward adultery and its implications for fitness as a custodial parent. In some states, adultery was enough to deny custody[30] and in others it was not.[31] Although more recently the advent of no-fault divorce has helped to diminish the significance of so-called immoral behavior in custody determination, parental actions remain "proper objects of inquiry"[32] and are particularly important when directly affecting the child's welfare (Kram & Frank, 1982). According to one source: In order to have effect on a determination of custody, the immorality must be of so gross a character that the morals of the child would be seriously endangered, and proof of a lapse from moral standards or of one immoral act does not prevent the parent from obtaining the custody of a child.[33] Nevertheless, vestiges of the old moralistic approach remain. In the Illinois case of *DeFranco* v. *DeFranco*,[34] custody was taken from a mother primarily because of her continuing adulterous relationship.

Intemperance or drug addiction provides another example of personal misconduct that could result in a determination of unfitness for child custody.[35] Cases consistently report situations involving alcoholic

---

[29]*State ex rel. Anderson* v. *Anderson*, 94 N.W. 681 (1903).
[30]See for example, *Hild* v. *Hild*, 157 A2d 442 (1960); *McCabe* v. *McCabe*, 114 A2d 768 (1958); *Parker* v. *Parker*, 158 A2d 607 (1960).
[31]*Bargeon* v. *Bargeon*, 153 So. 10 (1963); *Dixon* v. *Dixon*, 340 S.W.2d 230 (1960); *Stuber* v. *Stuber*, 244 P2d 650 (1952).
[32]*In re* Marriage of R.R., 575 S.W.2d 766 (1978) at 768.
[33]*Supra* note 22, at 248–249.
[34]67Ill. App. 3d 760, 384 N.E.2d 997 (1978).
[35]*Supra* note 22, at 244.

mothers who were denied custody[36] or who had custody decisions reversed against them.[37] Walker (1967) believes that this emphasis on mothers rather than on fathers was a function of the basic incompatibility of motherhood and alcohol. As with sexual misconduct, mothers seem to be at a severe disadvantage and are victims of a double standard.

Although an alcoholic parent can be considered unfit for custody, particularly if such behavior results in neglect of the child, legitimate employment in a bar[38] or the illegal sale of whiskey[39] are not sufficient grounds for denying a parent custody. On the other hand, taking minor children into a bar may be.[40] Recently, court decisions appear to be reflecting the belief that a parent's personal behavior should not have any bearing on parental fitness unless it directly affects the child and constitutes a hindrance to the proper care of children. In recent decisions involving a parent's consumption of alcohol, the occasional use of intoxicants in excessive amounts or even habitual use thereof, if it does not materially interfere with the parent's business habits or make his or her association dangerous to the family, is not of itself sufficient ground for denying such custody.[41] Unfortunately, no clear guidelines are available for deciding when or if a parent's behavior is "dangerous to the family."

Cruelty to or abuse of a child is definite grounds for a determination of unfitness, whether or not this unacceptable behavior is meant to discipline (Foster & Freed, 1964). In fact, a parent who is aware of the cruel treatment of his child at the hands of a stepparent and fails to intervene to protect his child can also lose the right to custody.[42] Similarly, a parent may permanently forfeit the right to custody of a minor child by abandoning, deserting, or failing to provide for the child.[43] Abandonment or desertion must involve the intention to sever "all obligations growing out of that relation"[44] and to "never again claim rights of a parent or per-

---

[36]See for example, *Floyd v. Floyd*, 129 S.E.2d 786 (1963); *Harris v. Harris*, 9 Cal. Rept. 300 (1960); *Lichtenberg v. Lichtenberg*, 130 P2d 371 (1942).
[37]*Usery v. Usery*, 367 P2d 449 (1961).
[38]*Gill v. Gill*, 363 P2d 86 (1961).
[39]*State ex rel. Burleigh v. Savoie*, 145 So. 285 (1933).
[40]*Davis v. Davis*, 63 N.W.2d 426 (1954).
[41]*Supra* note 22, at 299.
[42]*Id.*, at 244.
[43]*Id.*, at 245; *Benjamin v. Bush*, 67 S.E.2d 476 (1951); *Donoho v. Donoho*, 357 S.W.2d 665 (1962); *Schroeder v. Filbert*, 60 N.W. 89 (1804); *Vehle v. Vehle*, 259 S.W.2d 299 (1953).
[44]*In re* Bisenius, 343 P2d 319 (1959).

form duty of a parent."[45] Temporary neglect of parental duties is not sufficient to deny custody, nor is a failure to support, by itself, conclusive of intent to abandonment.[46] In fact, "the concept of abandonment is to be determined objectively, taking into account not only the verbal expressions of the natural parents but their conduct as parents as well."[47]

Other types of behavior that have been considered in the determination of unfitness for child custody include involuntary manslaughter,[48] child molestation,[49] poverty and instability of the home,[50] multiple sclerosis,[51] neglect of household duties, consorting with criminals, and attacks of temper and rage.[52] However, circumstances considered insufficient for the same purpose include remarriage,[53] interracial marriage,[54] advanced age,[55] gambling,[56] epilepsy,[57] illiteracy,[58] receipt of public assistance,[59] mental incompetence,[60] physical handicap,[61] or an unstable marital history.[62]

Evidently, a wide variety of circumstances will be considered in a determination of whether a parent is fit or unfit for the custody of the children. Thus far, we have see that only a determination of unfitness will topple the parental preference rule. However, Lord Esher cautioned long ago that such a decision should be evaluated carefully. Today's court decisions have taken note of Lord Esher's caution and have stated that "in order to justify depriving a parent of the custody of a child in favor of third persons, there must be substantial reasons or . . . the reasons must be real, compelling, cogent, weighty, strong, powerful, serious or grave."[63]

[45]*R.F.N.* v. *G.R.*, app. 546 S.W.2d 510 (1976).
[46]*Supra* note 22, at 246.
[47]*Id.*, at 247.
[48]*Yancey* v. *Watson*, 121 S.E.2d 772 (1961).
[49]*In re* Welfare of Bergin, 218 N.W.2d 757 (1961).
[50]*Clark* v. *Clark*, 234 S.E.2d 266 (1977).
[51]*McRae* v. *Lamb*, Civ. App., 233 S.W.2d 193 (1950).
[52]*Howells* v. *Howells*, 113 N.W.2d 533 (1962).
[53]*J.* v. *R.*, App. 446 S.W.2d 425 (1969).
[54]*Niles* v. *Niles*, App. 299 So.2d 162 (1974).
[55]*State ex rel. Brode* v. *Hatcher*, 97 So.2d 422 (1957).
[56]*Oraf* v. *Oraf*, 47 N.Y.S.2d 45 (1944).
[57]*Commonwealth ex rel. Shroad* v. *Smith*, 119 A2d 620 (1956).
[58]*State ex rel. Burleigh* v. *Savoie*, 145 So. 285 (1933).
[59]*Commonwealth ex rel. Gifford* v. *Miller*, 248 A2d 63 (1969).
[60]*Price* v. *Price*, 255 S.E.2d 652 (1979).
[61]*In re* Marriage of Carney, 598 P2d 36 (1979).
[62] *Ex parte* Ray, 537 S.W.2d 152 (1979).
[63] *Supra* note 22, at 222–223.

How is it decided whether a particular circumstance is sufficiently weighty? When does sexual misconduct become promiscuity or excessive drinking dangerous to the family? Who decides what are acceptable standards of personal morality? And, as we shall again question below, what does "the child's best interests" really mean? Thus far, the presentation of the issues surrounding child custody are consistent in their ambiguity, abstraction, vagueness, and lack of consistency. Further inquiry into this important subject, with its present reliance on the best interests of the child, the tender years doctrine, and other presumptions and assumptions, will show that the determination of child custody is insufficiently standardized and characteristically chaotic.

The Best Interests Doctrine

Judge Cordozo, in the 1925 case of *Finlay* v. *Finlay*,[64] is credited with affirming the *best interests doctrine* with the following opinion:

> The Chancellor in exercising his jurisdiction upon petition does not proceed upon the theory that the petitioner, whether father or mother, has a cause of action against the other or indeed against any one. He acts as *parens patriae* to do what is best for the interest of the child. . . . He is not determining rights as between one parent and another. . . . He "interferes for the protection of infants, qua infants, by virtue of the prerogative which belongs to the Crown as *parens patriae*."

However, the idea of deciding custody with the child's welfare paramount was presented long before Judge Cordozo in *Chapsky* v. *Wood* (1881).[65] In this case, the father was attempting to get custody of his 5-year-old daughter from a maternal aunt, who had raised the child from birth because at that time both parents were impoverished and unable to care for her. Subsequently, the mother died and the father acquired the means for caring for the child. The judge in this case denied him custody, explaining that "ties of blood weaken, and ties of companionship strengthen, by lapse of time." Although the right of the father must be considered,

> the right of the one who has filled the parental place for years should also be considered. . . . Above all things, the paramount consideration is, what will promote the welfare of the child? (pp. 653–654)

In addition to *Chapsky* v. *Wood*, the judgment of *Queen* v. *Gyngall*,[66]

---

[64] 148 N.E. 624 (1925).
[65] 26 Kan. 650 (1881).
[66] *Supra* note 17.

in which a mother wished custody of her 15-year-old daughter who had been placed with a legal guardian after her father's death, stated, "We must say to the mother, that, thru [sic] no fault or misconduct of her own, she is placed in such a position as to her child that we must supersede her natural rights."

Although these and other early cases used similar philosophy in the determination of custody, such decisions were the exception rather than the rule. Current standards, however, make the child's best interests primary.

Although *Finlay* v. *Finlay* and the Guardianship of Infants Act[67] proclaimed the importance of the "welfare of infants," it appeared that it was overshadowed by the parental preference rule (Derdeyn, 1976; Foster, 1972; Foster & Freed, 1964). Courts rarely awarded custody to a third party if two natural parents were involved. This practice reflected the belief that parents had a *prima facie* right to the custody of their children. Typically, the best interests of the child was determined by eliminating the less fit parent (Inker & Perretta, 1971). Similarly, when custody was to be decided between a parent and a nonparent, the best interest test seemed to be subordinate to the parental fitness test. That is, so long as a natural parent is a fit and proper person, he or she will be awarded custody over all other persons (Foster, 1972).

A most interesting case which demonstrates the freedom of interpretation under the best interests test is *Painter* v. *Bannister*.[68] Following the death of the child's mother and little sister in a car accident, Painter placed his son temporarily with his maternal grandparents on a farm in rural Iowa. The father lived in San Francisco in what was described as a Bohemian atmosphere. After he had reestablished a home and remarried, he returned for his son. Even though the father had never relinquished custody or abandoned the child, and although he was considered a fit parent, the court denied him custody, stating that a "stable, dependable, conventional, middle-class, middle-west background" was more in the best interest of the child than one perceived as "unstable, unconventional, arty, Bohemian, and probably intellectually stimulating." Security and stability in the home were considered to be more important to the proper development of a child than intellectual stimulation.

This case exemplifies the discretionary power of the judge, the

[67] *Supra* note 10.
[68] 140 N.W.2d 152 (Iowa), cert. denied, 87 Sup. Ct. 317 (1966).

influence his or her personal biases have over the future lives of individuals, and the breadth with which the best interests doctrine can be interpreted. There was no unfitness in this case as we have previously defined it, but there was an obvious value judgment made that one style of living was better for a child than another.

During the middle to late 1960s, the best interests doctrine was criticized by both legal and behavioral science writers. Phrases such as "conspicuously vague and unusually broad," "useful" but "inadequate," "indefinite," and of "questionable value" were commonplace. Some critics were especially disturbed by various presumptions and rules of thumb that seemed to go hand in hand with the best interests concept. Among these were the presumptions that the natural parent would best look after the child's welfare, that children of "tender years" belong with their mother (we will discuss this further later on), and that older boys belonged with their father and girls, regardless of their age, belonged with their mother. Such rules, it has been said, "tend to inhibit inquiry and thought" (Foster & Freed, 1964, p. 437), lead to "generalities becoming a substitute for the specifics of a case" (Derdeyn, 1975, p. 792), result in custody being made in a "stereotyped manner," and "encourage judges to avoid the hard task of weighing and balancing relevant facts in the determination of complicated custody matters" (Foster, 1972, p. 1). Most recently, there has been a movement sweeping the country aimed at incorporating a legal presumption of joint custody into our state statutes (see, e.g., California Civil Code §1600 and added section 1600.5, effective January 1, 1980). Such a presumption has been criticized for reasons similar to those just stated (Benedek & Benedek, 1979; Clingempeel & Reppucci, 1982; Felner & Farber, 1980; Foster & Freed, 1980; Group for the Advancement of Psychiatry, 1981; Miller, 1979).

Presumptions such as those mentioned were especially disturbing because courts continued to work under the attitude that "blood is thicker than water," although this attitude seems to be contrary to the spirit of the best interests doctrine. The Supreme Court of California, in *Roche* v. *Roche*,[69] examined this supposition and concluded that children were continuing to be viewed as chattel whereas the property interests of the parents were made paramount to the child's best interests.

Twenty years later, the California Assembly Interim Committee on Judiciary took seriously the spirit of the best interests doctrine and

---

[69] 25 Cal. 2d 141, 152 P2d 999 (1944).

queried, "Why should a court be deprived of the discretionary right to award custody to a third party if it is in the best interests of the child, without being required to find either or both parents unfit?" (California Assembly, 1965–1966, p. 156). This line of thought was reflected in *Painter* v. *Bannister*.

One justification for allowing third parties the custody of children despite the parental fitness of one or both parents came in the form of *psychological parenthood*. This term was popularized in the book *Beyond the Best Interests of the Child* by Goldstein, Freud, and Solnit (1973). The authors defined the terms as a child's "emotional attachment" that results from

> day-to-day attention to his needs for physical care, nourishment, comfort, affection, and stimulation. Only a parent who provides for these needs will build a psychological relationship with the child and become his psychological parent. . . . An absent biological parent will remain, or tend to become, a stranger. (p. 17)

In other words, it would not suffice merely to be a child's biological parent. The crucial factor is whether or not an individual has a psychological relationship with the child.

This concept and the best interests doctrine have been frequently criticized for their inherent subjectivity. Consequently, an effort was made to construct an acceptable definition. States began to write into law the criteria that should be considered in making custody determinations. One set of criteria is Michigan's Child Custody Act (1970). The following criteria are to be considered, evaluated, and determined by the court:

1. The love and affection between parent and child
2. The emotional ties between parent and child
3. The capacity of the parent to give the child guidance
4. The capacity of the parent to continue educating and raising the child in its religion and creed
5. The capacity of the parent to provide food, clothing, medical care, remedial care, and other material needs
6. The length of time lived in an emotionally or psychologically stable, satisfactory environment and the desirability of maintaining continuity
7. The permanence of the proposed custodial home
8. Moral fitness and mental and physical health of the parent

9. The home, school, and community record of the child
10. The child's preference for which parent, if the child is deemed of sufficient age by the court

Although these criteria are considered to be the most detailed of any similar American statute (Group for the Advancement of Psychiatry, 1981), the terminology is essentially general, ambiguous, and imprecise. The authors of this and similar state statutes are to be commended for their attempt to define the best interests doctrine operationally. Providing judges with some guidelines in making custody decisions is an important contribution. However, such criteria remain too broad and undefined to help the judiciary with these very difficult decisions. As Hirsch (1978) indicated, the future of the individuals embroiled in a given custody dispute "ultimately rests upon the clearsightedness, objectivity, and personal integrity of any given judge." She later suggests that the same case in the hands of three different judges is likely to result in three different determinations. This happens regardless of the personal integrity of the judge, and is more a reflection of the chaos and indefiniteness characteristic of the law and the criteria therein.

In a 1943 study by Kingly Davis concerning the attitudes of judges working in child custody adjudication, the findings were summarized as follows: "The welfare of the child rather than the claims of the parents is supposed to be the goal, but what is 'welfare' to one judge is apt to differ from what is 'welfare' to another."[70] Bradbrook (1971) conducted a survey of judges' attitudes in relation to child custody cases and his conclusions supported the findings of Davis. Each of the twelve judges surveyed in this study believed that he could choose the better custodian from the standpoint of the best interests of the child by "observing each claimant and relying on intuition" (p. 559). In fact, one justice stated in a letter to Bradbrook that "there is almost an intuitive aspect to the art (and indeed it is an art) of . . . judgery' " (p. 559). It would seem appropriate that more than the art of judgery should be employed in making determinations that so closely touch thousands of individuals each day. Unfortunately, the best interests doctrine, even with statutory guidelines, does not deliver our judges from the inherent subjectivity and anguish associated with making these decisions.

[70] *Supra* note 6, at 706.

One seriously questions whether the child's best interests are really being addressed in these matters. It has been pointed out that the child is essentially unrepresented during the hearing in most states and that the appointment of a guardian *ad litem*, if done, is not enough (Alternatives, 1963; Derdeyn, 1976; Foster & Freed, 1983). The position of the guardian *ad litem* is subordinate to the biases each parent, their lawyers, and the judge retain.

These and other conditions are reminiscent of feudal times and the parental preference rule, not the best interests test. Similarly, the numerous presumptions and assumptions that continue to be applied directly or indirectly to these cases appear contrary to the best interests doctrine. One such presumption has been the "tender years" doctrine.

The Tender Years Doctrine

Every year a large percentage of cases are decided on the basis of the tender years doctrine. The number of awards made to mothers in contested cases has been reported to range from 80% (Woody, 1978) to 95% (Slovenko, 1973). This doctrine simply establishes that the welfare of a young child—a child of "tender years"—is better served by the child's mother. The opinion given in the 1921 Wisconsin case[71] neatly summarizes the various rationales typically used under this presumption. The mother of three children (ages 8, 5, and 3) appealed a lower court's decision to place her children with their father. The court explained:

> The trial court erred in taking the youngest child from the custody of the mother. For a boy of such tender years nothing can be an adequate substitution for mother love—for that constant ministration required during the period of nurture that only a mother can give because in her alone is duty swallowed up in desire; in her alone is service expressed in terms of love. She alone has the patience and sympathy required to mold and soothe the infant mind in its adjustment to its environment. The difference between fatherhood and motherhood in this respect is fundamental, and the law should recognize it unless offset by undesirable traits in the mother. Here we have none so far as mother love is concerned. (p. 827)

The separation of custody from property ownership, the increasing interest in child development and children's rights, and the steady progression of women's status seemed to have been essential in the formation of the tender years concept. Not only were women becoming eco-

[71] *Jenkins* v. *Jenkins*, 173 Wis. 592, 181N.W. 826 (1921).

nomically self-supporting, but the needs of children as a distinct group, and not as miniature adults, were beginning to emerge. The role of motherhood in the fulfillment of these needs was seen as basic. The tables had been turned, and mothers, unless deemed unfit, were superior to fathers in obtaining child custody. The tender years presumption, despite its questionable validity, was directly responsible for this change.

Today, this presumption still remains very much a part of case law despite state statutes and court decisions equalizing parents' rights[72] (Foster & Freed, 1980; Miller, 1979). Although it is supposedly considered only when "all things are equal,"[73] as a "tie breaker" (Foster & Freed, 1980), this presumption is still being seriously questioned. A 1971 opinion[74] reads,

> the rule giving the mother preferential right to custody is considerably softened by the realization that "all things are never exactly equal" and is predicated upon the acts of motherhood—not the fact of motherhood.

Two years later, the New York State Supreme Court[75] upheld a family court's decision stating that "any presumption that mother should have custody of children of tender years violated state law and was unconstitutional," and that such a presumption was "based on outdated social stereotypes rather than on rational and up-to-date consideration of the welfare of the children involved." And finally, they stated that the tender years doctrine deprives one of the right to equal protection of law under the Fourteenth Amendment.

Despite all this concern with the tender years doctrine, no one seemed to agree on the age under which a child is considered of "tender years." Ages reported in relevant cases ranged from 7 years in Alabama[76] to 14 years in Pennsylvania,[77] with most such decisions involving children around 12 years of age.[78] Considering the lack of agreement in most areas of child custody, this situation comes as no surprise.

---

[72] *Supra* note 22, at 225.
[73] *Id.*
[74] *Garrett* v. *Garrett,*464 S.W.2d 740, 742 Mo. Appl. (1971).
[75] *State ex rel. Watts* v. *Watts,* 350 N.Y.S. 2d 285 (NY 1973).
[76] *Bosarge* v. *Bosarge,* 26 So.2d 73, 247 Ala. 667 (1946).
[77] *Williams* v. *Williams,* 296 A.2d 870, 223 Pa. Super 29 (1972).
[78] *In re* Carlisle, 310 A.2d 280, 225 Pa. Super 181 (1973); *Conway* v. *Conway,* 170 N.W.2d 169, 17 Mich. App. 564 (1969).

Joint Custody

Currently, the new issue of joint custody is being debated by professionals within and between the legal and mental health communities. It is nearly impossible to attend a workshop on child custody, read articles in professional journals on the subject, or converse with legal or mental health professionals involved in custody matters without encountering the phrase in one form or another. Although an exact definition of joint custody has eluded me and other writers as well (Benedek & Benedek, 1979; Clingempeel & Reppucci, 1982; Foster & Freed, 1980; Miller, 1979), the single most important element is that both parents have the legal responsibility and power to make important major decisions with respect to their child's education, religion, physical well-being, and general upbringing (Cox & Cease, 1978; Gaddis, 1978; Miller, 1979).

The message that joint custody advocates are attempting to communicate is that parents divorce each other and not their children; consequently, both parents should be directly involved in their child's life and upbringing after divorce. This position grew out of extreme dissatisfaction with various sole custody arrangements (the most common arrangement has been maternal custody with paternal visitation on alternate weekends, and on holidays and vacations). Such arrangements, it is argued, sever parent–child relationships and essentially turn fathers into "disposable parents."

Joint custody is being closely identified with the best interests doctrine, which historically has been used to justify other custody arrangements and presumptions, such as the tender years doctrine. Many facts have been used to challenge the arguments typically called upon to justify mother-only custody, the tender years doctrine, and personal biases, and legal assumptions made by the judiciary. These include pressure from fathers' rights groups, an increase in the number of fathers who seek custody, and evidence that the father's role in child development is significant (Lamb, 1976) and that he can be as competent as a mother in a sole custody arrangement (Orthner & Lewis, 1979). Furthermore, 82% of divorced mothers with children between 6 and 17 years of age and 66% with children under 6 were in the labor force in 1977 (Glick, 1979). The courts have begun to recognize that a presumption that favors mothers deprives fathers of equal protection under the law and is a violation of the Fourteenth Amendment (see *Watts* v. *Watts*), whereas the American Psychological Association has voted that discrimination against men in child custody matters is a violation of human rights (Council of Representatives Report of the APA, 1977). All of these factors have encouraged fathers to pursue custody either as the sole custodian or in a joint custodial arrangement with their ex-spouses.

Currently there appears to be a movement toward subdividing joint custody into two versions: joint *legal* custody, involving shared decision making only, and joint *physical* custody, adding shared residence (Miller, 1979). California's Law of Joint Custody provides a statutory precedent for defining joint custody with these two categories. Although recent case law awarding joint custody is rare, there are reports of such decisions,[79] and more are expected as a result of the new law in California, the recognition of joint custody as an alternative to sole custody in several other states including Iowa, Colorado, Oregon, North Carolina, and Wisconsin (Clingempeel & Reppucci, 1982), and the fact that at least 17 other states have statutes equalizing parental rights to child custody (Freed & Foster, 1979), thereby allowing a judge to make either a sole or joint custody determination.

Consistent with the historical development of child custody law, a new legal presumption—joint custody—is being entertained. In fact, California's 1980 custody statute presumes that joint custody is in a child's best interests and is therefore the court's first and preferred choice. If sole custody is ordered, the court must consider which parent is more likely to allow the child frequent and continuing contact with the noncustodial parent. Although much has been written concerning the advantages and disadvantages of joint custody, I agree with those who have argued against such a legal presumption. Not only is this a presumption lacking in empirical support (see, e.g., Clingempeel & Reppucci, 1982), but as with previous presumptions and preferences (e.g., parental preference and tender years), it may lack a careful, comprehensive evaluation of each child and his or her family's needs. Felner and Farber (1980) were correct when they wrote, "No single custody arrangement is equally suitable for all children and families. What we need to ask is what factors should be considered in determining the best

---

[79] *Hewitt v. Morgan,* 246 S.W.2d 423 (Ark. 1952); *York v. York,* 67 N.W.2d 28 (Iowa 1954); *Maxwell v. Maxwell,* S.W.2d 192 (Ky. 1961); *Ward v. Ward,* 353 P2d 895 (Ariz. 1960); *Reynolds v. Tassin,* 192 S.W.2d 984 (Ark. 1946); *Wheeler v. Wheeler,* 29 So. 2d 881 (Ala. 1947).

custody arrangement for each family on a case by case basis" (p. 346). Any presumption inhibits a case-by-case assessment. As such, a custody statute that allows a judge the option of making a joint custody determination based on the individual child and family circumstances appears to be more enlightened.

Mediation

Another recent trend that has received a lot of attention is divorce and custody mediation (Bienenfeld, 1983; Coogler, 1978; Doyle & Caron, 1979; Haynes, 1981; Irving, 1980; Milne, 1978). Mediation has been defined by Vanderkooi and Pearson (1983) as a

> cooperative dispute resolution process in which a neutral intervenor helps disputing parties negotiate a mutually satisfactory settlement of their conflict. It stresses honesty, informality, open and direct communication, emotional expressiveness, attention to underlying causes of disputes, reinforcement of positive bonds and avoidance of blame. (p. 557)

There has been continuous debate regarding whether or not custody decisions should be made by a judge in a court of law. Several writers have noted the escalating conflict and trauma that coexists with the traditional adversarial process (Bohannon, 1970; Mnookin & Kornhauser, 1979) and the fact that continued interparental conflict reduces a child's ability to adjust to the divorce (e.g., Anthony, 1974; Emery, 1982; Kelly & Wallerstein, 1976). Mediation advocates argue that this process can serve to lessen the hostility between former spouses and increase their cooperation in custody and visitation matters, thereby effecting better postdivorce adjustment for everyone. In one of the rare studies comparing the benefits of mediation and adjudication, Pearson and Thoennes (1982) found that mediation encourages settlement, leads to substantial satisfaction in the participants, results in more coparenting, increases visitation, improves communication and understanding, decreases the frequency of relitigation, results in more joint custody arrangements, and involves less time and money. With these kinds of results, it is not surprising that 13 states now have courts providing mediation or counseling services (Pearson, Thoennes, & Vanderkooi, 1982) and that California's Senate Bill No. 961 mandates mediation for all couples with children under the age of 12 who are experiencing custody and/or visitation disputes. Furthermore, Pearson, Thoennes, and Milne (1982) have compiled a directory of mediation services that includes over 400 public and private providers in the United States. Nevertheless,

Pearson, Thoennes, and Vanderkooi (1982) found that almost one-third of the women and one-fourth of the men who were offered free mediation, rejected it. Similarly, Pearson and Thoennes (1982) reported that about one-half of those offered mediation rejected it. Furthermore, in this same report, of the 125 individuals who participated in mediation, 64 failed to reach an agreement during mediation. In addition to situations in which parents refuse mediation or fail to reach agreement during mediation, four situations were identified by a family court as inappropriate for mediation (Salius *et al.*, 1978):

1. Cases involving children who allegedly have been or are physically abused or neglected
2. Most situations that involve multiple social agency and psychiatric contacts for adults or children
3. Postjudgment cases involving long-standing bitter conflict between parties and a history of repeated court appearances
4. Cases in which one adult (or both) has experienced serious psychological problems or has demonstrated erratic, violent, or severely antisocial modes of behavior

Clearly, mediation will not be able to solve all the problems inherent in custody disputes, although it is obviously a valuable strategy to consider in these situations. The data coming out of the Denver Custody Mediation Project (e.g., Pearson & Thoennes, 1982) attest to this. One should expect future research to continue to underscore the benefits of mediation. However, it will be important to separate those who will benefit most by this process from those who will not. Doing so will probably further reduce the cost and time required to generate a custody decision. Moreover, this may result in a reevaluation of the practice of forcing mediation on those persons involved in contested cases. As in so many areas related to divorce and child custody, there is a dearth of good research that would allow us to make any definitive statements regarding mediation. It will be important to evaluate all information as it becomes available and to adjust our procedures accordingly. At this time, it appears that we can be optimistic about the value of mediation for increasing the number of out-of-court settlements to custody disputes and consequently the postdivorce adjustment of children and parents.

Current Models and Strategies of Assessment

As the laws changed with respect to the custody of children, mental health professionals became increasingly more involved in assisting the courts in the decision-making process. Early in this history, the guidelines were very clear: fathers had an absolute right to their children, and therefore custody decisions were easily made by those in authority. Later, mothers superseded fathers in the frequency of obtaining custody, and unless there were extenuating circumstances, mothers were awarded custody almost exclusively. In accordance with another clear guideline, prior to the advent of no-fault divorce, children were routinely placed with the "innocent" party. In this situation there was little reason to involve professionals outside the legal system; one need only determine which parent was at fault and then give custody to the other. Although mental health professionals may have had some role, especially when there was question of mental illness, their involvement was infrequent by today's standards.

No-fault divorce laws resulted in many changes in how custody would be decided. Prior to these laws, legal presumptions and rules of thumb were followed by judges in making their decisions. But, with the introduction of the best interests doctrine and of statutory guidelines for deciding a child's best interests, mental health professionals entered the decision-making process more frequently. The publication of Goldstein, Freud, and Solnit's *Beyond the Best Interests of the Child* (1973) and their introduction of such concepts as "psychological parenthood" and "the least detrimental alternative" gave further evidence that custody decisions might become more efficacious if mental health professionals assisted the courts. Some writers even suggested that custody decisions might be made by mental health professionals and not by a judge in a court of law.

Lawyers and judges are turning to mental health professionals with the hope that difficult custody decisions can be made more easily. Given their general lack of knowledge of the behavioral sciences, they turn to the experts for assistance in elucidating the important issues to be considered when deciding the future of each family. This chapter briefly describes some of the current approaches taken by mental health professionals in evaluating families in custody disputes. I considered only those articles that relate directly to the evaluation process itself; I do not consider criteria suggested in works covering the broad area of child custody adjudication. Some current assessment strategies are identified, and the rationale for their use is described when it has been provided in the literature. Although I intended to present information on how the results of each procedure were used in making custody decisions within a specific model or orientation of evaluation, not one article presented this kind of information. Thus, I consider the overall goals of assessment (e.g., best interests), and a rationale for using these methods, but little information pertaining to how the outcomes of each method lead to specific recommendations (e.g., what themes on the Thematic Apperception Test are "good" for a parent?).

GOALS OF ASSESSMENT

Although there is some controversy about whether the mental health professional should recommend custody arrangements, there is no question that the ultimate objective of performing a custody evaluation is to assist the courts in making just this decision. However, my concern here is not with this obvious overriding goal, but with what the mental health professional uses as a guide in making a recommendation. The final recommendation merely follows from the achievement of other assessment goals that may vary from one evaluator to another. For example, Jackson, Warner, Hornbein, Nelson, and Fortescue (1980) indicated that they are attempting to assess "every possible alternative for meeting the children's individual needs and for providing the child with the most meaningful and stable psychological attachment" (p. 213). Their assessment is focused on making this determination, and their specific recommendation for custody follows from it. Similarly, Cogan,

Gottlieb, Meitus, Uslan, and Wilson (1982) attempt to "look at a number of factors to determine which parent is and will be better able to provide for the physical and emotional needs of the child now and in the future" (p. 62). Assessing a child's developmental needs is also important to Westman and Lord (1980), but beyond this, they wish to assess the capacity of each parent to meet those needs. Awad (1978) and Woody (1978) focus clearly on the parent and wish to determine which parent would provide the child with the best opportunity for growth and development. Levy (1978) and Gardner (1982) mention the psychological and emotional relationship between the parents and the children, although in addition Gardner is interested in each child's psychological relationships with "various adults with whom the child is involved" (p. 219).

The practice of including other adults and family members in the overall assessment goals appears to be very popular. For example, the Group for the Advancement of Psychiatry (GAP, 1981) and Gardner (1982) both emphasize the importance of the entire family system in deciding where a child should live following parental divorce, and they discuss decisions that would be "least destructive to the entire family interaction" or in the "best interests of the family." The GAP report (1981) notes, "There can be a number of different solutions which might be considered to serve the best interests of the child, but these different solutions need to be compared in terms of the total family interaction because the child will continue to relate to both parents and their family of origin" (p. 86). Assessing the child's opportunities for interaction with extended family members has also been stressed by Cotroneo, Krasner, and Boszormenyi-Nagy (1981): *"The best custodial parent is the parent who can most fully tolerate and cooperate in helping children maintain contact with all significant persons in their relational context"* (original italics, p. 476). The primary objective of completing a custody evaluation would be to select such a caretaker.

Although these and other writers identify different kinds of objectives, many of which seem to reflect important theoretical biases, all of them appear to be encompassed by three notions that in recent years have become prominent in child custody theorizing, adjudication, and evaluation and that guide both mental health and legal professionals in this area: (1) *the best interests of the child*, (2) *psychological parenthood*, and (3) *the least detrimental alternative*. Each of these concepts, individually or in combination, has been cited frequently by the legal and psychological communities as important conditions for determining child custody.

In Chapter 1 we noted that the best interests doctrine states that what is best for the child is of primary importance rather than what is best for the child's parents or others. Unfortunately, the meaning of this doctrine has been inadequately defined, and each judge or custody evaluator must decide what is or is not in the best interests of the child. The enormous amount of variability in the interpretation of this concept has drawn heavy criticism; as a result, individual states have enacted laws that define for the judge a set of criteria to be considered when evaluating and determining child custody placements (one set of these guidelines was presented in Chapter 1).

Although these criteria can assist judges by giving them guidelines for making their decisions, they are still sufficiently ambiguous to result in wide variations of interpretation (Foster, 1983; Oster, 1965). For the child custody evaluator, the same problem would seem to exist. For example, according to the Child Custody Act of Michigan (1970), the emotional tie between parent and child must be assessed. However, that which constitutes an emotional tie between a parent and child is subject to individual interpretation, and the signs hypothesized to reveal such a bond are usually undefined and idiographic (we will discuss this matter further below). Each assessor may have his or her own special understanding of why attachment is important and how it relates to the best interests of the child. Furthermore, without the empirical association between particular test responses, or patterns of response and the concept of emotional attachment, it would seem probable that there will be variation among examiners with respect to the particular test responses deemed critical as signs of the emotional bond between parent and child. As such this conceptualization of what is best for the child seems to be inadequate, being devoid of objective, operational definitions. Nonetheless, this concept appears to override all others as the ultimate objective of performing a custody evaluation.

These evaluations may also be directed at determining who in the child's environment is the "psychological parent" (see, e.g., Haller, 1981; Westman & Lord, 1980). Goldstein et al. (1973) first introduced this term to deemphasize the relative importance of blood ties when making child custody decisions. The important message they were giving to the legal and psychological communities was that there is much more involved in being a parent than biology and the successful fusion of egg and sperm. They wished to point out that the natural parents are not always the best suited to have custody of their child. The crucial concept on which psychological parenthood is based is the emotional attachment between the child and a third party. Goldstein *et al.* (1973) suggest that this attachment results from:

> day-to-day attention to his needs for physical care, nourishment, comfort, affection, and stimulation. Only a parent who provides for these needs will build a psychological relationship to the child on the basis of a biological one and will become his "psychological parent" in whose care the child can feel valued and "wanted." An absent biological parent will remain, or tend to become, a stranger. (p. 17)

They also point out:

> as the prototype of true human relationship, the psychological child–parent relationship is not wholly positive but has its admixture of negative elements. Both partners bring to it the combination of loving and hostile feelings that characterize the emotional life of all human beings, whether mature or immature. The balance between positive and negative feelings fluctuates during the years. (p. 19)

In addition to the serious criticism that has been raised against Goldstein *et al.* (1973), including criticism of the data on which they base their theory (e.g., Katkin, Bullington, & Levine, 1974), one must note that there is too great an opportunity for idiosyncratic interpretation of their notion of psychological parenthood. Goldstein and his colleagues stop far short of identifying the significant signs for determining whether an individual is indeed a psychological parent. The individual assessor, or team of assessors, is confronted with the same difficulty as before—deciding what constitutes psychological parenthood. What does one look for when assessing whether or not a 4-year old's needs for physical care, nourishment, comfort, affection, and stimulation are being met? If all "true human relationships" have a combination of positive and negative elements, and the "balance between positive and negative feelings fluctuates during the years," then what kind of mixture is appropriate at which ages? What kind of test responses or interactive behavior will indicate the proper balance? Unfortunately, the answers to these and many similar questions have not been given by Goldstein *et al.* (1973) or anyone else.

Consequently, the onus of making such decisions rests with each assessor, who does the best he or she can given the theory, clinical experience, personal biases, and gut reactions available to him or her. Again, the lack of clear and concise operational definitions allows extensive subjectivity and profession-wide ignorance of what precisely must be identified and measured in the context of a child custody evaluation.

The final guide available to those brave enough to undertake the task of completing child custody evaluations is the notion of the *least detrimental alternative* (see, e.g., Bentovim & Gilmour, 1981; Jackson *et al.*, 1980). Goldstein *et al.* (1973) proposed this concept to replace the standard based on the best interests doctrine. In their words, "placements should provide the least detrimental available alternative for safeguarding the child's growth and development" (p. 53). There are three major components to this new standard, as is evidenced in the following definition:

> The least detrimental alternative . . . is that specific placement and procedure for placement which maximizes, in accord with the child's sense of time and on the basis of short-term predictions given the limitations of knowledge, his or her opportunity for being wanted and for maintaining on a continuous basis a relationship with at least one adult who is or will become his psychological parent. (p. 53)

A thorough understanding of this definition requires an explanation of three important elements: (1) the child's sense of time; (2) short-term predictions given the limitations of knowledge; and (3) psychological parenthood, which has already been presented. The child's sense of time addresses the effects of parental separation given a wide range of ages and duration of separation. Goldstein *et al.* (1973) suggest that the younger the child, the shorter the amount of time required before the attachment to an object begins to be severed after separation. This notion is based on Freudian theory and pertains to the urgency of a child's instinctual and emotional needs. The older the child becomes, the more effectively he or she will be able to cope with delay and separation. Consequently, they suggest that the younger the child, the more quickly the law should act in making a permanent custody placement.

The second element within the definition of the least detrimental alternative states:

> our capacity to predict is limited. No one—and psychoanalysis creates no exception—can forecast just what experiences, what events, what changes a child, or for that matter his adult custodian, will actually encounter. Nor can anyone predict in detail how the unfolding development of a child and his family will be reflected in the long run in the child's personality and character formation. (p. 51)

The authors suggest that judges be less "pretentious" and "ambitious" in making custody decisions and focus on "a few even if modest, generally applicable short term predictions" (p. 52). Consequently,

> it should reduce the likelihood of their [the decision-makers] becoming enmeshed in the hope and magic associated with "best," which often mistakenly leads them into believing that they have greater power for doing "good" than "bad." (p. 63)

They submit that grandiose attempts to discover what is "best" for a child result in long delays which are especially harmful to a young child's sense of time. The application of this standard should result in the rapid determination of custody placements from the available alternatives, especially if the people involved are both psychological parents. When this occurs, and "if each parent is equally suitable in terms of the child's most immediate predictable developmental needs, the least detrimental standard would dictate a quick, final, and unconditional disposition to either of the competing parents" (p. 63), rather than an extensive and often futile search for the best.

Once again, the position represented by this concept is logical and seems to hold a great deal of merit. Unfortunately, the problems of definition and measurement discussed earlier are applicable here.

The theoretical espousal of these prominent concepts, namely, the best interests of the child, psychological parenthood, and the least detrimental alternative, may hold considerable promise for significantly increasing the awareness in the legal and mental health professions of the important issues for children and child custody. Consequently, there may be more rapid and efficacious decisions. However, unless someone clearly defines the various concepts discussed, their relationship to child custody, and most importantly, what precisely is to be measured, the application of these notions to the custody evaluation process will remain inconsistent and little more than an elusive ideal. Nevertheless, it is expected that custody evaluators will continue to use these concepts as a guide in the evaluation process.

WHAT IS ASSESSED

Although only a few major concepts seem to guide the clinician in completing a custody evaluation, the number of specific content areas assessed is multitudinous and frequently varies from one clinician to another. Unfortunately, rarely have the professionals writing on this topic stated specifically why they consider certain information important. Does the author include these data based on theoretical, empirical, or simply intuitive grounds? This lack of explanation often causes the impartial reader to question the usefulness of obtaining certain kinds of information, although, to those who espouse a similar theoretical viewpoint the rationale may seem obvious.

Parents

The most frequently cited area that is assessed during the course of a custody evaluation is parenting capacity. Regardless of how each evaluator labels it, he or she is concerned with what kind of parent a particular person can be for a particular child in comparison with other potential parent figures. Many aspects of the parental role have been addressed in the various approaches taken to evaluation. For example, Cogan *et al.* (1982) listed the following 12 points as critical for making an assessment of parenting abilities:

1. The capacity to tolerate separation
2. The capacity for empathy
3. The ability to set appropriate limits
4. The ability to maintain good impulse control
5. The ability to tolerate deprivation
6. The overall maturity
7. The nature and extent of attachment between parent and child
8. Strength of the parent's sense of identity
9. The capacity to love and be loved
10. The ability to tolerate frustration and postpone gratification
11. Basic knowledge of child development and ability to use such knowledge
12. The degree of reasonableness

Unfortunately, like many other authors, Cogan *et al.* stop far short of describing why these points are important in their system of evaluation and how they assess them.

Many other authors proceed in much the same manner (Awad, 1978; Chasin & Grunebaum, 1981; Levy, 1978). Jackson *et al.* (1980), for example, simply mention their interest in assessing each parent's "style, attitude, perception and understanding of the child," as well as their "empathy, emotional availability, capacity to stimulate appropriate interaction, and to establish and maintain bonds of affection" (p. 215). Emphasizing the significance of each parent's "track record," Haller (1981) assesses the use of discipline, the amount of time spent with the child, the ability to share activities, and the overall sense of the child as an individual.

Having a basic knowledge of child development, and, more importantly, being able to meet the child's developmental needs are considered very important by many custody evaluators (Chasin & Grunebaum, 1981; Cogan *et al.*, 1982; Everett & Volgy, 1983; Levy, 1978; McDermott, Tseng, Char, & Fukunaga, 1978; Westman & Lord, 1980). Moreover, Jackson *et al.* (1980) are concerned with each parent's own needs and how they meet them, as well as their "stability, internal consistency, and adaptive capacity or ego functioning" (p. 216). Furthermore, when parents describe their child, these assessors "watch for the balance of positive and negative feelings" (p. 217), implying that most parents have mixed emotions about their children, and that the evaluators should be alerted if this mixture is not present. Goldstein *et al.* (1973) were similarly concerned in their description of the psychological parent.

The Group for the Advancement of Psychiatry (1981), Levy (1978), Trunnell (1976), and Westman and Lord (1980) all appear to evaluate to some extent how well the parents will be able to get along with each other for the benefit of the child. Trunnell (1976) suggests interviewing the parents conjointly and attempting to answer the following questions:

1. How do their personalities mesh in terms of providing appropriate parenting as a dyadic unit?
2. How do their personalities mesh in terms of being minimally cooperative with their children?
3. How will future events affect them (e.g., remarriage of spouse)?

Each parent's relationship with his or her own parent provides useful information to many evaluators about the ability to parent (Gardner, 1982; Levy, 1978). Gardner (1982) suggests that if a woman's own mother was a poor parent then the woman may have incorporated her mother as a deficient role model and therefore have diminished parenting capacity herself. Working within a family systems model, Bentovim and Gilmour (1981) and Everett and Volgy (1983) also investigate parents' relationships with their own parents. The family history may reveal patterns that have been repeating themselves for many generations. This information may be valuable in describing current parent–child relationships, predicting future adjustment, and deciding a child's postdivorce living arrangements. Jackson *et al.* (1980) take this notion even further and refer to the possibility of each parent's "unconscious compulsion to repeat" (p. 217).

Consistent with a family systems framework, Everett and Volgy (1983) consider four "systemic issues":

1. The relative enmeshment or cohesion in each parent's family-of-origin loyalties
2. The relative degree of each spouse's success in structural decoupling
3. Patterns of "structural coupling" achieved by each parent
4. The parent's potential for healthy recoupling

According to these authors, if there is excessive enmeshment between a child's parents and grandparents, there is the chance that the grandparents will attempt to manipulate the situation. For example, they may actively encourage their child not to allow visitation with the noncustodial parent. Structural decoupling and recoupling involve the parents' capacity to disengage from each other and to reengage with other systems. These issues must be confronted by the parents in order for them to continue their parenting duties effectively, whether as single parents or within a new system, such as a stepfamily. If a parent is unable to accomplish these things successfully, there may be negative consequences for the child's future adjustment.

As part of their assessment, the systems theorists focus on many other facets of the family, including interactional and communicational patterns, patterns of enmeshment and disengagement, alliances, boundaries, triadic relationships, and circularities of interaction.

As one might expect, the family systems clinicians are not alone in their interest in family history. The majority of mental health professionals obtain information about courtship, marriage, and the causes of separation. Typically, a comprehensive social history is completed and includes such areas as education, occupation, marriage(s), and family. Because of the widespread concern about parental psychopathology, psychiatric histories are routinely taken. Current mental status may be investigated, as well as previous psychiatric treatment (inpatient and outpatient) and/or familial psychiatric history. It may be important to determine whether or not a person is psychologically or behaviorally disordered; however, a disordered person does not necessarily make an incompetent parent. Recognizing this, several evaluators point out the importance of evaluating how a given disorder affects the individual's ability to parent the child (Awad, 1978; Gardner, 1982; GAP, 1981; Haller, 1981; Jackson et al., 1980).

Finally, other matters that may be assessed include retardation, serious physical illness, and unresolved issues between the parents (Cogan et al., 1982), as well as the parents' "intrapsychic life" (Westman & Lord, 1980), unconscious material expressed in fantasy (Jackson et al., 1980), and "neurotic unconscious concerns about dependency, power, anger, sexuality, [and] defending against unhappiness using the child" (Trunnell, 1976, p. 124).

Children

The evaluation of children within the context of a custody dispute appears to focus on four major factors:

1. The child's attachment to his or her parents and/or other significant persons
2. The child's current developmental level and needs and the capacity of each prospective caretaker to meet these needs
3. The child's preference
4. The child's current mental status and level of adjustment

Each child's attachment to his or her parents is the most frequently cited factor that evaluators investigate (Awad, 1978; Bentovim & Gilmour, 1981; GAP, 1981; Levy, 1978; McDermott et al., 1978; Trunnell, 1976). If a child is not emotionally and psychologically attached to a parent, then the parent's chances of being given sole custody are diminished. Goldstein et al. (1973) suggest that such an individual would not be the child's "psychological parent." If, however, the child is attached to both parents, and this frequently appears to be the case, Gardner (1982) suggests that one must evaluate the "*depth* and *extent* of psychological parenting" (p. 219).

Determining whether a child is attached to a given individual does not appear to be related to any specific behavior that is identified by all or most professionals. Evaluators ask many different questions when making this decision. For example, McDermott *et al.* (1978) evaluate the child's "degree of comfort, initiative, spontaneity, fantasy expression, range of feelings, and separation behavior" (p. 111) during interaction with each parent. Levy (1978) appears to focus on different facets of the parent–child relationship. He writes:

> Attention is focused on the emotional and psychological relationships of children and parents with each other. Empathy, flexibility, understanding, fear, anxiety, trust closeness, appreciation and comfort can be clinically judged. (p. 195)

Furthermore, he investigates the child's "unconscious attitudes and feelings toward each parent," any statements the child makes about the parents, and his or her attitude in the company of the parents. Each of these factors assists in determining the level of attachment. Westman and Lord (1980) assess "the nature of the child's identification with each parent" (p. 260) and look for "signs of incorporating them in their personalities" (p. 261). When evaluating younger children, they consider the child's reaction to separation. When evaluating older children, they proceed on the belief that "the psychological imprints of parents become observable through their children's behavior and verbalizations" (p. 261). Unfortunately, they do not elaborate further. Similarly, other writers mention the importance of determining the degree of attachment between child and parent but fail to describe what criteria they use to make this determination (e.g., Awad, 1978; Bentovim & Gilmour, 1981; Trunnell, 1976).

The child's developmental level and needs and each parent's capacity to meet these needs are also discussed by the majority of writers. Although the significance of these factors is identified by several authors (Chapman, personal communication, February 27, 1980; Everett & Volgy, 1983; GAP, 1981; Purcell, personal communication, February 20, 1980; Trunnell, 1976), only Westman and Lord (1980) present a list of needs that apparently guide them in completing this assessment:

Developmental needs of children
  1. Social skills
      a. Ability to communicate

      b. Ability to relate to others
      c. Ability to be useful to others
      d. Ability to initiate self-expressive activity
   2. Self-control
      a. Ability to delay gratification
      b. Ability to tolerate frustration
      c. Ability to work
   3. Ability to learn
      a. About oneself
      b. About other people
      c. About the world
   4. Value system
      a. Commitment to adopt and adhere to social values
      b. Commitment to accommodating self-interests to social realities
   5. Ability to make decisions
      a. By accurate observing
      b. By objectively evaluating
      c. By expressing judgments
   6. Self-identity and self-esteem
      a. As a unique person
      b. As a unique gender
      c. As a unique personality

Westman and Lord (1980) indicate that if an individual develops the characteristics on their list, then he or she will be prepared for "self-reliant citizenship." In addition, these authors investigate several other areas that they believe are important to the child's development. They write:

> We are concerned about whether ecological factors, such as places, facilities, and neighborhoods in which the child could be raised, are oriented toward or are detrimental to the interests and development of a child.
> We are also concerned about a child's access to an expanding variety of life experiences: to peers, to appropriate schooling, to grandparents and to recreational facilities. Adequate economic sustenance is important, particularly for adolescents who have established lifestyles. (p. 264)

Westman and Lord (1980) consider these to be important skills for adults functioning in our society, and they consider specific environmental factors affecting child development. It is unclear what criteria others are using to assess developmental needs or, once they have identified these needs, what they look for to determine whether a parent is meeting them. One must suppose that each evaluator depends on whatever theory of child development he or she espouses (e.g., psychoanalytic, Eriksonian, ego development).

Determining the child's preference for the person with whom they will live is difficult. Although some evaluators ask the child directly for his or her preference (e.g., Jackson *et al.*, 1980; Levy, 1978), most mental health professionals avoid this question, believing it to be detrimental to the child given the child's loyalties to both parents (e.g., Chapman, personal communication, February 27, 1980; Gardner, 1982; Purcell, personal communication, February 20, 1980). They attempt to determine the child's preference indirectly (Chasin & Grunebaum, 1981; Gardner, 1982). Gardner evaluates the child's responses to a series of similar but "less anxiety-provoking" questions. For example, he might ask, "With which parent is it best for a boy (girl) to live, the mother or the father?" Of a 7-year-old boy he might ask, "With which parent should a 1-year-old baby live, the mother or the father? Why?" He may repeat this question asking about a 5-year-old, 6-year-old, 7-year-old, and so on. "If the judge asked your brother whom he would wish to live with, what would be his answer? When the judge asks you which parent you wish to live with, what are you going to answer?" Gardner believes that this line of questioning is much less threatening for the child but still elicits the preference. Jackson *et al.* (1980) ask the child about his preference both on a conscious and on a fantasy level. They believe that the child's play activities and interaction with the examiner will substantiate the child's preferences.

Levy (1978) supports asking the child directly. He writes:

> This question may seem to place a great deal of stress on the child, but in my experience it has usually been openly asked already by one or both parents. Even if it has not been asked, the question is close to the surface of the child's conscious thinking. (p. 194)

On the basis of 21 cases, he has placed children, according to their responses to the parental preference question, in one of the following categories:

1. The child who will not take sides
2. The child with an ambivalent preference
3. The child with a seemingly unambivalent preference
   a. The realistically unambivalent
   b. The pathologically unambivalent

Levy believes that these categories are important because they may be correlated with a number of factors relevant to making a custody determination, including aspects of the parent–child relationship, the parental stresses and pathology, and the parent's motives for desiring custody. For example, he suggests that both parents of children in the first group "relate well to their children and show an adequate degree of empathy, interest and flexibility . . . [and] demonstrate concern, knowledge and competence regarding the children's physical and psychological needs" (p. 198). In contrast, parents of children in the second group are unable "to recognize the developing child's need for two positive parental images and the child's inability to tolerate pressure to side with one parent against the other" (p. 201). Levy suggests that determining a child's preference and the category of his response can provide valuable information with respect to his future adjustment and may ultimately guide the evaluator in making recommendations.

Finally, the child's age, developmental level, and level of intelligence are often considered when weighing a child's preference. Generally, the older the child, the more weight given his preference, primarily because an adolescent, for example, plays a major role in determining whether or not the living and visitation arrangements are successful. It is assumed that younger children are equally attached to both parents and that they are not old enough to make an informed choice. In contrast, older and more intellectually sophisticated children are considered to be more prepared to make a choice that will be in their own best interests. At all times, however, the evaluator is cognizant of possible "brainwashing" by each prospective caretaker (see Gardner, 1982; Levy, 1978). If attempts to persuade are established, then the evaluator limits the weight given to the child's preference and may concentrate specifically on the parental behavior that led to the brainwashing (Levy, 1978).

The child's overall level of adjustment, current mental status, and presence or absence of psychopathology are important considerations for many evaluators (e.g., Cogan et al., 1982; Everett & Volgy, 1983; Haller, 1981). In the examination by McDermott et al. of 64 contested custody cases, 92% (59 cases) of the courtworker's written reports "generally" considered the child's adjustment in recommending custody, and 59% (38 cases) focused heavily on this area of assessment. Child adjustment was one of only four "emphasized" categories, the remaining three being caretaking arrangements (88%), parenting skills and commitment (72%), and the child's wishes (63%). Olson, Cleveland, Doyle, Rochcastle, Robinson, Reimer, Minton, Caron, and Cohen (1979) reviewed 40 articles that focused on custody criteria and grouped them into nine categories, one of which was the child's adjustment. In contrast to the study by McDermott *et al.*, only 6.3% of the articles mentioned this area. However, Olson *et al.* (1979) reviewed articles authored by both legal and mental health professionals who were concerned with child custody and "the best interests of the child." For the most part, these articles were not written by individuals actually performing custody evaluations. This may account for the small percentage of articles that focused on the child's adjustment in contrast to the McDermott survey.

Several writers have been interested in determining the child's level of adjustment in a variety of settings, including home, school, and community (see Olson *et al.*, 1979). For example, Everett and Volgy (1983) assess social and academic functioning, intellectual level, and general maturity, as well as developmental level and concomitant strengths and weaknesses in such areas as motor skills, communication, and self-help. McDermott *et al.*'s (1978) courtworkers also mentioned social and academic functioning, and Cogan *et al.* (1982) discussed cognitive processes, styles of thinking, and learning difficulties.

Mental status and the presence and extent of psychological disturbance have provided the focus of other child evaluations (e.g., Everett & Volgy, 1983; Trunnell, 1976). Frequently, the evaluator is interested in determining how well the child will cope with the stressors that inevitably accompany divorce. For example, Trunnell (1976) attempts to establish each child's "methods of coping; with particular attention to restoring missing parent and coping with grief" and the child's "ability to use substitute objects as resource in lieu of missing parent" (p. 123–124). Similarly, Cogan *et al.* (1982) examine coping and adaptive styles, emotional response styles, defensive flexibility, and self-images. They write, "Having a good idea of the child's abilities to cope with a variety of intense feelings can be of great aid in assessing how well the child will weather the emotional turmoil inherent in a divorce; and what special help the child might need to adapt to his new situation satisfactorily" (p. 68). Further, they attempt to assess "whether or not his coping mechanisms are sufficient to minimize the development of psychopathology either at the present time or the future" (p. 69). For many of these writers, knowing the child's level of adjustment, mental status, and extent of psychological distress, is important not only in making recommendations for custody, but also in recommending therapeutic interventions now or in the future (Haller, 1981; Jackson *et al.*, 1980; Trunnell, 1976).

Although many clinicians seem to be concerned with the child's adjustment and consider it to be important in making custody decisions, it is unclear how they use this information. Olson *et al.* (1979) write:

> Little of what is written in this area gives the clinician any clear guidelines about how the child's adjustment can be added to other factors to make a judicious and wise custody decision. For example, if the child shows poor adjustment in general, how is one to determine which parent is more responsible for that poor adjustment or which parent would help the child achieve better adjustment? (p. 41)

It is clear that mental health professionals are interested in assessing parents and children and other involved persons as well in a wide variety of settings and situations. Although there appears to be some overlap each assessor, or team of assessors, appears to have special interests resulting from professional training, theoretical perspective, and/or personal biases. That there is little standardization in what is assessed may reflect the broad, amorphous character of the standards that guide this field of psychology and the law (e.g., best interests standard). We will see that the same diversity exists across the professions with respect to how they measure and gather the data in which they are interested.

MEANS AND METHODS OF ASSESSMENT

Interviews

As one might expect, the predominant method of gathering information is the interview (e.g., Gardner, 1982). Although one might assume that the assessor structures his or her interviews in order to obtain certain kinds of information, this does not appear to be the case. With the exception of a few evaluators who obtain similar information from each parent (Gardner, 1982), interviews are mostly informal, or, at best, semistructured for content.

At some point during the custody evaluation, interviews are held with almost all of the principal parties in many different combinations. For example, each child may be seen alone, with each of the prospective caretakers, and with siblings. Each parent may be interviewed individually, with the other parent, and often with the entire family (e.g., GAP,

1981; Levy, 1978). Stressing the importance of intergenerational patterns, Everett and Volgy (1983) and Bentovim and Gilmour (1981) meet with each set of grandparents, as well as with new spouses and live-in companions. In addition to these family members, a full array of "significant network members" may be interviewed either by phone or in person. Such individuals include stepsiblings, teachers, neighbors, physicians, previous therapists, housekeepers, babysitters, and in some cases playmates or child relatives (Everett & Volgy, 1983). There do not appear to be any rigid guidelines for deciding who will be interviewed and in what order or combination, although Bentovim and Gilmour (1981) see certain combinations of family or system members "depending on the natural, recreated, therapeutic, decision making or significant past systems" (p. 69). Often included are social workers, attorneys, or other professionals. Unfortunately, Bentovim and Gilmour do not provide anything more specific concerning their selection process.

Observation

Observational assessments appear to be the second most frequently used method for evaluation. The primary purpose of observation is to investigate the interactions between the various individuals involved in the custody dispute. For the most part, this involves each child and each prospective caretaker. However, other individuals are often observed together, including siblings, stepparents, live-in companions, grandparents, and the divorced parents themselves. The mental health professional observes and evaluates these interactions throughout his or her contact with a family. This includes interactions that take place in the waiting room, playroom, to and from the waiting room, and during the various interviews. Occasionally, observations take place in naturalistic settings, for example, the home (Awad, 1978; Cooke, personal communication, March 12, 1980; Trunnell, 1976). As such, these observations are almost exclusively informal and unstructured. For example, Everett and Volgy (1983) ask the family to play together for one hour and purposely design the situation "to be unstructured, ambiguous in terms of expectations and positive in effect" (p. 349). Observations that are more structured have been reported, however (e.g., Bentovim & Gilmour, 1981; Chasin & Grunebaum, 1981; McDermott et al., 1978). Typically, these observations are structured around specific interactional tasks. For example, Bentovim and Gilmour (1981) ask the caretakers of infants to feed, change, comfort, and stimulate the children. If there are toddlers involved, situations are staged to investigate the setting of limits, separations, reunions and stranger reactions. Finally, with older children, the caretakers are asked to talk to the children about the divorce and custody situation, as well as about their own life histories. McDermott *et al.* (1978) developed the Parent–Child Interaction Test (PCIT), which requires the parent to work together with the child, to tell stories about a series of modified Children's Apperception Test (CAT) cards and to build a wooden block tower. M.A. Rodeheffer and C. Rhodes (personal communication, November 13, 1979) use a series of eight different activities that each parent completes with the child in an arranged playroom. Activities include sitting in a waiting room, playing with the child, being busy, teaching the child something, separating from the child, adapting to separation from mother, reuniting in the waiting room, and eliciting the child's obedience. Chasin and Grunebaum (1981) designed tasks to "elucidate the nature of the parent–child relationship" (p. 46). They may ask a parent to "guide a three-year-old in play to build a structure of blocks, or to make up a puppet play, or plan a vacation with older children" (p. 46). They write, "mostly we learn by directly observing the parents' attentiveness, understanding, empathy, capacity to talk and play with a child on the child's level, and capacity to allow spontaneity and maintain discipline" (p. 46). Although these evaluators structure their observations by having parents and children participate in specific interactional tasks, the observations cannot be considered more than semistructured. This point will be clarified in Chapters 10 and 11 on structured behavioral observations. Although these systems of observation are better than the informal waiting room variety, they do not meet the criteria for being structured. For the most part, they depend heavily on the observer's ability to make accurate clinical judgments. This ability will be discussed at some length in the next chapter.

Psychological Testing

Psychological testing appears to be a valuable component of the custody evaluation and is frequently mentioned by writers in this area (Alpern, 1982; L. Apperson, personal communication, February 6, 1980; J. Benedict, personal communication, February 18, 1980; J. Chapman, personal communication, February 27, 1980; Chasin & Grunebaum, 1981; Cogan *et al.*, 1982; R. Cooke, personal communication, March 12, 1980; Gardner, 1982; Levy, 1978; McDermott *et al.*, 1978; C. Purcell, personal communication, February 20, 1980; Rodgers, 1976; Trombetta, 1982; Trunnell, 1976; Westman & Lord, 1980; Woody, 1978). Unfortunately, understanding how psychological tests are used in the custody evaluation is not easy. Several writers merely mention that they use psychological tests but do not identify the tests or describe how they are used (e.g., Chasin & Grunebaum, 1981; Trunnell, 1976). Most writers identify the tests they use and then briefly discuss the reasons for their choice. None of the writers, however, explain how they use the resultant raw data. Questions such as the following are never addressed: Which TAT themes or figure drawing configurations are significant? Are there particular traits that identify a suitable caretaker? What is an appropriate $F+\%$ on the Rorschach, or a good MMPI profile ? And how does it all pertain to making decisions about the optimal living arrangements for a child following parental divorce? Although it is assumed that each investigator would have a reply to these and similar questions, nowhere could I find the answers.

Concerning the use of psychological testing, Trunnell (1976) writes:

> It may be highly germane to get baseline psychological testing data on one or all of the children, or on one or both parents. This might provide documentation of what has been a high degree of clinical suspicion of, e.g., the not visibly pre-psychotic parent who is likely to explode in the future to the obvious detriment of the child. Another example is the child whose current level of superficial functioning may not seem to be as disturbed as it is in fact, and in whom it would be important to document that if custody is not changed, additional psychonoxious stress will be accomplished by unfavorable developmental inhibitions. (p. 124–5)

Clearly Trunnell believes that psychological testing can tap something that is not visible to the naked eye. This view is similar to Levy's (1978) belief that testing can

> assist in determining the child's unconscious attitudes and feelings toward each parent. This is especially useful when the examination of parents and children has produced contradictory material or the force with which the child expresses his or her preference seems exaggerated. (p. 195)

Many different kinds of tests are currently employed in these evaluations. Although some writers caution against the use of projective techniques such as the Rorschach and the Thematic Apperception Test (TAT) (e.g., Barnard & Jenson, 1984; Gardner, 1982), many clinicians are using these and other projective devices. The Draw-A-Person (DAP), Children's Apperception Test, family drawings, and various forms of doll play and sentence completion, as well as the Rorschach and TAT, are all part of the evaluator's armamentarium (see, e.g., Apperson, personal communication, February 6, 1980; Benedict, personal communication, February 18, 1980; Chapman, personal communication, February 27, 1980; Cogan et al., 1982; Levy, 1978; Purcell, personal communication, February 20, 1980). Structured personality inventories such as the Minnesota Multiphasic Personality Inventory (MMPI), Edwards Personal Preference Schedule (EPPS), and Sixteen Personality Factors Test (16PF) have also been used in custody evaluations (Chapman, personal communication, February 27, 1980; Cooke, personal communication, March 12, 1980; Woody, 1978). Together, the projectives and structured inventories are viewed as a means of determining an individual's underlying personality structure and extent of psychopathology, as well as a child's true custodial preference and level of attachment. In addition to tests of personality, educational, intellectual, and neurological tests may also be used when appropriate (Cogan et al., 1982; Gardner, 1982). These are particularly important when evaluating a child with special needs, for example, a child with a learning disability. Gardner (1982) recommends the use of the Slosson Intelligence Test to assist in determining how much credibility to give to a child's expressed custodial preference. Furthermore, he suggests that a child's responses to the Comprehension and Picture Arrangement subtests of the WISC-R will tap the child's level of social sensitivity and values. If these subtest scores are high, Gardner believes, then the child's statements about parental preference should be given greater credibility.

Miscellaneous Methods

Other assessment methods that have been reported in the literature include genograms (Barnard & Jenson, 1984; Bentovim & Gilmour, 1981; Everett & Volgy, 1983); play interviews (Cogan et al., 1982; Trunnell, 1976); questionnaires given to those who furnish character references (Everett & Volgy, 1983) or to parents (Gardner, 1982); verbal projective questions (Barnard & Jenson, 1984; Gardner, 1982); projective games, such as the Talking, Feeling, Doing Game of Gardner (1982) and the "magic week" or "lifeline" of Chapman (1980); and records obtained from schools, mental health personnel, day-care operators, law enforcement officers, hospitals, and public agencies (Awad, 1978; Chasin & Grunebaum, 1981; Everett & Volgy, 1983; Rodgers, 1976; Westman & Lord, 1980).

Although it seems clear that ultimately each evaluator or evaluation team maintains the same goal of assessment (i.e., to recommend the postdivorce living arrangements of children), the means and methods by which they obtain this goal are wide ranging. Theoretical leanings, professional affiliation, and idiosyncratic preferences appear to permeate the field. For example, clinicians based in family systems theory are investigating intergenerational patterns, alliances, boundaries, and levels of enmeshment and disengagement (e.g., Everett & Volgy, 1983). They are interested in genograms and appear to do little if any testing. Other investigators appear to be interested in unconscious motivation and underlying personality structure. Accordingly, they give or recommend the use of projective and objective personality tests. Another group of professionals may have no training in psychological testing and therefore must rely primarily on interviews and observations or refer their clients to someone who is trained to do the testing. Truly, this field of investigation encompasses many diverse viewpoints which are reflected in the number of different professions involved and the myriad of approaches to and methods of assessment.

Foundations for a Behavioral Assessment Alternative

In this chapter, I will lay the foundation for the model of assessment to be proposed and presented throughout the remainder of this text. This model grew out of two closely related areas of research, personality and psychological assessment. Understanding personality and the prediction of behavior and how they directly relate to theories of assessment and their associated strategies is vitally important in the development of any evaluation model. After reviewing the research on personality and on the person–situation controversy, I will explain how this research led to my espousal of a behavioral assessment model and to my dissatisfaction with and dismissal of the more commonly used trait-oriented and psychodynamic models of assessment. Furthermore, because traditional assessment strategies are frequently used within the context of child custody evaluations, I shall raise some important questions about their current status as methods of personality assessment.

The Foundations of Assessment: Personality and the Person–Situation Controversy

Within the past 15 to 20 years, and especially since the publication of Mischel's 1968 book, *Personality and Assessment*, theorizing and research in personality have been embroiled in controversy. The cornerstone of the debate is whether or not social behavior is determined primarily by a variety of underlying predispositions (i.e., "person" variables), or by situational factors, namely, the environment.

Currently, there are four major approaches to the study of personality: trait psychology, psychodynamics, situationism, and interactionism (Endler & Magnusson, 1976). Trait theorists posit global underlying predispositions as the primary determinants of behavior. Although they recognize that an individual's behavior may vary in different situations, they maintain that the rank order of individuals with respect to specific traits is transsituationally consistent. They identify various trait signs that are additive. Thus, the strength of a given characteristic is linearly related to the number of signs present. As the number of observed signs for a particular trait increase, the observed person is said to possess more of that trait. Consequently, two individuals can be compared and ranked on the basis of the number of signs. Although proponents of the psychodynamic position also believe in underlying predispositions that emanate from a basic personality structure, they believe that the relationship between predispositions and overt behavior is much less direct. Psychodynamic theory implies a continuous interaction and conflict between the id, ego, and superego. Furthermore, this theory suggests that the behavioral manifestations of these underlying causal agents may not be cross-situationally consistent because they are often distorted and displaced by the operation of an individual's defense mechanisms (e.g., repression, displacement, reaction formation, and denial). Situationists are primarily concerned with the stimulus properties of the environment. They believe that situational stimuli, rather than underlying hypothetical entities, are responsible for the evocation of behavior. Their position grew out of the radical behaviorist position characterized by the writing of B. F. Skinner (1953). They do, however, recognize the reciprocity between the person and the situation and believe not only that the individual responds to the environment but also that the environment can be changed by the person. Proponents of an interactionist perspective currently hold that the question of whether person or situation variables are more important in understanding and predicting behavior is a "meaningless," "pseudo issue" (Ekehammar, 1974). Endler and Magnusson (1976) define interactionism in the following manner:

> Behavior involves an indispensable, continuous interaction between individuals and the situations they encounter. Not only is the individual's behavior influenced by significant features of the situations he or she encounters but the person also selects the situations in which he or she performs, and subsequently affects the character of these situations. (p. 958)

Thus, interactionists believe that without knowing the specific person and the environmental context in which he or she will be acting, predicting how that person will behave is a futile undertaking.

The principal difference between situationism and interactionism is in the relative importance attributed to cognitive–perceptual factors as determinants of behavior; proponents of the former dismiss their role, and the latter see them as indispensable. The significant ways in which cognitive–perceptual variables interact with the environmental context were elaborated by Mischel (1973) in conjunction with his cognitive social learning perspective. In other important ways, situationism and interactionism are compatible with each other but are incongruous with both the trait and psychodynamic positions. The crucial issue that divides these four positions concerns the transsituational consistency of behavior. Trait and psychodynamic theorists believe that, relative to other individuals, each person's rank order with respect to specific traits, impulses, needs, motives, and other similar genotypes is consistent across situations. The one exception to this belief, found within the psychodynamic model, involves cases in which a person's defenses are operating. In contrast, the situationist and interactionist positions state that cross-situational consistency is not to be expected. Whereas the traditional trait and psychodynamic approaches explain observed inconsistencies in overt behavior in terms of measurement errors and/or defenses, the current theorizing and research of situationists and interactionists views the situation as a significant and vital factor in understanding and predicting behavior.

Although the important role of the environment has been recognized for many years (see Ekehammar, 1974), the trait and psychodynamic models have reigned supreme for decades. The overwhelming majority of our most widely used personality assessment measures, including a wide variety of projective and objective tests, are directly tied to their underlying assumptions. The interactionists and situationists have commenced a frontal assault on these models and their assumptions, thereby challenging the reigning Zeitgeist, that has been supported by thousands of mental health professionals.

In Support of Interactionism

Several prominent researchers have reviewed the scientific literature that addresses the core assumption of the trait and psychodynamic models of personality but they have unearthed very little empirical support (Argyle & Little, 1972; Bowers, 1973; Endler, 1973, 1975a, 1975b; Mischel, 1968, 1969, 1976; Pervin, 1968; Peterson, 1968; Vernon, 1964). This conclusion, reached repeatedly by these writers and others, has been particularly disconcerting, not only because years of theorizing have been seriously questioned but also because the principal assumption underlying the construction and employment of psychological assessment methods has been similarly challenged.

Hartshorne and May's (1928) classic studies on the trait of honesty dealt the consistency assumption its first blow and simultaneously laid the groundwork for a strong argument in favor of situationism. Children were given the opportunity to lie, cheat, and steal in several different settings, and although they consistently expressed the same attitudes and opinions concerning cheating on questionnaires administered in the same setting, their responses on alternate forms completed in different settings, as well as their observed behavior, varied greatly across settings. The authors noted a progressive lowering of correlations between measures with increasingly greater changes in the situation. They suggested that honesty is primarily a function of the stimulus situation to which a child is exposed. Their studies elevated the situation to an important position in which it could not be easily ignored.

Endler, Hunt, and Rosenstein (1962) provided further evidence that challenged the tenets of trait psychology. This study used the *S–R Inventory of Anxiousness,* a self-report questionnaire that makes it possible to ferret out the relative contributions of persons, settings, modes of response, and their simple interactions to overall variance in behavior. The most significant finding was that, in one sample, situations contributed 11 times as much as persons to the overall variance. The authors concluded that it was much more important to know the situation than to know "personal idiosyncrasies" when predicting behavior.

Although these results strongly supported situationism and cast considerable doubt on the importance of individual differences in understanding behavior, the results were criticized for being determined by an inappropriate statistical model (Ekehammar, 1974; Wiggins, 1973). Endler and Hunt (1966) reanalyzed their original data using a more appropriate model and discovered that indeed person variables contributed only a very small proportion to the total variance—approximately 5%. Surprisingly, however, situations contributed approximately an equal amount. The largest proportion contributing to overall variance was nearly 30%, accounted for by the simple interactions. These results were highly stable across the original two samples, and across a newer third sample. Two years later, the same authors published a third report in which they investigated hostility. Using the newly constructed *S–R Inventory of Hostility,* they again found that the largest portion of variance was accounted for by the three simple interractions. As a result of these early studies, Endler and Hunt shifted their support from situationism to interactionism.

Several years prior to the work by Endler and Hunt, Raush and his coworkers (Raush, Dittmann, & Taylor, 1959a, 1959b; Raush, Farbman, & Llewellyn, 1960) presented evidence that also supported an interactional model. They investigated the influence of six social settings on interpersonal behavior. Six "hyperaggressive" preadolescent boys living in a residential setting were observed during two phases. The initial phase occurred when the boys were at an average age of 10 years, and the second phase occurred 18 months later.

During both phases, each boy was observed twice in each of six settings: breakfast, other meals, structured game activities, unstructured group activities, arts and crafts, and snacks at bedtime.

The results indicated that a knowledge of the setting in which a particular boy was observed contributed substantially to the understanding and prediction of this boy's social behavior. Differences were observed in the type of behavior each boy exhibited in specific settings. As in the work done later by Endler and Hunt, Raush and his coworkers found that most of the variance in the aggressive behavior of these boys was accounted for by an interaction between subjects and situations. These boys did not behave consistently across the six settings with respect to aggressive behavior. To permit the most accurate prediction of a boy's behavior, it was necessary to identify both the boy and the setting in which he was to be observed.

In 1973, Bowers analyzed and criticized the situationists' position and reviewed 11 articles published since 1959 that evaluated the relative contribution of persons and situations in the determination of behavior. In the 11 studies there was a mean of 12.71% of the total variance accounted for by person variables, 10.17% by situations, and 20.77% by their interaction. In fact, the interaction effect reported in these 11 articles was the highest percentage in 14 of the 18 possible comparisons and in 8 of the 18 was higher than the main effects combined.

Evidence has consistently supported an interactional framework and has raised serious questions concerning the validity of the primary assumption of both trait and psychodynamic psychology, that is, transsituational consistency. The previously mentioned studies represent only a small portion of the investigations that have addressed the person–situation controversy. In fact, four independent research projects have investigated the subject: Endler and Hunt (1966, 1968, 1969; Endler, 1966, 1973, 1975a and 1975b; Endler & Hoy, 1967; Endler, Hunt, & Rosenstein, 1962; Endler & Magnusson, 1976; Endler & Okada, 1975; Endler, Wiesenthal, & Geller, 1972; Hunt, 1965; Wiesenthal, Endler, & Geller, 1973), Moos (1967, 1968, 1969, 1979; Moos & Clemes, 1967; Moos and Daniels, 1967), Magnusson (1971, 1974; Ekehammar & Magnusson, 1973; Ekehammar, Magnusson, & Ricklander, 1974; Heffler & Magnusson, 1979; Magnusson & Ekehammar, 1973, 1975; Magnusson, Gerzén, & Nyman, 1968; Magnusson & Heffler, 1969; Magnusson, Heffler, & Nyman, 1968), and Raush (1965, 1972; Raush et al., 1959a, 1959b; Raush et al., 1960). These researchers have studied a variety of traits and behaviors, including anxiety, hostility, cooperative ability, self-confidence, leadership, conformity, talking, smiling, smoking, and social behavior. Other researchers have investigated altruism (Rushton, 1976), honesty (Burton, 1963; Nelsen, Grinder, & Mutterer, 1969), introversion–extroversion (Newcomb, 1931), social perception (Argyle & Little, 1972), rigidity (Applezweig, 1954; Wrightsman & Baumeister, 1961), conditionability (Eysenck, 1965), assertiveness (Hersen & Bellack, 1977; Kazdin, 1974a), leisure time activities (Bishop & Witt, 1970), and friendliness and conscientiousness (Mischel & Peake, 1982). They have used self-report questionnaires, direct observations and reports from significant others, and different populations from different countries, and they have statistically analyzed their results using correlations, factor analyses, or analyses of variance. Despite so many variables, there is a consistency of findings across these projects with respect to the primary role of person–situation interaction in the understanding and prediction of behavior.

There have been some recent attempts to breathe life back into the trait model (Bem & Allen, 1974; Bem & Funder, 1978; Epstein, 1979, 1980). As Mischel and Peake (1982) have pointed out, these studies arose from a frustration with what they have referred to as the "consistency paradox." The paradox exists because an overwhelming majority of the findings in personality research say that there is little consistency in behavior across settings, whereas each and every day we ourselves observe behavioral consistencies in other people. Bem and Epstein have suggested that this paradox exists as a result of the research methods used to study the question of consistency and not because generalized global traits are fictions. They have proposed the "reliability" solution (Epstein, 1979), the "idiographic" solution (Bem & Allen, 1974), and the "template-matching" solution (Bem & Funder, 1978) as more valid methods for demonstrating the existence of traits (see Mischel & Peake, 1982, for a full discussion). However, Mischel and Peake reviewed these studies and presented new data from the Carleton Behavior Study and the Mischel–Peake Study that strongly suggest that these methodological "solutions" do not solve the consistency paradox. The controversy continues to rage, however, as Epstein (1983a,b) and Funder (1983a,b) have replied to Mischel and Peake (1982) and Mischel (1983) continues to expound his position. Mischel and Peake present their own resolution using Mischel's cognitive social-learning conceptualization of behavior (e.g., Mischel, 1973) and a cognitive prototype view of person categorization (e.g., Cantor & Mischel, 1979). Having accepted the lack of generalized cross-situational consistencies in behavior, the authors focus on the *perception* of consistency. Mischel and Peake (1982) write:

> congruent with a cognitive prototype approach, . . . the judgment of trait consistency is strongly related to the temporal stability of highly prototypic (but not of less prototypic) behaviors. In contrast, the global impression of consistency may not be strongly related to overall or average cross-situational consistency, even in prototypic behaviors. Thus, the perception and organization of personality consistencies . . . will depend more on the temporal stability of key features than on the observation of cross-situational behavioral consistency, and the former may be easily interpreted as if it were the latter. (p. 753)

Although, as the authors suggest, replications and extensions of their studies will be necessary before any firm conclusions can be advanced with respect to their reconceptualization, there does appear to be ample evidence supporting the interactional model of personality. In view of this evidence, disregard of the environmental context in any attempt to understand and predict behavior appears to be an inexcusable omission. The traditional trait model of personality appears to make just such an omission. Consequently, its utility has been seriously questioned. Endler and Magnusson (1976) wrote:

> Personality validity coefficients range from .20 to .50, with an average of .30 [citations omitted]. The results . . . indicate the limitations of the trait model as a general basis for personality research, and also as a general basis for the use of personality data for predicting and describing behavior in actual situations. (p. 966)

Implications

The significance of this area of research for those of us assisting families and the legal community in determining the postdivorce living arrangements of children is immense. In fact, it is my opinion that no other body of research is more important for the accomplishment of the task before us. The assumptions we hold about personality guide us in our understanding and prediction of human behavior and consequently shape the types of questions we ask and the assessment methodologies we construct and employ. The theorizing of personologists, for example, has been based on one major premise: that our behavior is determined by underlying predispositions that exert generalized effects transsituationally. From this premise, trait constructs arose that in turn led to the construction of assessment devices intended to identify and measure predispositions in persons. Ultimately, predictions are made based on a person's performance on these tests. We looked inside the person to make predictions of overt behavior.

Our entire tradition of personality assessment follows from our theorizing and, we hope, from our empirical investigations. If we assume that human behavior is a function of person variables that lie within, then through our assessments we will look for underlying factors. If these factors exert generalized effects across situations, then the particular situation in which we conduct our assessment is of little significance. If a knowledge of various genotypes is sufficient for predicting how an individual will behave, then the determination of the optimal living arrangements for a child will be based on the underlying predispositions of each person involved, our knowledge of how various dispositions interact among people, and which dispositions are most important for an individual in a parental role. However, if the underlying assumptions of both the trait and psychodynamic models of personality are shown to be of little use, and I believe this to be the case, then the assessment devices that have been constructed and employed on the basis of these two models can be similarly criticized. Unfortunately, the overwhelming majority of our most prized evaluation methods are theoretically based on these models. Peterson (1968) states:

> If behavior is a joint function of situation and internal disposition, no *standard* stimulus situation can possibly represent the diversity of circumstances in which behavior occurs. However valid a test may be in its revelation of intrapsychic characteristics, behavior continues to vary with stimulus change and logically, not just empirically, *the stimulus conditions must be taken into account* [italics added]. No psychodiagnostic test designed along traditional lines can do this. (pp. 138–139)

If the task at hand is to determine the optimal living arrangements for a given child after the divorce of his or her parents, then we are asking ourselves to predict. If the trait and psychodynamic models and their assessment methodologies are of questionable value for this purpose, then they should not be used. If they are not discarded, we will be frustrated continually by our inability to make accurate predictions and useful recommendations, and we will be justifiably criticized for practicing our profession with blinders on (i.e., with disregard of our own body of scientific evidence). We must look for guidance from that body of research in order to develop and make use of new, more empirically verifiable methods.

If we are to banish current practice in this matter, then what are our alternatives? A more fruitful approach would be to use those currently available assessment devices (and/or those that can be developed) that evaluate the person(s) in question with respect to the environment(s) for which we wish to make predictions. In other words, we need a comprehensive assessment that addresses the person–situation interaction. Predictions will be made concerning a particular child and his or her family and surrounding environment. In order to predict accurately, we must know as much as possible about the cognitive social-learning history of that child and the alternative environments in which that child may be placed. Only with this information can we begin to predict his or her future behavior and adjustment. Mischel (1983) states:

> Predictions of behavior generally are more likely to be supported when the behaviors to be predicted are adequately sampled and when there is a careful and relatively close match between the content of the predictor and that of the criterion. (p. 600)

TRADITIONAL PERSONALITY ASSESSMENT

Conceptually, there are many objections to the use of traditional, trait-oriented assessment strategies. Nevertheless, as I noted in Chapter 2, many such devices are currently being used by mental health professionals completing child custody evaluations. Unfortunately, not one of the articles I reviewed concerning the use of psychodiagnostic assessment strategies was empirically based. The reliability and validity of the instruments reported were not mentioned once in any of them. In fact, to my knowledge, no such research exists. The reliability and validity of these devices have never been investigated in the context of a child custody evaluation. Although this fact alone raises serious questions about their continued use, especially when coupled with the previously discussed conceptual objections, other concerns should also be mentioned.

Projective Assessment Strategies

The use of projective techniques (e.g., the Rorschach, TAT, and figure drawings, such as the DAP) is one method of assessing personality within a trait-psychodynamic conception and, as we have seen, may frequently be employed in the child custody evaluation. Despite the continued use of projective techniques in a large percentage of clinical settings (Levy & Fox, 1975; Lubin, Wallis, & Paine, 1971), they have been severely criticized through the years. The Rorschach, for example, although in the midst of a comeback through the efforts of Exner (1974, 1978), has been criticized continuously for many years. In 1959, McCall reviewed the Rorschach literature published until that time and had the following comment:

> Though tens of thousands of Rorschach tests have been administered by hundreds of trained professionals . . . and while many relationships to personality dynamics and behavior have been hypothesized, the vast majority of these interpretive relationships *have never been validated empirically*, despite the appearance of more than 2,000 publications . . . . This holds not only for the claims made by Rorschach himself, but equally for extensions and modifications of those advanced by Klopfer, Beck, Piotrowski, Rapaport, Loosli-Usteri, Schafer, and others. (original italics p. 279)

Six years later, Jensen's (1965) review of the matter continued the indictment against the Rorschach, only a bit more strongly:

> Put frankly, the consensus of qualified judgment is that the Rorschach is a very poor test and has no practical worth for any of the purposes for which it is recommended by its devotees. (p. 501)

In later years, opinion has not changed:

> The bulk of evidence . . . has shown the Rorschach to have serious limitations as a psychometric instrument based on a formal scoring system for the perceptual determinants as associations to the inkblots. (Reznikoff, 1972, p. 446)

And

> The general lack of predictive validity for the Rorschach raises serious questions about its continued use in clinical practice. (Peterson, 1978, p. 1045)

In 1980, Widiger and Schilling wrote, "After more than fifty years of research, most questions concerning the validity of the Rorschach remain unanswered" (p. 450).

The TAT and DAP have not been spared either. Jensen (1959) claimed that the TAT's validity was "practically nil," and other writers attacked this test for its inability to provide a profile of personality traits or to measure reliably any specific trait (Adcock, 1965; Eron, 1972). By far the most serious indictments against the validity of human figure drawings in general and against the DAP specifically, have come from Swensen (1957, 1968) and Roback (1968). In Swensen's (1957) review article, 8 years after the publication of Machover's *Personality Projection in the Drawing of the Human Figure* (1949), data were presented that compared experimental research findings with Machover's hypothesis concerning body parts and with structural and formal aspects of the DAP. Of the 40 different hypotheses mentioned, only one was supported. Swensen (1957) concluded:

> The evidence presented . . . does not support Machover's hypotheses about the meaning of human figure drawings. More evidence directly contradicts her hypotheses than supports them. (p. 460)

Although in his 1968 review Swensen believed there was more empirical support for using the DAP, especially as a gross screening device, he still concluded:

> Aside from global judgments for the DAP, the base rates would suggest that the use of the structural and content signs of the DAP for clinical assessment is not likely to provide any improvement in the clinician's judgmental accuracy. (p. 40)

Roback (1968) also reviewed the post-1956 literature on the DAP and commented:

> Many clinicians apparently entertain grandiose delusions that they can "intuitively" gain a great deal of information from figure drawings about the personality structure and dynamics of the drawer. . . . Perhaps in individual cases, they may provide insight into the drawer's perceptions of himself and others, but in these instances the cases are usually so extreme or the patient is so disorganized that one could easily have gotten the same information from a multitude of other sources which would not have necessitated a testing situation. (pp. 16–17)

In addition to the general criticisms that have been made against projective methodologies, questions have also been raised because of the overwhelming number of situational and interpersonal variables that affect the testing situation and its subsequent outcome and interpretation. Examiner characteristics, examiner behavior, order of test battery administration, the reason for the assessment, and probably other unknown variables contribute to the data obtained from the Rorschach (Dana, 1972) and TAT (Masling, 1960). Several studies have demonstrated the effect of different examiner–examinee sex combinations on the number and kind of responses given on the Rorschach (Harris & Masling, 1970; Hersen, 1970; Tuma & McCraw, 1975) and the TAT (Masling & Harris, 1969; Milner, 1975). Age (Mussen & Scodel, 1955), social class or ethnicity (Haase, 1956; Koscherak & Masling, 1972; Levy, 1970; Levy & Kahn, 1970; Mason & Ammons, 1956; McArthur, 1955; Mussen, 1953; Riesman & Miller, 1958; Rychlak & Boland, 1973; Trachtman, 1971), subtle differences in phrasing instructions (Klinger, 1966), and the order of test administration in a battery (Bespalec, 1978; Magnussen, 1967) have all been shown to affect results. Also, the examiner's verbal and nonverbal behavior result in reinforcement of certain types of examinee test responses despite the examiner's lack of awareness (Dana, 1982; Dinoff, 1960; Gross, 1959; Hersen & Greaves, 1971; Magnussen, 1960; Simmons & Christy, 1962; Stewart & Patterson, 1973). Even the examiner's mere presence in the examining room can inhibit certain kinds of responses (Bernstein, 1956), as can the reason for testing or the expectation and demand characteristics of the situation (Dinoff, 1960; Marwit, 1971; Marwit & Strauss, 1975; Zubin, Eron, & Schumer, 1965). With such a variety of factors impinging on the testing situation, ferreting out the affects of each one on the resultant protocol would appear to be an almost insurmountable task. This situation obviously contributes to the poor validity of these projective tests.

Overall, there appear to be major problems with projective techniques. Not only have their basic underlying assumptions been seriously challenged, their soundness from a psychometric standpoint has also been questioned (see, e.g., Anastasi, 1976). Although adequate levels of reliability and validity can sometimes be obtained with certain procedures and variables, the consistency with which this is accomplished is far from adequate (Marafiote, 1981). Davids (1973) suggests that the "findings in regard to projective personality assessment have been especially controversial, contradictory and confusing" (p. 451). Concerning the future of projective techniques, he writes:

> If those who have devoted much of their time and energy to the development and utilization of projective methodologies in the recent past do not soon begin to convincingly demonstrate their efficacy and value, it seems likely that the coming generation of clinical psychologists will continue to perpetrate ideas that they find to exist solely in the thoughts (fantasies) of their predecessors, with little relationship to the facts of behavior in real life. (p. 451)

A recent survey of clinical psychologists in academic settings reported that 62% considered these techniques to be unsupported by the research (Cleveland, 1976). The results of this survey provide a powerful statement concerning the lack of confidence in these instruments within the psychological community. This profession-wide controversy over the use of projective methods has been emphasized by Ziskin (1975, 1977), a lawyer and psychologist who makes a rather convincing case against the use of these (and other) psychological tests in courts of law, simply basing his argument on the tests' controversial status within the field of psychology. Summarizing his assault on projective tests, he writes:

> It is clear that opinions based upon projective tests should no more be admitted into evidence than opinions based upon psychiatric interviewing, polygraph data, or any other clinical method. The research does not establish satisfactory reliability or validity. In view of the disputes that exist and the negative statements of so many authorities, it cannot be said that any of the more commonly used tests meet the criteria of established scientific principles or general acceptance by the scientific community. (Ziskin, 1975, p. 180)

This controversy and the disdain for projective tests held by legal professionals may explain why some professionals in the child custody field strongly recommend against their use (Gardner, 1982).

Structured Personality Assessment

Structured personality inventories are also subject to considerable criticism, mostly relevant to test construction and standardization. Although such tests as the Minnesota Multiphasic Personality Inventory (MMPI) the Edwards Personal Preference Schedule (EPPS) yield high reliabilities in scoring because of their relative objectivity and the advent of computer scoring, the MMPI, for example, has been shown to have serious problems in its original sampling procedures (Marafiote, 1981). The overall sample was extremely narrow geographically and was too small to present useful data by sex, age, socioeconomic status, or ethnic group (Anastasi, 1975; Hathaway & McKinley, 1980). Because of these problems, the utility and validity of the test for the general public is questionable. For example, it cannot be assumed that parents in the midst of divorce and custody proceedings are similar to people who are not in that situation. Although norms have been established on many populations, including adolescents and college students, I am not aware of any that have been developed for use with parents under the stress of a child custody dispute. This concern exists for other structured inventories as well. Every time the MMPI or any other similar inventory is used to evaluate an individual, a rather large but obviously questionable assumption is being made, that he or she is represented in the standardization sample with respect to age, sex, SES, ethnic group, and geography, thus allowing appropriate comparisons to be made. This appears to be an assumption that can be readily questioned.

Beyond the controversy that appears to surround the interpretive significance of structured inventories, response sets and response styles impact heavily on the completion of structured inventories and their subsequent scale scores and profile analyses (Jackson, 1973). Response sets are defined as response consistencies having little or nothing to do with the substantive content of the item. Among the most common response sets reported in the research are the tendency to answer items in the most socially desirable direction (social desirability—Edwards, 1953, 1961); the tendency to answer only items keyed in a "true/agree/yes" or "false/disagree/no" direction (i.e., acquiescence—Couch & Keniston, 1960; Jackson & Messick, 1958, 1962; Messick & Jackson, 1961, 1966); and the tendency to respond in the most unusual or deviant manner (i.e., the deviation hypothesis—Berg, 1967). These sets occur irrespective of actual item content, thus eliciting considerable suspicion regarding the validity of the resultant scores and of the profiles and personality descriptions that they generate.

The complexity of these structured personality inventories is magnified when one incorporates the impact of moderator and situational variables. According to Anastasi (1976), a *moderator variable* is "some characteristic of persons that makes it possible to predict the predictability of different individuals with a given instrument" (p. 178). These variables enhance the predictive validity of a test because of the variations that may exist between persons on a given characteristic. Typically, moderator variables are demographic characteristics, such as age, sex, educational level, socioeconomic background, or ethnic group; knowing these variables may substantially increase the accuracy of prediction and change the interpretation of test results.

The MMPI, for example, is notorious for the influence that moderator variables have on the outcome of profile scores on the basic scales. Dahlstrom, Welsh, and Dahlstrom (1975) report relevant research on the effects of age, race, socioeconomic status, education, intelligence, religious affiliation, family birth order, national origin, urban or rural residence in various regions of the country, profession or occupation, and different degrees of physical integrity. For example, blacks consistently score higher on specific scales, thereby heightening a deviant or antisocial image (Erdberg, 1969; Harrison & Kass, 1967; Strauss, Gynther, & Wallhermfechtel, 1974). Consequently, profile interpretations must be adjusted for these consistent differences.

In addition to the person variables that appear to alter significantly an individual's responses to MMPI items, there are other components that contribute to overall variance such as the testing situation, the reason for testing, and instructional sets. It has been reliably documented, for example, that individuals are able to dissemble on self-report personality inventories (Jacobs & Barron, 1968; Radcliffe, 1966; Stricker, 1969; Wiggins, 1966) and that they will vary their responses depending on the reasons for the test administration (Braginsky, Grosse, & Ring, 1966; Green, 1951). Rodgers (1972) comments on the MMPI:

> It has some but such more limited utility in assessing emotional upset in an evaluation situation such as an employee screening program, in which the client's best interests are served by concealing emotional upset rather than, as in a patient–doctor context, by openly revealing it. The test is dependent for its power on self-description. It was empirically developed from patient populations that were reasonably cooperative and reasonably motivated to reveal upset. In a differently motivated population, the test and its standard norms are not valid and can be grossly misleading. (pp. 243–244)

In sum, there are a great many variables that must be considered when interpreting the results of an MMPI. Unfortunately, in only a few instances have special norms been developed to assist in the appropriate comparisons of subgroups. Consequently, individuals are being compared to general adult norms that as we have indicated, are less than adequate. Moreover, the examiner must be able to ferret out the various factors impinging on the test results, including any moderator variables, response sets, or other situational considerations. This is an extremely complex task and has led one reviewer of the MMPI (Rodgers, 1972) to suggest:

> The test is valid and safe only in the hands of an MMPI expert and in my estimation is not, contrary to what has been suggested often enough in the literature, useful for the physician or psychiatrist who is psychometrically naive or the psychologist or psychiatrist who wants to use the test for only an infrequent assessment and who has not taken the time and effort both to become thoroughly familiar with the literature on the test and to become clinically experienced in its actual use. Paradoxically, considerable clinical sophistication in the use of the MMPI is necessary before its actuarial power can be appropriately utilized. (p. 244)

Familiarity with the literature alone is a formidable obstacle. At the time of the publication of Buros's *Eighth Mental Measurement Yearbook* (1978), there were over 6,000 references to the MMPI, with over 200 books and articles published annually, and more scales than items on the inventory (Butcher & Tellegen, 1978). Certainly, to know this material would require more than a day or two of reading. In light of all the problems inherent in the MMPI with respect to test construction, standardization, norming, response sets, moderator variables, and situational determinants, it is little wonder that Rodgers (1972) referred to this test as a "projective device" and a "psychometric nightmare":

> In effect, then, the scales are often given personality-dimension meanings, the meaning for a given scale perhaps varying considerably depending on other scale elevations, on the particular level of elevation of that particular scale, and on the particular interpreter or interpretive program. Used in this fashion, the MMPI can approach the Rorschach and TAT as a projective device that allows remarkably wide latitude for professional interpretation and that is lacking to a surprisingly large degree in the safeguards of actuarial tables and clearly established validity that the empirical tradition of the test would suggest exists. (p. 248)

The question of the validity of the MMPI is one laden with both complexity and simplicity. The complexity is associated with the amount of time and effort necessary to interpret adequately the massive quantity of validation research that has been compiled on the MMPI with the individual client being tested. The simplicity is a function of the empirical nature of the scales and their ability to differentiate and identify special groups of people. As Wiggins (1973) has pointed out, the empirical nature of the scales "guarantees" a certain amount of success in predicting the chosen criteria. This success is a function of careful scale construction and cross-validation. However, Wiggins also points out one very important and serious drawback in this procedure. Successful prediction is likely to occur only with similar populations in similar circumstances, and even then success is not a foregone conclusion. All one need do is administer the MMPI to two groups who differ on some characteristic (e.g., alcoholics versus nonalcoholics), note any consistent systematic differences between them, and determine a profile. Then one identifies traits, dispositions, and behavioral characteristics of that group and pairs them with the profile that identifies them. Special scales may be developed to assess individual personality traits or other criteria. However, once the scale or profile has been validated on a specific population, its ability to predict across different populations is doubtful. For instance, if an alcoholic scale is developed with a male population in a rural area of southwest Virginia, then the scale may do little to predict alcoholism in a female population from an urban area such as New York City. In fact, scales may not predict criteria outside the hospital or clinic in which they have been developed, although they may predict exceptionally well in that environment. In sum, empirically constructed scales may be extremely limited in their generalizability. This is why there has been so much research done on the MMPI. Local norms and scales are constantly being developed in an effort to increase the utility of the test. Wiggins (1973) explains:

> Empirically constructed scales faithfully mirror differences that existed between the original criterion and control groups. Minor variations in the populations studied, the criterion employed, or the conditions under which the test is administered may result in drastically reduced validity coefficients. (pp. 393–394)

In fact, for our purposes all the research that has been done on the MMPI, with the piling up of its incredible record of group identification and differentiation, matters little without empirical evidence that demonstrates its ability to do the same with the population being considered here—parents involved in child custody disputes. It would be unreasonable to challenge the incredible amount of evidence that has accumulated with various groups and settings, but because of the narrowness of scope and limited generalizability demonstrated with these findings it may all be for naught. In perusing over 6,000 citations in the most current *MMPI Handbook* (Dahlstrom *et al.*, 1975), I found none that addressed the topic of child custody. Needless to say, despite the MMPI's position of high esteem in the world of personality testing, its current value for child custody decisions is questionable.

Expertise in Clinical Judgment

Clinical psychologists and other mental health professionals are frequently called upon to assist in making very important decisions. Because of the years of training involved in becoming a psychologist, the nature of the field, and the certification process through which the professional must proceed, one would assume that their judgments are superior to those of the layman. One would further assume that a linear relationship exists between the amount of training and experience that a clinician has and the degree of accuracy of his or her judgments and clinical predictions.

Assessment methodologies employed during a child custody evaluation are highly dependent on the evaluator's clinical judgment (see Chapter 2). Not only do interviews and informal observations require the clinician's expertise in judging a series of interpersonal events, but the interpretations of psychological tests, especially the projectives, also demands clinical judgments. For these reasons it is extremely important to investigate the validity of these assumptions in greater detail. Does accuracy of judgment and clinical prediction increase with greater amounts of clinical training and experience? Are mental health professionals more accurate than professionals in unrelated disciplines or than nonprofessionals? Unfortunately, studies that address these questions as they pertain to child custody are unavailable. Therefore, it is necessary to review studies concerning clinical judgment and prediction tasks as applied to other areas.

   Expertise and Level of Training. Studies have consistently demonstrated the lack of a direct relationship between the amount of training and experience and the degree of judgmental accuracy (e.g., Arnoff, 1954; Fisher & Fisher, 1950; Heaton, Smith, Lehman, & Vogt, 1978; Horowitz, 1962; Oskamp, 1967; Sarbin, Taft, & Bailey, 1960; Silverberg, 1976; Steiner, 1978; Watson, 1967). Moreover, Sarbin *et al.* (1960) reviewed ten studies that compared the judgmental accuracy of students with minimal training in psychology with that of students or graduate trainees with extended training. Only two of the ten studies demonstrated superiority of the more extensively trained judges. Of the eight remaining investigations, two demonstrated the superiority of judges with less training, and six found no difference as a function of amount of training. Arnoff (1954) found that the accuracy of judgment on a task in which the degree of disorganization of thinking in schizophrenics was rated on the basis of vocabulary responses decreased as a function of increasing experience. Judges were 60 undergraduates who had completed an abnormal psychology course, 60 graduate interns, and 60 professionals with four or more years experience. The undergraduates were the most reliable in their judgments. Oskamp (1967) reported that psychologists and trainees did not differ significantly in their ability to decide if a patient was psychiatrically or medically hospitalized on the basis of MMPI profiles. Watson (1967) and Fisher and Fisher (1950) found that the ability to make accurate judgments from figure drawings did not differ substantially between groups with various amounts of training and experience with the test. Horowitz (1962) reported that clinicians were unable to make stereotype predictions based on biographical data any more accurately than freshman and sophomore introductory psychology students. More recently, Heaton *et al.* (1978) asked ten judges with eight weeks to 18 years experience with neuropsychological test batteries to attempt to classify correctly patients either as faking believable deficits or as truly impaired. The relationship between total correct classification rates and amount of experience in neuropsychology was not significant.

Not only has it been demonstrated that a direct relationship between experience and training and accuracy of judgment is not to be expected, it has also been demonstrated that an inverse relationship may occur (Cline, 1955; McDermott, 1980; Schinka & Sines, 1974; Stricker, 1967). Stricker investigated the ability of clinical students and experienced psychologists to discriminate between 87 pairs of figure drawings from 37 normals and 50 psychiatric patients. In addition to comparisons made between students and clinicians, comparisons were also made with an actuarial formula. The judges were divided into three groups: 6 Ph.D.'s with a mean of 14 years experience, 10 third-year clinical students, and 12 first-year students. Results were expressed in terms of percentage of "hits," or correct classifications. The performance of both groups of students was superior to that of the experienced clinicians. Third-year students had a hit rate of 73%, first-year students 72%, and clinicians 66%. The data demonstrated that not only was the amount of experience and training not helpful in increasing judgmental accuracy between students and clinicians, but, again, experience appeared to *worsen* accuracy (students versus clinicians) or have no effect (first-year students versus third-year students).

Schinka and Sines (1974) investigated the relationship between seven indices of professional training and experience, and judgmental accuracy. Twenty-two graduate clinical psychology students with 1 to 6 years of training and three clinical faculty, two with five years postdoctoral experience and one with more than 30 years experience, served as judges. They were asked to rate subjects on a 5-point scale, from "indicative" to "contraindicative" for 125 items pertaining to diagnosis, prognosis, and personality dynamics and characteristics, after viewing a videotaped diagnostic intake interview completed by a psychologist with over 15 years of postdoctoral experience. There were two subjects, a female and a male, 18 and 24 years of age, respectively. The criteria consisted of a Q-sort completed by the patient's therapist at the end of treatment and an empirically established key based on 2-point codes from the MMPI (i.e., the two scales with the highest evaluations).

Only one of the seven indices, amount of graduate training, was shown to have a significant relationship to accuracy with the empirically established key. However, this relationship was a significant *inverse* relationship. The relationship between graduate training and the therapist's key was also *inverse*, although nonsignificant. In other words, increased training and experience did not enhance accuracy of clinical judgment with this sample using these criteria. In fact, it appeared that the more graduate training a judge had, the *worse* his or her judgments were.

McDermott (1980) investigated the diagnostic accuracy of three groups of school psychologists: students, interns, and experts with two or four years of experience. They were given complete case history information on three children; for each child they received 10 pieces of information, including educational and psychological test data, behavioral observations, and demographic and social history data. The results showed a decrement, rather than an increment, in levels of diagnostic congruence based on increasing amounts of training and experience.

It appears, then, that the accuracy of clinical judgments does not increase with greater amounts of experience or training and may in fact decrease. Furthermore, others have demonstrated that confidence in judgment is either not related to accuracy (Oskamp, 1965; Twaites, 1974) or is inversely related (Cohen, 1976; Fero, 1976; Holsopple & Phelan, 1954). These findings present serious questions about clinicians doing child custody evaluations who use clinical judgment as a primary assessment tool and point to their level of training to validate these judgments.

Expertise and Professional Training. Although one might expect clinical judgments made by experienced mental health professionals to be more reliable and more accurate than those of other professional groups or nonprofessionals, again the research does not support this expectation. Sarbin *et al.* (1960) reviewed 14 studies that compared psychologists with nonpsychologists. They cited three studies in which the nonpsychologists were more accurate, six in which there was equality, and five in which psychologists were superior. However, the authors suggested that the superiority of the psychologists in these five studies was confounded by biased tasks or criteria. In addition, in one study the superiority of psychologists was credited to the nonclinical psychologists rather than to the clinical psychologists, who receive more relevant training.

Goldberg (1959) explored the relationship between accuracy in diagnosis of organic brain damage using the Bender-Gestalt test and level of training, and the degree of confidence in clinical judgment and accuracy. The test protocols of 30 patients were obtained from the testing files of a Veterans Administration general medical and surgical hospital. One-half of the patients had had brain damage diagnosed on the basis of neurological examination, and one-half of the patients were without neurological problems. Sets of 10 were given to judges to diagnose as either organic or inorganic, and to rate the degree of confidence in their own diagnoses on a 5-point scale. Three groups of judges were used: (1) four psychology staff members, all Ph.D's with four to nine years experience with the Bender; (2) 10 psychology trainees with master's degrees and one to four years experience; and (3) eight hospital secretaries with no training or experience with Bender.

The results demonstrated a slight tendency for the trainees and secretaries to do better than the staff psychologists, although the differences were not significant. Only 12 of the 22 judges exceeded chance accuracy, and the highest proportion of these 12 were from the group of secretaries. Moreover, there was no significant relationship between confidence and accuracy, although the staff psychologists were least confident and the secretaries more confident in their selections.

Cline (1955) had five groups of judges make real-life predictions of the verbal and social behavior of nine male subjects observed in a filmed stress interview. The 316 judges included 109 undergraduates, 106 professionals (i.e., psychologists, psychiatrists, and trainees), 47 adult members of a church congregation, 43 nursing trainees, and 11 advanced engineering trainees. The results demonstrated that although the professionals were most accurate in their predictions, they did not do significantly better than the nursing trainees, who were the second most accurate. Also, there was a considerable amount of variation within groups, as evidenced by the fact that two housewives were the most accurate of all judges. Finally, with increasing lengths of professional experience, the accuracy of predicting the real-life social behavior diminished.

In an investigation using the DAP, Schaeffer (1964) found no significant differences between groups of psychologists, clinical trainees, and nonpsychologists (i.e., social worker, vocational counselor, and secretary) in their ability to rate level of adjustment and to discriminate between protocols of normals, neurotics, and psychotics. Hiler and Nesvig (1965) found psychologists and nonpsychologists (i.e., attendant, EEG technician, lab technician, electronics technician, photographer, secretary, and librarian) to discriminate equally well on a similar task.

Voelz (1970) asked groups of trained and untrained judges to predict events that had actually occurred on the basis of two factual case-study tests, each consisting of 27 three-choice items. The untrained judges were 34 biological science graduate students, 33 undergraduate students who had scored high on the American College Test, and 49 randomly selected undergraduate students. Thirty-nine clinical and counseling psychology graduate students served as the trained judges. The accuracy levels of the trained judges were not significantly greater than those of the untrained judges and again accuracy was not associated with amount of professional training. Finally, Steiner (1978) gave 32 Bender-Gestalt protocols, 16 by organic and 16 by nonorganic children, to 20 clinical psychologists, 20 doctoral students in clinical psychology, and 20 doctoral students in other fields of study. They were asked to classify the children as organic or as emotionally disturbed. The results showed no relationship between the type or amount of training, level of experience, and accuracy of clinical judgment.

The evidence has demonstrated that amount of training and experience in psychology is unrelated to accuracy of clinical judgment. Even when experienced clinicians were better than nonpsychologists, brief training was enough to increase the layman's accuracy up to par with that of the highly experienced professionals. (Goldberg, 1968; Oskamp, 1962).

In view of the impressive literature available on this topic, it would appear that Taft's (1955) 29-year-old summary still applies today:

> Physical scientists, and possibly other nonpsychologists, e.g., personnel workers, appear to be more capable of judging others accurately than are either psychology students or clinical psychologists. . . . There is also evidence that suggests that courses in psychology do not improve ability to judge others and there is considerable doubt whether professional psychologists show better ability to judge than do graduate students in psychology. (p. 12)

Clinical Judgment and the Child Custody Evaluation. Although studies that directly investigate clinical judgment in the context of a child custody evaluation are nonexistent, the implications of the research cited here are cogent and weighty. The exercise of subjective inference and clinical judgment appeared to permeate every facet of the evaluative process and in some cases is the only mode applied. In addition to psychological tests, most of which are highly dependent on clinical judgment, interviews and informal observations appear to be of equal importance to the mental health professionals who do these evaluations. Both procedures are wrought with clinical judgments. The professional observes the parents and children, separately, together, and in different combinations during the interview process (see, e.g., Jackson et al., 1980; Levy, 1978; Trombetta, 1982; Westman & Lord, 1980). Occasionally, informal parent–child interactions are noted in the waiting room, or a parent is given tasks to complete with a child (e.g., teach your child something) and is observed from behind a one-way vision mirror (e.g., Cogan et al., 1982; McDermott et al., 1978). How does the parent act with the child? Who is in control? How do the parents interact? What does the child do when the parent leaves the room? How open is the parent with the child? How flexible and adaptive is the parent in getting the child to cooperate? How well does each parent know his or her child? To whom does the child turn to get his or her coat or to go to the bathroom? How does the child adjust to the strange new environment? Is any negative behavior apparent? How does the parent respond to this behavior?

The answers to these questions and to many others are extremely important to the evaluator. These data are supposed to provide insight into parent–child relationships, underlying personality traits and characteristics, and ultimately the question of who will be the most suitable custodian for a given child or children. Unfortunately, the practice of using informal observations and/or unstructured interviews is riddled with problems inextricably linked to the use of clinical judgment. For example, depending on the theoretical bias of the observer or interviewer and on what factors he or she believes are important in determining the optimal living arrangements for a child, different questions will be asked, and different interpretations will be made about observed behaviors (see, e.g., Snyder, 1981). Operational definitions with clear, identifiable behavioral referents are rarely available, leaving ample room for each observer to interpret parent–child interactions subjectively. What does it mean for a parent to be "flexible" and "adaptive" or for a child to "cooperate"? How do we know when a child is "adjusting" to the new environment, and what exactly is "negative behavior"? Because there are no clear, objective criteria by which different observers can evaluate these behaviors, evaluation is left to clinical judgment.

Another major problem with the present system of interview and observation is what happens to the data once generated. Consistent with the trait and psychodynamic models of personality assessment, both verbal and nonverbal behavior are interpreted with respect to an underlying personality structure. Each behavior means something about, or is a sign of enduring genotypes that have caused the observable behavior (see Goldfried & Kent, 1972). Notwithstanding the research presented earlier in this chapter that seriously questioned the existence of enduring traits, establishing exactly what certain behaviors mean appears to vary from examiner to examiner, depending on theoretical persuasion and personal biases (see Chapter 2; also, e.g., Arkes, 1981; Ebbeson, 1981). Again, the judgment of the individual professional impinges on the observation and interpretation process. Not only will different assessors look for different signs, but each will elicit different behavior from which to interpret underlying structure through the selection of questions and tasks developed for parent–child observations. This lack of standardization means that different parents, children, and combinations thereof will be assessed on different behavior. The lack of standard objective stimuli to which each person involved can respond provides ample reason for questioning the appropriateness of making interindividual comparisons. Behaviors observed, questions asked, and interpretations proffered are all lacking in objectivity and standardization and essentially follow from what appears to be unsubstantiated personal bias and individual clinical judgment.

In sum, the usefulness of any assessment method that greatly depends on the custody evaluator's ability to render accurate clinical judgments is seriously questioned. Certainly the use of inference in any evaluation procedure is unavoidable. However, the pertinent issue here is to what extent the procedures are dependent on the evaluator's ability to judge accurately. Clinical judgment is probably the most widely used assessment device in child custody evaluations. Not only does it constitute the basis on which interviews and informal observations are evaluated, but it also permeates much of the interpretations of psychological tests, particularly projectives. The value of such judgments in a court of law seems to rest with a determination of expertise. Traditionally, expertise is associated with the amount of training and/or experience an individual has with respect to the area of interest. In this case, we are concerned with the mental health professional's ability to make accurate judgments about the personality characteristics of the individuals involved in a child custody dispute and to predict future behavior. A logical assumption is made that the more training and experience the professional has, especially in the area of child custody evaluations, the more accurate he or she will be, and therefore the more faith we can put in his or her judgments. Logical as it may seem, a substantial amount of research invalidates this assumption. Not only does judgmental accuracy fail to increase with increased training or experience, it may actually diminish. Furthermore, nonprofessionals may be as accurate, if not more, in their ability to judge personality and predict behavior.

The issues presented in this chapter, from the person–situation controversy to the questionable utility of traditional, trait-oriented assessment methods, serve as the foundation of and the impetus for the remainder of this volume. The research that has been presented makes several points clear: First, if mental health professionals are to provide the court with the most accurate predictions of future adjustment for a family undergoing a custody evaluation, then their assessments *must* address, as much as possible, the interaction of the person and environment. An assessment that focuses on person variables alone is doomed for failure. Second, most assessment strategies developed along traditional lines are inadequate to evaluate these interactions and therefore remain of questionable value for the purposes of prediction in this context. And third, every assessment method employed during the course of a custody evaluation must not only be consistent with the research on interactionism but must also be as independent of the clinician's subjective judgments as possible and must focus on increasing objectivity and standardization and consequently on reliability and validity. For these reasons, I have become dissatisfied with most current practice and will propose a new model of assessment in child custody disputes based on a behavioral construct system. Prior to discussing the model itself, the next chapter will delineate the important conceptual differences that exist between the behavioral and traditional models of assessment.

CHAPTER 4

A Comparison of Behavioral and Traditional Assessment

Several authors have written about the similarities and differences between behavioral and traditional approaches to assessment in personality (e.g., Goldfried & Kent, 1972; Hartmann, Roper, & Bradford, 1979; Mischel, 1968; Stuart, 1970). Goldfried and Kent (1972) delineated three major areas on which the two approaches can be compared: (1) personality assumptions; (2) selection of test items; and (3) interpretation of test responses. This chapter will address each of these areas in turn and will then compare and contrast the two approaches with respect to the levels of inference involved and the methodological assumptions inherent at each level.

CONCEPTION OF PERSONALITY

The major point of departure between traditional and behavioral assessment methodologies is the basic assumption of the former to explain human behavior in terms of an enduring and underlying personality structure and dynamics. As explained in Chapter 3, this personality structure is hypothesized to consist of a number of different predispositions that maintain a causal role in the manifestation of overt behavior and exert generalized effects over time and across diverse settings. Within this framework, person variables are believed to account for most of the variance in behavior. Furthermore, traditional conceptions of personality assessment either ignore the effects of environmental factors in the etiology and prediction of behavior or overlook their effects by explaining them as error. In contrast, behavioral assessment not only refuses to ignore the important impact that situational variability exerts on human behavior, but it also takes special care in identifying behavior–environment relationships. Primary emphasis is placed on the interaction between the person and his or her environment. It is believed that the causes of behavior, rather than resulting from unobservable genotypic entities within the individual, are to be found by identifying each individual's social learning history and the current environmental antecedent and consequent events that function to elicit and maintain the behavior. Within this framework, personality can be viewed as a conglomeration of learned behaviors or capabilities that are exhibited only if elicited and reinforced by certain situational factors (see Wallace, 1966, 1967).

Behavioral assessment, as a result of the essential role it attributes to environmental events in the causation of behavior, and because of the relative impermanence or diversity of events, neither expects nor requires behavioral consistency across settings. In fact, if the greatest portion of variance in behavior is found in the interaction of person–situation factors, then behavioral variability from one situation to another may be predicted. Mischel (1968) suggested that even slight stimulus variations may have a significant effect on behavior. In contrast, a trait conception of personality predicts temporal and cross-situational stability and invokes mediating constructs such as defense mechanisms, conflicts, and displacements to explain observed inconsistencies in overt behavior. A behavioral system has no need for such special constructs. "Inconsistencies" are not interpreted as such. They are considered to be response variations under the control of different environmental stimuli.

It is possible, however, to observe similar behaviors across dissimilar environments. Mischel (1968) pointed out that behavioral generality across a wide range of situations can be expected if the behavior has received similar consequences across the different environments. Furthermore, Nelson and Hayes (1979), drawing from both Mischel (1968, 1973) and Staats (1971, 1975), have suggested the following naturalistic circumstances in which stimulus conditions do remain similar and that therefore offer an explanation of why behavior can demonstrate good temporal consistency:

1. A person may live in a fairly stable environment with repetitive and discriminative eliciting and reinforcing stimuli.

2. Intermittent reinforcement with combined schedules character-
   izes most socialization, thus making behavior highly durable
   and resistant to extinction.
3. Learned cognitive encoding strategies may remain constant.
4. A person's gender and physical appearance remain fairly constant, serving as a discriminative stimulus for others.
5. Physiological needs (e.g., for food, drink, sleep) continue over
   time.
6. Current behavioral repertoires set limits on situations to which
   a person is exposed, on additional responses that a person is
   capable of making, and on rewards that are available to him or
   her. (p. 9)

The role of environmental stabilities of this kind will later be shown
to be important in determining the living arrangements for a child after
his or her parents divorce. For the present, however, it suffices to note
two characteristics of behavioral assessment: the lack of consistency expected in behavior and the significance attributed to environmental variables when consistency occurs. It is believed that the greater the similarity between two environments (or in the same environment over time)
in terms of stimulus conditions and the like, the more likely it is that
behaviors will exhibit stability.

SELECTION OF TEST ITEMS

The theoretical conception of personality espoused by a test devel-
oper is the foundation of his or her assessment method. As such, it has
major implications for the selection of test items, the manner in which
these items are conceptualized, and how a subject's responses are subsequently interpreted. A comparison of the test item selection of
behavioral and traditional assessment methods is understood most easily through the differentiation between the sample and sign approaches
first delineated by Goodenough (1949). Traditional tests such as the
Rorschach, TAT, and MMPI are based on the sign approach, which is
founded on the belief that all test responses are merely superficial signs
of some underlying personality disposition. The reponses themselves
are important only with respect to their association with the underlying
personality structure. For example, if a child frequently tells TAT stories
in which the protagonist accomplishes many feats in the face of great

adversity, the assessor may interpret these responses as signs of an underlying need for achievement. Similarly, a parent who reports seeing more monsters than humans in the Rorschach cards may be said to have a great deal of underlying hostility. As the number of these signs increases, so does the amount of that trait said to be possessed by the individual in question.

Behavioral assessment, however, uses a sample approach to item selection. In this approach, each item is a direct subset of the population of behaviors in which the assessor is interested. In other words, the test items are drawn from the population of criterion behaviors. For example, if one wished to assess how well an applicant would perform in a new job, let us say as a machine operator, the test used to predict actual job performance would include samples of the types of behavior or skills needed to perform the job adequately. The applicant might be tested in knowledge of the machine, reaction time, or any other relevant set of skills. Similarly, a secretary might be given a time-test on a typewriter or be required to demonstrate competence with a particular filing system. With respect to a behavior assessment measure, let us say of children's social skills, the test would include items directly assessing a representative sample of behaviors identified as important for children's social skills. The behaviors sampled might be drawn from such areas as conversation skills, responding to teasing, and entering an ongoing activity.

The critical element in the sample approach used in behavioral assessment is the maximization of congruence between the test responses and the criterion behaviors. As such, the concept of content validity is critically important in the development of behavioral assessment methodologies. This is in direct contrast with most traditional tests, especially the projectives, for which test responses are insignificant except as signs of what lies beneath the surface. Because the underlying personality dispositions are hypothesized to manifest themselves, either directly or indirectly, across time and place, the specific content of the items in these tests is irrelevant. If a child is dependent, it is expected that this dependency will manifest itself regardless of the situation (i.e., test or test item). In fact, projective test developers appear to make a special effort to disguise their content. This camouflage is thought to increase the probability that underlying personality characteristics will be revealed. However, because content validity lies at the heart of behavioral assessment, in this approach the direct sampling of a wide variety of situations is very important. The extent to which one can safely generalize from the testing situation and test performance to other nontest situations increases with the representativeness of the sample of test items.

Thus, behavioral assessment is a direct sampling method that attempts to measure a representative group of items drawn directly from the population of criterion behaviors to which the test is designed to predict. In contrast, traditional assessment is generally indirect, uses a sign approach, and involves a greater degree of inference and judgment on the part of the assessor.

INTERPRETATION OF TEST RESPONSES

The final important way in which traditional and behavioral assessments differ is in the interpretation of an individual's responses to the test items. Here again, the difference between the sign and sample approaches is relevant. Test responses generated from behavioral assessment devices are interpreted directly from the test to the criterion. As previously indicated, the test is a subset of the criterion and test interpretation is therefore direct. For example, an individual's responses to a set of analogue situations requiring the refusal of requests are said to be a direct measure of how this individual would respond in similar criterion situations. The test situation and the criterion situation are the same or very similar. Of course, it is assumed that the situations used are a representative sample of the population of situations requiring refusal responses.

When individual responses are interpreted as signs, as they are in most personality tests, a more indirect route is taken. As Wiggins (1973) has pointed out, whether the test is based on an empirical relationship (as in the MMPI) or on a more informal, intuitive approach (as in the projectives), test responses are interpreted as indirect, symbolic manifestations of some underlying characteristic(s). The predominance of color responses on the Rorschach, for example, is hypothesized to be a sign of emotionality; the drawing of large ears and eyes on the DAP is thought to be symbolic of suspiciousness or paranoia. In structured inventories, to the extent to which the present examinee responds similarly to those in the original sample, he or she is said to *have* the same personality characteristics as that original group of individuals. So although an empirical relationship is used initially, the end result, as with other traditional measures, is an interpretation based on an underlying personality structure.

LEVELS OF INFERENCE

In an often cited paper, Goldfried and Kent (1972) compared traditional and behavioral assessment by considering the three levels of inference that seem to characterize all personality assessment (see Figure 1). Each inference entails certain methodological assumptions that, if met, increase the reliability and validity of both the interpretation of the test responses (an inductive process) and the prediction of criterion behaviors from these test responses (a deductive process). At each level, the inferences become farther and farther removed from directly observable behavior (i.e., test validation). The first and fundamental inference identified is that the test responses observed are true responses (i.e., accurate observations of a special event or criterion behavior). This inference entails basic assumptions concerning the method being employed. The test responses observed are assumed to have been reliably observed and recorded and therefore to be unaffected by the method of measurement itself. However, Campbell and Fiske (1959) have demonstrated

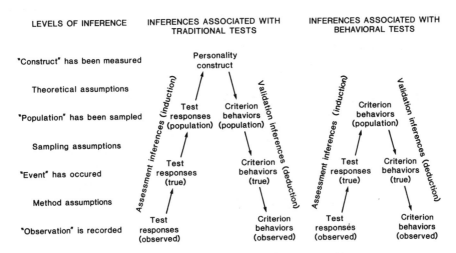

Figure 1. Levels of inference in traditional and behavioral tests. *Note.* From "Traditional versus behavioral personality assessment: A comparison of methodological and theoretical assumptions" by M. R. Goldfried and R. N. Kent, 1972, *Psychological Bulletin, 77,* p. 416.

that the method used to measure a given phenomenon can contribute considerably to the overall variance. They found, for instance, that the measurement of a particular phenomenon with the same method (e.g., self-report inventories) could lead to high correlations, but when two different measures of the same phenomenon (e.g., observations and self-report inventories) were compared the correlations were diminished considerably. The first level of inference, therefore, assumes that the variance accounted for is due to the phenomenon itself and not to the measuring device. This assumption applies not only to the inductive steps involved in the testing process but also to the deductive steps, establishing and measuring behaviors that will serve as the criteria. In the latter case, it is assumed that the observed criterion behaviors are an accurate measurement of the true criterion behaviors and are not affected by the measurement process itself (e.g., Q-sort or peer ratings).

The relationship between the test responses and the population of possible responses comprises the second level of inference. The test responses measured are supposed to be a subset of some larger population of responses. This inference entails certain assumptions with respect to the sampling procedures used in the development of the instrument. It is assumed that the responses given by the examinee in the testing situation are a representative sample that adequately reflects the larger hypothetical population of such test responses, and it is further assumed that if the test were to be extended, it would include other responses from this larger population. In addition, test responses are assumed to include the relevant aspects of the event or characteristic. Also, it is assumed that the criterion behaviors measured are representative of the population of such behaviors or characteristics and that other criterion behaviors within that larger population could easily be substituted for the ones presently being used.

Once one assumes that a representative sample of the population of responses has been measured, then inferences are made with respect to what personality construct these responses reflect. This is the third and final level of inference and is relevant only to traditional personality testing. This level of inference entails theoretical assumptions that vary from theory to theory but that nonetheless include inferences for both the inductive and deductive processes. First, there are the inductive inferences of test interpretation that generate the unobservable personality constructs from the test responses. Second, there are the deductive inferences of the validation process that result in the selection of criterion events in which the personality construct is hypothesized to be reflected. Therefore, the third level of inference entails theoretical assumptions that relate the construct to both the population of test responses and the population of criterion behaviors. It has been pointed out, however, that the rules for translating these test responses into an individual's position on some trait dimension are not always precise (Wiggins, 1973). Not only is it difficult to specify exactly which attributes are being attended to in the measurement process, but the linguistic transformation from the test responses to the unobservable construct typically requires the examiner to interpret these observed attributes so that he or she may categorize them as traits. Unfortunately, the interpretation involves the judgment of the human observer, who is notoriously biased and prone to err (see Chapter 3). In contrast, behavioral assessment is primarily concerned with what Wiggins (1973) refers to as "performance recording," in which the attributes of interest are not traits but physicalistic properties of the stimuli and responses (e.g., amplitude, frequency, and duration). These properties, which can be reliably recorded by either mechanical or human means, involve a minimum of human judgment in the translation process. Operational definitions with clear and definable behavioral referents are used to translate the properties into stimulus conditions and response patterns.

In order to demonstrate how these viewpoints are applied in practice, a specific behavior will be traced through the levels of inference characteristic of both traditional and behavioral assessment. For convenience, the assessment and prediction of an individual's assertive behavior with persons in a position of authority will be described.

First, traditional personality tests assume that the examinee's test responses are only minimally affected by the measurement process, if at all. These responses, which might include themes of deference on the TAT, monsters on the Rorschach, and a high elevation on the social introversion scale of the MMPI, are assumed to be true responses. Second, these observed events are considered to be a representative sample of the larger pool of possible responses on these particular tests and to be indicative of some underlying personality characteristic that causes the examinee to behave in a specific manner in response to authority figures. These underlying personality characteristics will vary from theory to theory and may include such constructs as an unresolved oedipal conflict, a need for deference, basic insecurity, or a predominance of one's child (àla TA theory).

Having identified these constructs at the third level of inference, the deductive validation process is begun. The theoretician hypothesizes that the examinee's trait or other underlying characteristics will be manifested in some specific manner in the population of criterion situations. How the characteristics will be exhibited and in which situations may vary depending on the theory generating the constructs. For instance, one theory may expect our examinee to express himself or herself directly to an authority figure as a result of an underlying trait of aggression, whereas another theory might expect the examinee to be passive and submissive with authority figures despite the underlying aggression (in the latter case, the examinee would be defending against these underlying aggressive impulses). In this particular example, the criterion situations would probably include those in which the examinee makes contact with an authority figure and an assertive response is appropriate.

Finally, the examinee's behavior is measured in a sample of such situations derived from the hypothetical population of situations, and specific behavioral responses that are thought to be indicative of assertiveness (e.g., eye contact, verbal responses) are recorded using specific measuring devices (e.g., ratings by judges, direct observations).

Despite the similarity of methodological assumptions, the prediction of specific behavior with a behavioral assessment device is considerably different from that done with a traditional device. In a behavioral test, the examinee would be asked to respond to a set of situations requiring an assertive response to authority figures. These situations could be presented in a number of different ways, including actual situations, role-played analogues, or paper-and-pencil inventories. As in traditional tests, it is assumed that the observed responses are only minimally affected by the measurement process and that they are therefore true responses. Additionally, the responses given to the test items are assumed to constitute an adequate and representative sampling of the relevant aspects of the population of assertive responses to authority figures. If the test were extended, or if current test items were replaced with other items from the population, it is assumed that there would still be a representative sample.

In contrast to traditional assessment, however, and because those situations sampled are derived directly from the population of criterion behaviors, behavioral assessment has no reason to invoke underlying personality constructs. Therefore, the two processes of inference at the third level are avoided. Furthermore, Goldfried and Kent (1972) explain that the behaviors sampled are derived directly and established empirically through the sampling of the criterion situations (in this instance, the situations are those in which an assertive response is called for in the presence of an authority figure such as a parent, employer, or teacher).

FINAL REMARKS

The major point being advanced here is that behavioral assessment attempts to maximize the similarity between test response and criterion behavior. As such, in comparison with traditional assessment, the amount of inference required is substantially diminished, thereby reducing the number of assumptions that underlie behavioral assessment and making it more comprehensible and more amenable to empirical testing than is traditional personality assessment.

Goldfried (1977) explains that, although there is indirect evidence of the greater predictive accuracy of behavioral tests (Goldfried & Kent, 1972), "the acceptance of a behaviorally oriented approach to assessment by clinical psychology in general is not likely to occur until it can be shown that it does a better job than the available techniques" (p. 18). Despite the relative lack of empirical data that presently supports the greater predictive accuracy of behavioral assessment methodologies, there appears to be considerable optimism with respect to the potential inherent in this approach. For example, Goldfried and Kent (1972) concluded their important paper with the following hopeful comments:

> The assessment of personality by means of behavioral tests . . . is more consistent with the findings that human functioning is due to both the individual's behavioral repertoire and the demands of the specific stimulus situation. Further, relatively fewer assumptions are associated with this approach to test construction, and those that are involved can more readily be subjected to direct experimental investigation. By allowing a more systematic elimination of erroneous inferences when validity coefficients are unsatisfactory, the behavioral approach to personality assessment would appear to have greater potential for the development of procedures that may enhance our ability to predict human behavior. (p. 419)

This optimism was echoed by Wiggins (1973) when he compared the predictive strategies of tests involving an R–R analysis (e.g., MMPI) with the traditional functional S–R analysis (best characterized by Kanfer and Saslow's (1969) "behavioral diagnosis"). He explains that whereas instruments such as the MMPI, which are based on the empirical relationships between test responses and signficant nontest behavior, provide predictions of "typical" behavior under a variety of criterion environments, a functional analysis, which involves the empirical relationship between specific environmental conditions and samples of criterion response classes, predicts an individual's response capabilities under *specific* criterion environments. Wiggins (1973) believes that a functional analysis has the advantage because it can specify which aspects of the environment are important in making predictions and how to adjust these predictions with environmental variability. As indicated earlier, other tests, including the MMPI, are able neither to identify the salient aspects of the environment nor to tell us how an individual will behave in a given set of circumstances.

However, Wiggins (1973) went on to say that his belief in the greater predictive ability of functional analyses is based on conviction rather than on fact. Functional analysis in behavioral assessment has not been used for prediction but rather for identifying stimulus–response relationships in the present in order to develop treatment programs for the alleviation of human suffering. Consequently, there have been few data generated to permit the evaluation of behavioral assessment's predictive potential in terms of such conventional indices as standard error of prediction, proportion of the variance accounted for, and number of correct decisions.

Other authors have written optimistically about behavioral assessment. For example, Anastasi (1976), in the fourth edition of her text on psychological testing, had the following to say about the behavioral approach to personality assessment:

> Social-learning theory and behavior-analytic approaches are undoubtedly exerting a salutary influence on personality assessment as a whole. Their focus on direct sampling of the behavior of interest, their exposure of circular reasoning involved in hypostatizing traits as stable, underlying causal entities, and their rejection of remote and untestable psychoanalytic (or "psychodynamic") explanations of behavior are helping to clear away some psychometric cobwebs. (pp. 525–526)

And Mischel (1968) wrote.

> Behavior assessments *do not* label the individual with generalized trait terms and stereotypes, sort him into diagnostic or type categories, pinpoint his average position on average or modal dimensions, or guess about his private reasons and motives. Instead, the focus is on sampling the individual's relevant cognitions and behaviors. In this sense, behavioral assessment involves an exploration of the unique or idiographic aspects of the single case, per-

haps to a greater extent than any other approach. Social behavior theory rec-
ognizes the individuality of each person and of each unique situation. This is
a curious feature when one considers the "mechanistic S–R" stereotype not
infrequently attached by critics to behavioral analysis. (p. 190)

Although it has yet to be empirically demonstrated that behavioral
assessment is the panacea of personality measurement, it does appear
that assessment methodologies based on the principles of cognitive social learning possess a greater potential for predictive accuracy than do
traditional methodologies. The value of this approach for providing answers to questions generated during a child custody dispute can be
tested empirically, as can the comparative utility of traditional and
behavioral approaches. Traditional approaches appear to have had ample time and opportunity to develop reliable and valid methods of assessment and, in general, have not fared well. Thus, it is worth considering the possibility that the assessment of persons involved in a child
custody dispute may best be approached from a behavioral perspective.

PART II

A BEHAVIORAL MODEL

WHAT TO ASSESS

CHAPTER 5

Determining the Postdivorce Living Arrangements for Children

A BEHAVIORAL MODEL

Within a behavioral model, the concept of the best interests of the child maintains its position of importance. It is suggested that a child's interests are best served if he or she is placed in an environment in which it is most likely that his or her interaction with it will result in the acquisition and maintenance of patterns of behavior that hold the greatest promise for good future adjustment. The environment would include people, places, and material objects; adjustment would include physical, psychological, and intellectual factors. Although this description is somewhat broad, it advances the position that a child's environment shapes and develops his or her thoughts, feelings, and actions and that the living arrangement which is most likely to result in the greatest number of positive outcomes for a child and in the least number of negative ones is the arrangement that should be selected. The search for this environment seems to suggest five possible areas of assessment:

1. the capacity of all potential caretakers to parent the child (i.e., parental competence)
2. the child's behavioral repertoire in relation to the environment
3. the prospective caretaker as a model for the child (i.e., observational learning)
4. the potential postdivorce environments (i.e., a functional analysis of the criterion environment)
5. the self-ratings and prediction of potential caretakers and children

Each of the areas listed is directly related to identifying the most appropriate type of placement for a given child and therefore addresses the question: What is to be measured in the child custody evaluation and why? Two of these five areas will be discussed in this chapter.

PARENTAL COMPETENCE

The most important consideration when making the decision to place a child, whether it be in regard to foster care, adoption, or, in this case, divorce, is the suitability of the individuals petitioning for custody. How good would *this* person be as the primary caretaker for *this* child? Although many factors enter into the answering of this question, the critical factor is the capacity of the individual to perform the duties and responsibilities inherent in the job of caretaker–parent. In other words, does he or she possess parental competence? If one person demonstrates the capacity to be more effective as a parent than another person, one of several significant pieces of data has been obtained that can then be used to make the most efficacious decision concerning the optimal living arrangements for a child after parental divorce.

Consistent with a behavioral conception of human functioning, parental competence is considered to be a function of an individual's previous learning history and the present situation rather than of some underlying predisposition. The prototype for this notion involves what Wallace (1966, 1967) referred to as "response capabilities." According to this position, individuals are not predisposed to respond in certain ways but instead learn certain response capabilities or skills that can then be elicited by the stimulus cues of the given situation. A person is either capable or incapable of making certain responses in specific stimulus situations. If a person does not exhibit a particular behavior, Wallace posits that this is the result of either a learning deficit or of a response inhibition. He makes a distinction between response capability and response performance, underscoring the importance of the stimulus situation in the elicitation of behavior. In order for a specific response or pattern of responses to be performed, not only is it necessary for the person to have learned that response pattern (i.e., be capable of responding), but he or she must also be in contact with the stimulus situation (i.e., environment) that will provide the cues that elicit that response. In a sense, a person may learn a response but never be presented with the appropriate cues for making that response. The emphasis in this conception of human functioning is on the interaction between the person (i.e., his or her learning history) and the current (or prospective) environment.

Within this framework, then, parenting would be construed as a group of learned capabilities. Either a person is capable or incapable of certain responses in specific life situations that are identified as parenting situations. The significance of this viewpoint in determining child custody placements is enormous. Does a given individual have the learned capabilities within his or her behavioral repertoire that are adjudged to be important and possibly necessary in making an effective caretaker–parent? Given these capabilities, will the individual use them, and, if so, when or in what circumstances? Finally, what are the response capabilities needed for becoming a competent parent, and who decides the answer to this question? Goldfried and D'Zurilla's (1969) behavioral–analytic model for assessing competence greatly assists in answering these questions.

The Behavioral-Analytic Model of Assessing Parental Competence

What constitutes parental competence? The answer to this question will also guide us in answering the more general question, what is to be measured? Is a parent demonstrating competence with the knowledge of a child's shoe size, of how long it has been since the last dentist appointment, or of the immunization shots received? Is competence defined as knowing likes and dislikes—that hamburgers are terrible without mustard and that the Philadelphia Eagles are the greatest? What about being able to respond consistently to undesirable behavior with discipline or being able to attend to and praise desirable behavior? All of these factors probably have something to do with parental competence, depending on how the term is defined. Goldfried and D'Zurilla (1969) have developed a model for assessing competence that defines competence in relation to Wallace's abilities conception of personality. Consequently, they continue the avoidance of trait explanations of behavior and define competence operationally, by the manner in which an individual interacts with the environment. Generally, they define competence as effective functioning within a person's own environment. More specifically, they suggest that it is "the effectiveness or adequacy with which an individual is capable of responding to the various problematic situations which confront him" (p. 161).

The basic unit of their behavioral definition of competence is a person's "effective response" to a variety of specific life situations. In order for a response or pattern of responses to be considered effective in dealing with a problematic situation, it must "alter that situation so that it is no longer problematical, and at the same time produces a maximum of other positive consequences and a minimum of negative ones" (p. 158). A "problematic situation" is one that requires a solution to a problem or some decision for appropriate action. Effective responding can occur in any one or combination of the three response systems—verbal-cognitive, physiological, and overt-behavioral—and a person's ability to respond effectively depends heavily on his or her previous learning history.

The competent parent, therefore, can be identified as a person who is capable of responding effectively to specific parenting situations that are problematic in nature and who does so by maximizing the positive consequences and minimizing the negative ones. This definition makes it possible for many people to be competent parents, that is, to make effective responses to problematic parenting situations. Goldfried and D'Zurilla made it clear that any given situation can have more than one effective response. However, they went on to explain that effectiveness can be thought of as a continuum on which responses are placed. Any situation can produce responses that range from extreme ineffectiveness to superior effectiveness. They suggest that

> maladaptive behavior may be viewed as more or less "ineffective behavior," because the individual is not capable of resolving the problematic nature of the situation, and/or because his behavior results in negative consequences that create additional problematic situations. (p. 161)

Figure 2 graphically represents the continuum of responses that can be given to a problematic situation (Sp).

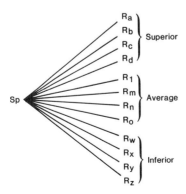

Figure 2. Diagrammatic conception of a problematic situation with varying levels of effective responses. *Note.* From "A behavioral-analytic method for assessing competence" by M. R. Goldfried and T. J. D'Zurilla. In *Current Topics in Clinical and Community Psychology,* Vol. 1 (p. 161) edited by C. D. Spielberger, 1969, New York: Academic Press.

From this diagram it can be seen that, although many responses can be effective in resolving the problematic situation, some are identified as being much better than others. Hypothetically, if a measuring device could be developed that assessed a person's ability to respond effectively to a wide variety of problematic parenting situations, and if that person consistently responded within the inferior range, this would be a valuable piece of information for use in determining the ultimate living arrangements for a child. Certainly, any custody decision that rested solely on this one area of assessment would be inadequate. Although such an assessment is critical to the overall objective in that it gives some indication of the person's capabilities as a parent, no information directly related to this person's interaction with the target child is provided. The assessment of this important area will be considered below.

In sum, the behavioral-analytic model for assessing parental competence would help to identify the response capabilities of each potential caretaker, to assist in the overall search for the most effective environment for the child, and to identify the specific areas in which each individual is either competent or incompetent. Such information provides the assessor with the opportunity to plan possible future interventions to increase competence and diminish incompetence.

The development of a measure within a behavioral-analytic framework that yields a valid assessment of competence requires a procedure that emphasizes the importance of person–situation interactions and obtains a representative sample of situations that are a subset of the population of situations relevant to the target area of competence. Such an approach would be consistent with the literature on interactionism, the functional analysis of behavior, and the sample approach characteristic of all behavioral assessment measures.

Goldfried and D'Zurilla (1969) proposed using the behavior–environment interactions identified through a criterion analysis as the foundation of the measuring instrument. In other words, the test items of the measurement device would be a direct reflection of the criterion environment or of the environment to which one would like to predict from performance on the instrument. They cite Wing (1968), who made the following observation which Goldfried and D'Zurilla believe comes closest to the philosophy of their behavioral-analytic approach to assessment.

> An important key to improving the predictive efficiency, or empirical validity, of many personality measures lies in developing uniformity between the

measurement environment and the criterion environment. The hypothesis
we put forth here is that the greater the similarity between criterion environment and measurement environment, the greater are the chances of
achieving high empirical validity. (p. 341)

There are five steps in the development of the assessment measure,
of which the first three constitute the criterion analysis. They are (1)
situational analysis (2) response enumeration (3) response evaluation (4)
development of the measuring instrument format and (5) evaluation of
the measure. Each of the first three steps, the criterion analysis, will be
considered first as a general procedure and then as it pertains to the area
of parental competence.

The first step of the behavioral-analytic model, the "situational analysis," requires a comprehensive survey of the situations relevant to the
area under study. If competence is to be assessed, the gathering of all
kinds of potential problematic situations must be attempted. The situations must be specific and operationally defined. According to Goldfried
and D'Zurilla (1969), "The situational analysis that is appropriate to our
method of assessment must involve those specific, but meaningful situations with which most individuals in the particular environment must
cope effectively in order to be considered 'competent'"(p. 164). What are
the specific problematic situations with which a parent must cope effectively if he or she is to be considered competent? The "particular environment" that is referred to may vary depending on the region of the
country, city, or social class for which the assessment is being developed, since different kinds of problematic situations may be encountered in each. The age of the children may also have to be systematically
taken into account. Regardless of the parameters characteristic of the
chosen environment, a wide range of situations must be collected.

The primary reason for completing a situational analysis in the area
of parental competence is to gather a large, representative sample of
concrete problematic situations which are likely to confront most parents. As such, it would seem that there are several valuable sources for
obtaining situations. They can be divided easily into two groups: parents, and relevant others, such as teachers, social workers, judges, child
and family therapists, and doctors.

There are a number of possible procedures for obtaining these situations, thereby increasing the likelihood of developing a content-valid instrument. These include direct observations in the natural environment
where a detailed account of the problematic situations is taken, inter-

views with those persons who are most likely to observe the situations in progress or who have had direct or indirect experience with them in the past, or self-monitoring by those who actually experience the problematic situation when they occur. From the responses to these situations it should be possible to differentiate those potential caretakers who are most effective in coping with the parental environment from those who are less so.

In the original article, Goldfried and D'Zurilla (1969) illustrated the application of each step of the criterion analysis in relation to a research project designed to assess the effective behavior of college freshmen. In that example, the subjects were given a blank record form upon which to record problematic situations, a set of instructions of what was required, and examples of three problematic situations to function as a model for comparison. Furthermore, they were given a list of 14 different areas in which problematic situations could occur in their lives as freshmen in college. This list was used to sensitize the subjects to those areas in which the investigators were interested. A similar format could be used with a random sample of parents in a given city or community.

A list of situational areas to which the parents could be sensitized includes: discipline, physical care, morals, peer relations, sexuality, academics and school behavior, adult–child relations, personal appearance and hygiene, sibling relations, alcohol and drugs, and money management.

A large number of problematic situations should result from this procedure, with some from each of the areas listed. Once these situations have been assembled, situations identified as "redundant, trivial, or improbable" are dropped from the pool, and the remainder are refined and rewritten into a more suitable form. This process helps to shape situations which were originally too vague, too general, too short with not enough information, or too long with irrelevant details. This phase of the situational analysis is designed to discard unnecessary information and mold the important data with sufficient detail and specificity so that the problematic situation could apply to any person in a similar environment. In other words, the stimulus conditions have to be presented in such a way that future respondents have enough information to make an appropriate response, but not so much information (i.e., trivial details) that the situation then becomes unfamiliar.

The final phase of this component of the criterion analysis continues the shaping process through which the test situation will emerge. Although a sample of problematic situations is available, the frequency with which these situations are encountered by parents in general is unknown. It is possible that these situations are not a representative sample of the population of situations experienced by a parent. The present information simply tells us that at least one parent from the original sample of parents has encountered the problem. If only one or two parents in a relatively large sample has had to respond to such a situation, then it is not consistent with the goal of collecting a large, representative sample of specific, meaningful problematic situations which are likely to confront *most* parents.

Consequently, in order to assess the representativeness of the obtained situations for most parents in a similar environment, a survey would be conducted on a new sample of parents, who would be asked to indicate which of the situations or similar situations they had personally encountered and how often. *Similar* has been defined as differing "only by unimportant details which did not alter its basic problematic aspects" (Goldfried & D'Zurilla, 1969, p. 174). For example, refusing to sweep the floor rather than refusing to take out the garbage are similar.

The results of this survey would then be analyzed and a cutoff applied for deciding whether a given problematic situation is to be retained or eliminated. Goldfried and D'Zurilla included only those situations which were found to occur one or more times for at least 50% of the sample surveyed, therefore considering these situations to have a "high likelihood" of occurrence in the target population. The shaping and refinement process during the situational analysis resulted in retaining 30% of the original sample as useful problematic situations.

The second step of the criterion analysis is "response enumeration," which constitutes a multiphase response sampling procedure with three stated goals. First, the process helps insure that only those items which can potentially discriminate between individuals with different levels of effectiveness be retained. Second, the problematic items which continue to be identified as ambiguous and vague will be clarified and further defined. Finally, after all the ambiguities are removed, and the exceptionally easy or difficult nondiscriminating items are withdrawn, the situations are presented to a group of target individuals and a sample of potential responses is obtained for each situation. These responses will be important in the last step of the criterion analysis in which criterion judgments will be made of each response's individual effectiveness.

In order to evaluate how well each situation will discriminate, two levels of assessment can be used. First, a group of parents or adults would be asked to respond to a subsample of the total pool of problematic situations generated by the situational analysis. They would be asked to give every possible reaction they could imagine themselves giving. Two purposes would be served by this initial screening; those items which only elicited a few different responses could be immediately dropped as nondiscriminating, and those items which continued to be ambiguous could be further clarified, thereby increasing the likelihood of a variation in future responses.

The second screening would be more detailed, would be completed on a new sample of parents, and would informally evaluate the range of response effectiveness to each situation, thus continuing the assessment of the potential discriminability of each item. In the college freshmen study (Goldfried & D'Zurilla, 1969), 280 freshmen males were administered the questionnaire and approximately 20 responses were generated for each situation. Following an elaborate instruction format with detailed examples, the subjects were asked to give a detailed account of their likely reactions to each of the situations. Once the responses were gathered, the effectiveness of each was judged informally (i.e., not by the criterion judges to be used in the response evaluation phase) by two independent judges on a 7-point scale. The criteria used were derived directly from the definition of *effectiveness*. To obtain a superior rating (6 or 7), the response would have to resolve the problematic situation with the maximum of positive consequences and the minimum of negative ones. It was critical that each situation generate a full range of responses, from inferior to extremely effective. Without this full range, the item would probably be ineffective in discriminating between persons at different levels of effectiveness. Consequently, a rule of thumb was used by Goldfried and D'Zurilla which eliminated any item which did not have at least 10% of its responses on the effective end of the continuum and 10% on the ineffective end. This did away with items that could be considered too easy or too difficult.

Following the second screening and further modifications to enhance clarity, the final version of the instrument would be administered to yet another sample of parents, but this time their responses would be considered typical in that they could be expected from others in future administrations of the instrument. Therefore, these responses would be subject to the evaluation of significant others (i.e., criterion judges) for their level of effectiveness.

Response evaluation is the final step of the criterion analysis and is probably the most important because in essence it defines what is effective and what is not. The future responses of persons administered this measure will be identified as competent or incompetent on the basis of the criterion judgments established by this response evaluation procedure. The relative effectiveness or ineffectiveness of each potential response to each problematic situation in terms of its likely positive and negative effects will be determined by a group of significant others. Considering the importance of these judgments, the definition and selection of the significant others is critical. These influential individuals have been defined by Goldfried and D'Zurilla (1969) as those who:

> a. have frequent contact with the people to whom the assessment technique will be applied;
> b. have an important role in labeling or judging behavior as effective or ineffective in the environment; and
> c. whose opinions are likely to be respected by others, particularly those toward whom the assessment will be directed. (p. 166)

"As experts in their particular environment, it is then their task to supply judgment as to which specific behaviors are effective, and to what degree" (p. 166). The most relevant standards and guidelines for a particular environment need not necessarily be explicit. In fact, the implicit expectations of the significant influential people in a particular environment may play a more significant role in defining and governing behavior. Typically, they are the people who serve society by evaluating conformity to some set of societal standards and expectations.

A list of potential judges in the area of parental competence would include psychologists, psychiatrists, social workers, teachers, juvenile and domestic relations court judges, and child development specialists. Each group of professionals has been trained within the institutions of our society to evaluate parental effectiveness either directly or indirectly, and all currently make judgments as a part of their job in the natural environment. Their combined judgments would be used as a criterion for this instrument.

The judges are provided with a set of detailed instructions which include not only an explanation of the project and a definition of the concepts involved (e.g., competence, effective response) but also an explanation of the scale they are to use in making their judgments. Each situation is presented to the judge with a full range of effective responses, but if for some reason they do not rate any of the responses on either extreme end of the scale, they are encouraged to add additional responses of their own reflecting these extremes.

The final phase requires that a concensus be made between the various judgments to determine whether a particular response is more or less effective. In this regard, Goldfried and D'Zurilla (1969) categorized the various responses into three general levels of effectiveness. The middle range of responses, 3, 4, or 5, was considered average effectiveness, the responses at the lower end (1 and 2) were inferior, and ratings of 6 and 7 were identified as superior. Then, depending on the number of times a given response was placed in one of these three categories, it was identified as an inferior, average, or superior way of coping with the problematic situation. If wide disagreement was found between the judges concerning the effectiveness of any given response, that problematic situation would be eliminated. The authors point out that the elimination of such an item in the behavioral-analytic approach should reduce error variance and increase reliability and validity.

The criterion analysis is completed once the response evaluation phase is finished. What remains is a representative sample of problematic situations with which most parents would have to cope effectively to be considered competent in their particular environment. In addition, each situation carries with it a sample of effective responses in each of the three ranges, inferior, average, and superior. These responses can then serve as the criterion with which all responses from subsequent administrations of the instrument can be compared.

Final Remarks

As part of a child custody evaluation, this instrument should be able to tell which person is more competent in which areas. It may well be that a prospective caretaker demonstrates the capacity to make superior effective responses in one area and only average responses in another. The implications of these findings are enormous and especially important when combined with the rest of the evaluation. This portion of the overall evaluation will permit the identification of an individual's strengths and weaknesses, which can subsequently be evaluated with respect to a particular child. Does the child's environment present other opportunities for obtaining the appropriate experience and learning in the area in which the prospective custodian is deficient? If not, can the child be given the opportunity for such instruction or the parent be taught the requisite skills? If a parent demonstrates enormous capacity in most areas of parenting as defined by this instrument but is somewhat deficient in the area of discipline, what are the possibilities for child management classes? Not only could this instrument be used to assess present abilities, but also it could provide the basis for planning an intervention strategy to assist in postdetermination adjustment either on a volunteer basis or as a condition for a specific living arrangement.

Despite the fact that the development of this instrument would appear to have addressed sufficiently the issue of content validity, several questions remain. Although we can begin to answer the question concerning what is to be measured in the child custody evaluation, several other questions arise. *How* do we measure? What is the specific format of the measuring device? Do we use naturalistic observations, an analogue method, or a behavioral interview? Given a procedure for completing the measurements, how reliable is it? Assuming no significant changes, will its administration over time or on several different occasions yield similar findings? Will two different independent examiners obtain the same results using the same method? These are important questions with respect to the psychometric properties of the measuring device.

There are also important validity issues. Does the instrument really measure what it purports to measure, that is, does it have construct validity? If so, it should be able to differentiate groups of people identified on some independent variable as competent or incompetent. For example, the measure should be able to identify parents who have been denied custody of their children for reasons such as abuse, neglect, or abandonment and differentiate them from so-called model parents or those identified by the community as such. If this cannot be accomplished, then the measure does not adequately measure parental competence or effectiveness (or the criterion groups are not validly selected). Similarly, this procedure should be sensitive to changes following an intervention program designed to increase a person's skills or capabilities in a particular area. For example, if an initial assessment reveals skill deficits in a prospective caretaker's ability to cope effectively with discipline, then the successful completion of an intervention program designed to increase effective discipline should be reflected by an improvement in that area on a postintervention adminstration of that measure. At the same time, however, improved effectiveness ratings in other areas, such as sexuality or peer relationships, would not necessarily be expected. The degree of change to expect in other areas would depend on the extent to which the two areas overlapped with respect to their stimulus characteristics. The more similar the stimulus cues, the more one would expect changes in responses in one area of intervention to generalize to other areas. These expectations are consistent with the principles of stimulus generalization and discrimination, reemphasizing the importance of the person–situation interaction.

The question of reliability and validity raised in this section can be answered only through an extensive research project. The selection of a measurement procedure will be considered in two later chapters which will describe a few of the available behavioral assessment methods along with their advantages and disadvantages, and potential utility in determining the postdivorce living arrangements of children. In the meantime, however, the question of what should be measured has only been partially answered. Up until this point, consideration has been given to the prospective caretaker and the capacities he or she may have acquired that identify him or her as capable of effective responding in problematic parenting situations. Although this bit of data is vitally important, it is not sufficient to make the most efficacious decision. In the next section, the child and his or her interaction with the surrounding environment will be addressed.

A FUNCTIONAL ANALYSIS OF BEHAVIOR: THE CHILD

Our primary concern remains with the selection of one living arrangement from among the available alternatives which has the greatest probability of providing the child with the best possible living situation. Ideally this environment will have the necessary conditions for the child to acquire and maintain a behavioral repertoire which will result in the greatest number of positive outcomes and the least number of negative ones. These behaviors would be effective in their relationship to the environment either immediately or in the near future. *Effective* as defined previously refers to the positive consequences which follow any given response or behavior. Concurrently, this environment would provide the necessary conditions for the inhibition or redirection of maladaptive or noneffective responding, that is, undesirable, inappropriate, and/or socially unacceptable behaviors. To proceed in this direction, a comprehensive assessment of each child's behavioral repertoire must be completed. The focus of this assessment would be twofold: the identification of specific behaviors or patterns of behavior deemed appropriate or inappropriate, and the determination of how each of these behaviors may have been acquired and is presently maintained, with an emphasis on the child's previous learning history and the current environmental contingencies. The prototype for this component of the behavioral assessment model being advanced here is Kanfer and Saslow's (1969) "behavioral diagnosis."

The S-O-R-K-C Model

The functional analysis of behavior stresses the importance of five factors which play an important role in the acquisition, maintenance, and modification of behavior. These factors are represented by the letters S-O-R-K-C, which are defined as follows:

1. *Stimulus events (S)*. These are events antecedent to the behavior of interest and can include physical stimuli, such as a sink full of dishes, an enclosed space, or a monthly bill; social stimuli, such as praise or verbal "putdowns"; or internal or interoceptive stimuli, such as "butterflies" in the stomach or rapid heartbeat. These stimuli set the occasion for or elicit certain behavior responses.

2. *Organismic variables (O)*. These include the biological condition of the organism, involving such factors as physical handicaps, hormonal imbalances, or drug-induced states. All of these variables must be assessed because they might affect an individual's ability to acquire, maintain, or modify behavior.

3. *Responses (R)*. These can occur within one or more of the following modes: verbal-cognitive, physiological, or motoric-behavioral. These response systems include behaviors which are either directly observable or reliably reported and can be overt, such as verbal behavior and motor responses, or covert, such as thoughts, feelings, and internal physiological reactions.

4. *Contingency relationships (K)*. This component refers to the schedule of consequences for a given response. For instance, what is the relationship between a child's picking up his or her toys and parental attention (i.e., reinforcement)? This relationship or schedule of reinforcement, can be *continuous*, occuring each time the child picks up the toys, or *intermittent*, occurring either after a certain number of similar responses of a specific amount of time (e.g., at the end of each day). Also, the amount of time between parental praise and the number of times the child has to respond before he or she is praised can remain constant (*fixed*) or be continuously changing (*variable*). In other words, the child may be praised only at the end of each day (*fixed interval*) or following every third response (*fixed ratio*). Or, the consequences will oc-

cur after different intervals of time (*variable interval*) or different numbers of response (*variable ratio*). The contingency relationship specifies the environmental conditions under which a behavior is likely to be reinforced.

5. *Consequences (C).* These are events which follow the behavior. They can be positive or negative, environmental or organismic. When Samuel is told that he cannot eat an entire pint of ice cream, he falls on the floor, kicks his feet and screams, "I want it, I want it, I want it!!" The consequence is that his father sends him to his room. Similarly, when René thanks her mother for fixing her toy truck, she gets a smile and a hug.

The functional analysis of behavior, which is defined by the S-O-R-K-C model, permits the behavioral assessor to describe the relationship between the particular behaviors under investigation and the environment in which they occur. This method of analysis seeks to discover the unambiguous environmental and historical variables which control the observed behaviors (Bijou & Peterson, 1971; Ferster, 1965; Kanfer & Saslow, 1969). These relationships are described in objective terms enabling two or more individuals to observe them at the same time, and ideally are measured with a direct sampling method (i.e., the observation of actual interactions between the target individual and other persons in their natural environment). As a result of this procedure, the assessor will be able not only to suggest how specific behaviors are presently maintained but also to plan an intervention strategy for the modification of undesirable behavior and/or the enhancement of behavioral assets. The significant contribution of the functional analysis of behavior is its consistency with the literature on person–situation interaction. The behavioral-analytic approach permits the description of behavior as it varies from situation to situation, as well as the determination of the conditions or environmental factors which covary with the occurrence, maintenance, and change of behavior across different or similar stimulus situations.

Analyzing each child behavior using the S-O-R-K-C model will yield information valuable for determining the future living arrangements of a child. Such an assessment should allow the investigator to hypothesize which environmental conditions are currently supporting the continued occurrence of specific desirable and undesirable patterns of behavior. More specifically, this portion of the behavioral assessment has the potential for determining the appropriateness of one prospective living arrangement over another on the basis of each parent's apparent role in the acquisition and maintenance of specific child behaviors. In other words, which person appears to be more instrumental in the child's learning or maintaining specific desirable patterns of behavior, for instance, those associated with academic achievement? Also, who appears to be supporting, albeit unknowingly, stealing or antagonistic behavior? A functional analysis of these behaviors can assist in discovering which environment would be more conducive to the postdivorce adjustment of the child.

Kanfer and Saslow (1969) suggest that behaviors be categorized as either problematic or nonproblematic, with the former being defined as either a behavioral excess or deficit and the latter as a behavioral asset. Behaviors might also be the result of inappropriate stimulus control as suggested by Bijou and Peterson (1971). A behavior can be problematic because of excessive frequency, duration, intensity or occurrence in circumstances in which the behavior is socially unacceptable, even if occurring once. Examples of behavioral excesses include noncompliance, too much time on the telephone or in front of the television, punching one's sibling, or swearing at the teacher. Behavioral deficits are those responses which do not occur with sufficient frequency or adequate intensity, in an appropriate form, or when expected. When a child does not respond to the teachers or other adults, is unkempt or unable to make friends, he or she can be said to have behavioral deficits.

Nonproblematic behavioral assets were originally intended to refer to a child's special strengths and talents, but other positive behavior can be considered in this context. What can the child do well? How and when does he or she behave most appropriately? Is he musically talented or a good student? Does she always go to bed on time or come home when expected? Are there assets in the areas of sexuality, morals, and religion, or peer relationships? What about physical skills or interpersonal relationships? It is essential that this information be secured and subjected to a functional analysis. By understanding how these nonproblematic behaviors were acquired, as well as how they are presently being maintained, the advantages of each potential living arrangement can be properly assessed. The analysis of behavioral excesses, deficits, and assets, if done correctly, will take into consideration not only the parent and child but also the entire relevant environment, including parents, siblings, peers, and other school-related relationships. The development and support of behavior is infrequently under the control of one dyadic relationship. Usually included are many other persons and places. Consequently, in order to decide in which living environment a child will have the greatest opportunity to develop new positive capabilities and maintain those already within the behavioral repertoire, all relevant environmental conditions must be taken into account.

The functional analysis must be tailored to the problem at hand (i.e., the living arrangements of a child following his parents' divorce). There appears to be one major difference between the purpose for completing a S-O-R-K-C analysis as it is typically done and doing it in conjunction with an overall child custody evaluation, that is, its relationship to treatment. Behavioral diagnosis is typically directed at the development of strategies of intervention for the modification of maladaptive behavior patterns. In contrast, a child custody evaluation is not necessarily concerned with intervention, although this possibility presents an important secondary function. The question is one of current interactions and their relative value in deciding what is best for or least detrimental to a child, and not one of changing their interactions to make them more suitable. The emphasis, then, is on describing and evaluating current patterns of interactions rather than changing those patterns. This contrast of emphasis would appear to have a large impact on deciding what kinds of information are most important in the functional analysis.

The seven areas suggested by Kanfer and Saslow (1969) can provide the necessary information to complete a comprehensive behavioral analysis as defined by the S-O-R-K-C model. However, Stuart (1970) disagrees with the "broad informational requirements" of their approach and is concerned with both the necessity and accessibility of such information. The assessment of a child's behavioral repertoire without bypassing any component of the S-O-R-K-C model, while at the same time avoiding unnecessary, inaccessible information is probably both feasible and sufficient.

Functional Analysis

A functional analysis characterized by questions similar to the following is completed on each of the behaviors identified earlier as a behavioral excess, a deficit, an asset, or a behavior under inappropriate stimulus control.

Stimuli (S). The primary focus of this component in the functional analysis is to ascertain the stimulus conditions in response to which the target behavior occurs. The information obtained on this point constitutes the situation in the person–situation interaction. What are the specific stimulus conditions which furnish the occasion for the occurrence of this response? Where and when does the behavior occur? Where and when does it not occur? Who is usually present when the behavior is exhibited? What are the exceptions, if any? In what circumstances does it occur most frequently? When was the last time it happened? Describe the circumstances that led up to it. Have there been any changes in this behavior recently in terms of frequency, intensity, or duration? If so, what were they? In what circumstances did these changes occur? Where did these changes take place and in whose presence or absence? Have any of these new behaviors generalized to other environments (e.g., home to school)? When, where, and in whose presence? Are there specific groups or categories of people which appear to increase the likelihood that this behavior will occur (e.g., young, women, policemen, old people)?

Organismic variables (O). What are the biological conditions of the child which have a direct impact on the target behavior? Does he or she have any diseases, physical or mental handicaps, hormone imbalances, drug-induced states, or learning disabilities which appear to elicit, inhibit, or maintain their behavior? Have there been or are there any biological developments which place this child far from the norm (e.g., facial hair, early menstruation, etc.)? When and how did these conditions develop and what were their immediate effect on the child's behavior and attitudes? What were or have been the long-term effects? How did or are specific people in the child's environment responding to this deviation? In general, are there any biological conditions that must be considered in order to understand the development, maintenance, or inhibition of the target behavior?

Responses (R). This component of the functional analysis will answer the question: What is the problematic or nonproblematic target behavior under consideration? The primary focus is in revealing a description of the behavior in operational terms instead of vague summary labels. For example, a child who "does not mind" may be one who fails to respond when her mother asks her to help with the dishes, runs out the front door when told to set the table, or verbally responds, "No, I won't. Do it yourself!" The functional analysis of behavior requires that responses be described with specific behavioral referents which can be either directly observed or reliably reported. Responses can either be external, as with overt behavioral manifestations, or internal, such as physiological reactions or cognitions. Frequently, it may be important to obtain information about all three response systems, motor-behavioral, physiological and verbal-cognitive, although internal components may not be available or necessary (say, from a very young child). Questions in this section might include: What do you mean by "withdrawn"? If I were able to observe this behavior surreptitiously, what would I see and hear? When you behave in this way, how do you feel? How does your body react? What kind of thoughts do you have associated with this behavior and your bodily reactions? And describe for me, step-by-step, exactly what happens.

Contingency relationships (K). The relationship between the target behavior and the consequences which follow that target behavior is the focus of this area of investigation. Do the consequences, positive or negative, follow the behavior every time it occurs? If so, how frequently does it occur? If not, how often are the consequences delivered? And, does it depend on the amount of time that elapses (e.g., a report card) or the number of times the behavior occurs (e.g., not answering when called for dinner)? When the behavior is not followed by the same consequences, what other consequences follow, and how often? Whenever a consequence does follow a response, how soon after is it delivered?

Consequences (C). What are the positive and/or negative consequences which follow the behavior of interest? Describe exactly what happened the last time this behavior was either directly observed or reliably reported. Who responds to this behavior and how? What exactly do they say or do? How do other people in other environments reinforce or respond to this behavior (e.g., friends, teachers, siblings, neighbors)? How does the child feel, physically, as a result of this behavior? What about any cognitions? Does the child deliver consequences to himself after this response? If so, of what sort, and how? If the child no longer exhibited this behavior, what would she have to lose or to gain? How do the people in the child's environment behave as a result of this behavior? What would they have to gain or lose if the child no longer behaved in the same fashion? Are there people who respond positively (negatively) to this behavior when everyone else responds negatively (positively)? Who? How?

Once completed, the functional analysis of the child's behavior should permit the assessors to explain how particular child behaviors or patterns of behavior are being maintained or inhibited and what role each person in the prospective living environment appears to have or has had in this respect. Certainly, the issue is a complex one, and at this point the ability of the investigator to make such statements with confidence is speculative and rests solely on the theory which underlies the analysis. The functional analysis of the child's behavioral repertoire, with specific emphasis on specific excesses, deficits, assets, and behaviors under inappropriate stimulus control, adds more data to assist in answering the question *what* are we to measure in deciding the living arrangements of a child?

Observational Learning

THE PROSPECTIVE CARETAKER AS A MODEL

Observational learning refers to the acquisition of behavior through contiguity without direct external reinforcement to the learner for that behavior (Mischel, 1968). Also known as modeling, this concept implies that learning occurs by observing the environment and the people in it. Observational learning can be used to explain the vicarious acquisition of responses not previously within an individual's behavioral repertoire, as well as the inhibition or disinhibition of behaviors already learned (Bandura, 1969, 1971a).

MODELING EFFECTS

Bandura and his associates are responsible for a large portion of the research findings on the effects of modeling. In one of his early studies (Bandura, Ross, & Ross, 1963a), nursery school children were exposed to either a real-life aggressive model, a model acting aggressively on film, a cartoon character behaving aggressively, or no model at all. The victim of the aggressive acts was the famous Bobo doll. Soon after observing their various models, the children were mildly frustrated in a playroom situation and their imitation of aggressive behavior on the Bobo doll was measured. The children who had observed the aggressive model responded most aggressively when frustrated, whereas the children who had not observed a model were hardly aggressive at all. In addition, there were equal amounts of aggression exhibited by the children whether they had observed a real-life model or the filmed model, which suggests the importance of symbolic models (e.g., movies, books).

Research has demonstrated that other kinds of behavior can also be acquired through modeling, for instance, self-control (Bandura & Kupers, 1964; Bandura & Mischel, 1965; Bandura & Whalen, 1966; Mischel & Liebert, 1966) and self-criticism (Bandura, 1971b; Grusec, 1966; Mischel & Grusec, 1966). Bandura and Kupers (1964) investigated the acquisition of self-reinforcement through imitation. Two groups of children observed either peer or adult models praise and reward themselves with freely available treats for performance during a bowling game. One group observed models reward themselves for only high levels of performance while denying themselves rewards for poorer performance. The other group, however, adopted a lower criterion for self-reward and disapproval. A control group observed no model. Surreptitious observation of the child's own self-reward criteria after exposure to the models revealed closely matching patterns between the child's self-reinforcement and that of the observed model.

In another study, Bandura and Mischel (1965) demonstrated that children would adopt a self-imposed delay of reward determined in part by the patterns of delay modeled by adults. In the initial phase of the experiment, children were placed in either a low-delay or high-delay condition depending on their selections from a series of paired rewards—one which was smaller but immediately available, and another, larger but available only after a waiting period. During the treatment phase, children were exposed to either a live or symbolic model who demonstrated delay behavior in opposition to their own pattern of behavior as established in the initial phase. Immediately after exposure to the models, the children were administered an alternate form of the delay-of-reward measure and one month later were readministered the original measure but in a different setting with a different experimenter. The results demonstrated that those children who had exhibited a predominately high-delay pattern of behavior changed their preferences by choosing the more immediate, less valuable rewards after being exposed to adults modeling immediate gratification. Similarly, the low-delay children later increased their preferences for larger, contingent rewards having observed high-delay models. These effects were maintained one month later and the effects were similar for those children who were exposed to the symbolic model, although less pronounced and less generalized. The findings of this study and the others mentioned previously support the importance of live and/or symbolic models in the social transmission of behavioral responses in children.

In a very interesting study by Mischel and Liebert (1966), the effects of modeling were investigated with respect to the consistency between what the model asks the observer to do and what he does himself. In essence, this study addressed the effects of the child-rearing philosophy frequently called upon by parents and others—"Do as I say, not as I do." Will the observer response be consistent with the model's "preaching" or with her behavior in the situation? In order to answer this question, children were exposed to one of three treatment conditions in a bowling game in which the scores were experimentally controlled. The model in this task was a woman who, along with the subject, had free access to a large supply of tokens which could be exchanged later for desirable prizes. In one condition, the women modeled a stringent criterion for self-reward but imposed a very lenient criterion on the child; the second condition had the model using a very lenient criterion and imposing a stringent one; and in the third condition, a stringent criterion was both modeled and imposed. Following ten trials, the model left, and the self-reward behavior of the child was recorded from behind a one-way mirror. One-half of the children performed alone and then demonstrated the game to a younger child, and one-half demonstrated first and then performed alone.

The effects of discrepancies and consistencies in observed and imposed reward criteria received strong support. When there was consistency between what was observed and what was imposed, all children adopted and maintained the criteria. The children who had been led to be lenient in obtaining self-reward while observing a stringent model chose the lenient criteria for themselves; of those who had had stringent criteria imposed on them while their model was lenient on herself, half remained stringent and half became lenient. The patterns of self-reward acquired by the children in the three groups were the same patterns demonstrated and imposed on their own young observers, thus transmitting their previously learned self-reward criteria.

Apparently, if a parent "practices what he preaches," the child is quite likely to acquire the desirable behaviors. However, if there is a lack of consistency and the child is allowed to gain rewards with little effort while being shown a more stringent criterion for reward, the child will take the easier method of obtaining the reward. For instance, if a child is allowed to have a messy room even though parents keep a clean room, the child is likely to keep the room the way it is because it takes the least amount of effort. In contrast, however, if the parents keep a messy room but require the child to keep his or her room clean in order to obtain rewards, then this study would predict that approximately one-half of those children would keep their rooms clean and one-half would not.

Although modeling alone can result in the observer's acquisition of a pattern of behavior, the effects are enhanced if the observer views the model being rewarded for the observed behavior. Similarly, if the model is punished for exhibiting a particular pattern of behavior, the observer's performance of that behavior is inhibited. In general, seeing an individual rewarded for a behavior increases the chances that the behavior will be displayed by the observer, whereas observing the model being punished for a behavior will decrease this probability (Bandura, 1977; Mischel, 1968). The observation of a model being rewarded or punished for a behavior can increase or decrease the likelihood that a behavior will be acquired, inhibit behaviors that have been previously acquired and displayed, or disinhibit behaviors that have been learned but not exhibited. For example, if a child observes his older sister receiving a nice big piece of chocolate cake after she says "please," the probability that he will learn this verbal behavior is increased. With respect to the other two examples, let us say that a child has the capacity within her behavioral repertoire to steal small toys from a department store. In the first case, she has stolen a few times from this store without negative consequences; however, on a similar occasion, her best friend is caught, verbally reprimanded by the manager, picked up by her parents and severely punished in the observer's presence. This vicarious punishment would increase the likelihood that her own stealing behavior would be inhibited in the future. In contrast, if this young girl had never stolen before but was obviously capable of it, and observed her friend being rewarded with the fruits of her escapades, then it would increase the likelihood that her stealing behaviors would be disinhibited. Of course, the prediction of this girl's future behavior is a function of many variables other than observational learning (e.g., strength and intensity of the consequence, schedule of reinforcement), but one must be aware of the probabilities which result from observational learning. In essence, the observer learns what to expect from certain behaviors by observing the consequences delivered to other people in the environment.

Research in the area of modeling and the effects of observed reward and punishment of behavior have yielded some very interesting findings. A group of studies (Bandura, 1965; Walter & Parke, 1964; Walters, Parke, & Cane, 1965) have clearly demonstrated that when observers see people go unpunished for enjoyable behaviors which are usually inhibited because of societal prohibitions, they are as likely to behave similarly in the future as if they had witnessed the models being reinforced for the behavior. Furthermore, witnessing aggressive behavior being punished will result in far less imitation of aggression than if the behavior was either reinforced or followed by no apparent consequences (Bandura, 1973). Walters and Parke (1964) and Walters et al. (1965) demonstrated that the effects of punishment to a model on an observing child are similar with respect to the transgression of social prohibitions such as aggression. Children who observe a model being punished for transgressing are less likely to transgress themselves than if the model was either rewarded or ignored for the behavior. In addition, Benton (1967) found that under some conditions punishment was equally effective in reducing transgressive behavior whether it was directly experienced or observed.

Similar results have been found under conditions of self-reward and punishment. Porro (1968) found that 80% of children who witnessed a model praising herself for violating prohibitions transgressed themselves, whereas only 20% engaged in the forbidden activity after having observed the model responding self-critically toward her own violation. Finally, the observation of rewarding and punishing consequences for self-denying behavior displayed by a model resulted in increases and decreases, respectively, of self-denying behavior of the observing child (Bandura, Grusec, & Menlove, 1967; Rosekrans & Hartup, 1967; Walters & Parke, 1964; Walters, Leat, & Mezei, 1963; Walters et al., 1965).

A classical conditioning model can also be used to explain learning within the modeling paradigm. Intense emotional reactions can be learned from watching the reactions of others to specific eliciting stimuli. For instance, children can easily learn to fear ants, dogs, a particular race of people, or an ideology without ever directly experiencing aversive stimulation in their presence simply by repeatedly observing the same or different people responding emotionally to a stimulus (Berger, 1962). In this way, a previously neutral stimulus will evoke an intense emotional response. A parent who consistently responds to the dentist or stimuli associated with going to the dentist with fear (e.g., repeated cancellations, statements of fear) is likely to teach his or her child to be afraid of going to a dentist without the child's ever having had any direct experience with one. Emotional reactions can be acquired vicariously to many kinds of stimuli including people, places, animals, objects, ideas, words (Mischel, 1968).

The value of this information and its importance in deciding what to measure in determining the optimal living arrangements for a child should by now be apparent. Given the kind of learning that takes place in a child's life simply by his opening his eyes and perceiving what happens to others in the environment, some attempt should be made to assess what it is that the child is or will be exposed to. Certainly, there is no evidence that concludes that a child will learn everything he sees others doing. The acquisition of behavior is much more complex. However, there is evidence, some of which has been presented, which demonstrates that observational learning does take place and that witnessing the positive and negative consequences following other people's behavior increases or decreases the likelihood that the observing child will conduct himself in a similar manner in similar circumstances. Therefore, knowledge of the kinds of models to which the child is exposed or will be exposed should theoretically increase the predictive accuracy of a given child's future behavior in similar circumstances and therefore assist in deciding which of a number of alternative living arrangements would maximize the probability that appropriate patterns of behavior (i.e., socially effective) will be acquired and maintained, while inappropriate, socially ineffective patterns will not be acquired or will be disinhibited.

IDENTIFYING IMPORTANT MODELS

There is no question that as a child grows and develops she is exposed to a wide variety of models, including parents, siblings, grandparents, teachers, and peers. All may have a role in teaching the child through their actions how to behave and what consequences to expect for certain behaviors. However, the child's parents are his or her most potent models. Mischel (1976) cites three reasons for believing this. First they are the earliest models in the child's environment. Second, they are the most enduring models, being a part of the child's environment longer than any other social agent. And third, they are the most powerful persons in the child's life, providing nurturance and controlling most of the resources. For these reasons, the behavior of both parents must undergo close scrutiny to determine what kind of models they have been or will be for the children in question. In the special circumstances of this evaluation, persons other than the natural parents may be included. As such, the prospective caretakers will be evaluated with respect to their performance as models for this child in the past and/or their potential as models in the future. For example, if a grandparent is attempting to acquire custody of a recently deceased son's child, then that grandparent, as well as the current mother-custodian, would be evaluated as a model for this child.

Beyond the assessment of each of the prospective caretakers, the child's current or future environment must be surveyed for other potent models, who should then be evaluated. If there is a particularly appropriate and potent model in the child's present environment other than one of the natural parents (e.g., an uncle), and that model will not be available to the child in one of many possible living arrangements, then this becomes valuable information for making the most efficacious decision.

To decide who warrants investigation as a potent model, three factors have been identified which can assist in determining the extent to which a child takes on herself the attitudes and behaviors of the various models to which he or she is exposed throughout development. They are: (1) the model's nurturance or rewardingness; (2) the model's power or control over the resources; and (3) the similarity of the model to the child.

Rewardingness

Although the relationship between the model's rewardingness and the observer's imitation of that model is not entirely clear (Martin, 1975), there is some evidence to suggest that a child will imitate a nurturant model more often than a nonnurturant model (Bandura & Huston, 1961; Bandura, Ross, & Ross, 1963b; Mussen, 1961). In the Bandura and Huston study two groups of nursery-school children were exposed to a highly nurturant woman model bestowing rewards liberally or to the same model behaving in a distant and nonnurturant manner. In the second group, the model was with each child for the same amount of time but did not play warmly with the child. Subsequent to this initial phase, all of the children observed the model being either aggressive or nonaggressive in the course of a game. Although all of the children imitated the model's aggressive behavior (i.e., hitting a doll) equally as often, the children who had been exposed to the nurturant (i.e., rewarding) model adopted her nonaggressive behavior much more frequently. Similarly, Grusec (1966) found that children imitated the self-critical behavior of a nurturant model more often than that of a nonnurturant model. On the other hand, however, other studies have indicated that little relationship exists between levels of nurturance and imitation of altruistic behavior (Grusec & Skubiski, 1970; Rosenhan & White, 1967), delay of gratification (Mischel & Grusec, 1966), or sharing behavior (Grusec, 1971), although, as suggested elsewhere (Martin, 1975), rewards tend to be given out noncontingently in these studies and the child may learn that rewards can be expected without engaging in the modeled behavior. In other words, since the child does not have to exert any energy in order to receive rewards, why share or wait for treats when there are costs for doing so and none for not? It would appear that although rewardingness is not a prerequisite for emulation, it may enhance imitation, especially when it interacts with power and similarity.

Control over Resources

The degree to which an individual has control (power) over a child in the form of both rewards and punishments is clearly associated with the tendency of that child to adopt the behavior displayed by the model and be influenced by her. Several studies provide evidence for this association (Bandura *et al.*, 1963b; Grusec, 1971; Hetherington, 1965; Hetherington & Frankie, 1967; Mischel & Grusec, 1967). Bandura *et al.* investigated the relationship between the degree to which a child imitates and adopts the behavior of a model and the amount of power or control over resources that individual has over the child. Nursery-school boys and girls each became part of a triadic relationship consisting of a child and one man and one woman. Three roles were assigned to the various participants: (1) "controller" was that person who was in the position of power and could dispense or withhold the available resources (i.e., attractive games and treats). This role was played by only one of the two adults, being designed to represent a parent. (2) The "consumer," any of the three participants was that person to whom the treats were dispensed. (3) The "onlooker," who could also be any one of the three, was ignored and participated only by watching the controller–consumer interaction. The sex of the three roles was systematically varied so that the man and the woman were able to play each role in each condition.

After these initial sessions were completed, each of the child-subjects participated in a new game with the adults. The adult model emitted new, distinctive behaviors, and the degree to which the child imitated these and other behaviors was assessed. In general, the results demonstrated that the child imitated the adult who was controlling the rewards much more frequently than the adult who played the role of the consumer. This result lends support to the notion that power or control of resources increases the tendency for imitation of that person.

Mischel and Grusec (1966) also investigated the variable of control but in addition attempted to discover how the characteristics of the model influence the rehearsal and transmission of aversive and neutral behaviors when observed and directly experienced by the child. Subjects were 52 nursery-school children, boys and girls, who were exposed to a woman model. These children were randomly assigned to one of four treatment conditions which varied in both rewardingness and future control. Within the reward condition, the adult either delivered a high rate of noncontingent tangible and intangible rewards (e.g., attractive toys, treats, interest, praise, and warmth) or a low rate of noncontingent rewards (e.g., less attractive, broken toys; child left alone while the adult was busy). The control manipulation consisted of informing the child that the woman was going to be his or her new teacher (high future control) or was a visiting teacher who would be leaving in an hour and not be seen again (low future control). The four groups were: (1) high reward/high future control; (2) high reward/low future control; (3) low reward/high future control; and (4) low reward/low future control.

After this initial 20-minute play session, the child was reminded of the model's role and taken to another room where child and model engaged in a special game which involved playing store with a cash register and making change and similar activities. During this interaction, each child was exposed to two kinds of adult behavior, neutral and aversive. The neutral behaviors were very explicit verbal comments and overt actions. For example, the model would hit the cash register, say "bop," and march around a table twice saying, "March, March, March!!" There were three kinds of aversive behavior which were delivered as direct consequences to the child's behavior. The child could be subjected to an imposed delay of reward, receive verbal criticism for his behavior, and/or have a reward taken away. After playing with the model, the child was left alone for three minutes and observed through a one-way mirror and scored for imitation (i.e., "researsal") of any of the model's behaviors.

In the final phase of this investigation, the child was allowed to show someone else (a woman dressed as a clown) how to play the register game. The game and all of its consequences were reviewed with the child, as was the model's role (i.e., control). The child was then observed with the clown and assessed for the amount of imitation demonstrated by the child in transmitting the game to the clown.

The results indicated that significantly more children rehearsed both aversive and neutral behaviors when the model was high in both rewardingness and future control than when both were low. Furthermore, the amount of control was particularly important in the child's rehearsal of aversive behavior. The authors report that not a single child rehearsed an aversive behavior when the model's future control had been low. However, the two groups with models manifesting high rewardingness significantly affected the level of rehearsal of neutral behaviors and not aversive behaviors, whereas there was just the opposite effect of rewardingness and the transmission of neutral behaviors. There were significantly more *aversive* behaviors transmitted than neutral behaviors when rewardingness was high. Curiously, the amount of future control did not affect the transmission of any behavior.

Mischel (1968) made the following remarks concerning the results of this study:

> Observed behaviors may be reproduced and transmitted to others without external reinforcement for their actions, even when the observer was the object of the modeled behaviors and received aversive consequences from the model. Indeed, the percent of aversive behavior transmitted exceeded the percent of neutral behavior transmitted. Moreover, the extent to which the models' behavior was reproduced was affected by her rewardingness and her future control over the subject. The overall results support the view that the rewardingness of a model and his power are determinants of the degree to which his behavior is adopted. (p. 156–157)

Bandura *et al.* (1963b) and Mischel and Grusec (1966) provide support for the contention that the more control over resources (power) a given individual has for a child, the greater the impact he or she will have on the child and the greater the likelihood that the child will imitate that person's behavior.

Similarity

The third factor which appears to enhance imitation is the similarity between the model and the observer. Characteristics which have been shown to increase the likelihood of emulation given a similarity between the observer and model are: age (Bandura & Kupers, 1964; Hicks, 1965; Jakubszak & Walters, 1959), sex (Bandura et al., 1963a; Hetherington & Frankie, 1967; Maccoby & Wilson, 1957; Rosenbligh, 1959, 1961), and ethnic status (Epstein, 1966). If learning is to occur as a result of observing another person and not directly experiencing the consequences of behavior, then this other person should be as similar to the observer as possible. These similarities can exist in reality or be perceived as such (Rosekrans, 1967; Tannenbaum & Gaer, 1965). If the model is not perceived as similar, then the observing individual is more likely to discount the model and the consequences of her behavior as irrelevant to himself, not attend to the situation, and therefore not change his behavior in concordance with the model's.

Although a variety of model–client similarities have been found to be important for enhancing the therapeutic effects of modeling procedures (Kazdin, 1974b, Kornhaber & Schroeder, 1975; Thelen, Dollinger, & Roberts, 1975), the most potent variable in child development appears to be gender similarity (Bandura et al., 1963a; Hetherington & Frankie, 1967; Maccoby & Wilson, 1957). Maccoby and Wilson had male and female seventh-graders watch a film in which the protagonists were a male and a female adolescent. The two characters in the film exhibited a variety of social behaviors, but differed from each other. After one week, the children who had observed the film were asked questions concerning the various characters in the film (who was most like them, etc.). The investigators were attempting to measure how well the children could remember what they had observed and heard.

The results demonstrated that the children identified with the character of the same sex. In addition, they tended to recall the verbal and overt behavior of their same-sex models better than that of the opposite-sex models. This study appeared to support the hypothesis that children tend to observe the behavior of a same-sex more closely. These results were later supported by Hetherington and Frankie (1967), who found that boys tended to imitate their fathers more than their mothers, and girls their mothers more than their fathers.

This finding may be important in attempts to decide which persons in a child's environment constitute important models. However, there is research to indicate that as the child grows older, peers, rather than adults, begin to be the objects of potent modeling effects (e.g., Devereux, 1970; Fremouw & Harmatz, 1975; Nelson, Worrell, & Polsgrove, 1973). Commenting on an earlier review of the peer-model research (Hoffman, 1970), Hoffman (1979) suggested:

> Exposure to a peer who behaves aggressively or yields to temptation and is not punished increases the likelihood that a child will do the same; if the model is punished, the subject behaves as if there were no model. These findings suggest that if children deviate from adult moral norms without punishment, as often happens outside the home, this may stimulate a child to deviate; if they are punished, however, this may not serve as a deterrent. The immediate impact of peer behavior may thus be more likely to weaken than to strengthen one's inhibitions, at least in our society. (p. 960)

It would appear to be important, then, to look more closely at the child's peer group for modeling effects as the child gets older if a thorough evaluation of his environment is desired. This would not be as important with younger children.

IMPLICATIONS

Obviously, when deciding who other than the prospective caretakers should be evaluated as current or potentially important models for the child, the three factors discussed above should be considered in combination. How rewarding is this person to the child? Are there demonstrations of love, affection, and nurturance? Does the child spend a great deal of time in the company of this person? What is the quality of this time together? Does the person have control over the events that are significant in the life of the child? Does he or she have the power to protect, reward, and punish the child? What do the child and this person have in common?

The social environment of the child can be scanned for potentially potent models. For example, what about the school environment? Are there any teachers who can be considered potent models? Coaches? Does the child engage in any extracurricular activities? If so, do any of the group moderators provide a significant modeling effect for the child? How about the Little League, Girl Scouts, or church? The child's environment can be subdivided and briefly examined for signficant others. Bandura (1969) noted:

The affective valence of models, as mediated through their attractiveness and other rewarding qualities . . . may augment observational learning by eliciting and maintaining strong attending behavior. At the social level one's organizational affiliations and living circumstances, which affect associational networks and preferences, will also determine to a large degree the types of models to whom one is repeatedly exposed, and consequently, the modes of behavior that will be most thoroughly learned. (pp. 136-137)

Consequently, if a thorough evaluation requires that the assessor make recommendations concerning the appropriateness of potential living arrangements for a child, then it would seem prudent to examine the effects (past or potential) of modeling in those environments. One might find through such an investigation that a child's support system, in the form of highly rewarding models, would be seriously weakened if he were placed out of the mother's custody simply because the child's most potent models are associated with the mother (e.g., maternal grandparents) and that if the father were to get custody the child would be torn away from these sources of learning. Of course, cases of such clarity are probably rare. Nonetheless, this area of investigation is important and can add substantially to the overall evaluation and subsequent decision concerning a child's future living arrangements by identifying important social factors in the child's environment.

Once the models have been identified, what behaviors are selected for further analysis? Recognizing the interdependence of many of the areas previously targeted for assessment (parental competence, the child's repertoire, etc.), a significant number of parental behaviors will be identified simply through the process of assessment. For example, a functional analysis of specific adaptive and maladaptive child behaviors will reveal parental responses to the child. From such an analysis, it may be possible to determine, for example, that a child's father consistently responds to the child's misbehavior with severe criticism and belittlement or that the maternal responses to a child's enuresis are comfort and understanding. Similarly, the responses of other persons to the child's behavior can be considered a sample of behavior modeled for the child. If it is revealed that this response frequently occurs in the child's presence, strong statements can be made about their potential effects on the child. And if the child has demonstrated similar behavior, that is, if he or she is already imitating the parent's behavior, then even more support would seem available for statements concerning the effects of modeling on the child.

Information derived from the assessment of parental competence can be utilized in much the same fashion. The prospective caretaker's responses to the various problematic situations are suggestive of the kinds of behavior modeled for the child in those specific situations. As such, some determination can be made of what the child is learning with reference to how to respond to these particular situations. For instance, if responses are elicited to children's request for information about sexuality, and one parent responds with a scornful look and ignores the question and another parent answers the child in a simple, matter-of-fact tone, then it is suggested that each child is provided with information on how to respond in similar situations. Both parents have modeled a sample of behavior which reflects their attitudes about sexuality, and each child has learned something different. It is likely that the child will learn the same thing regardless of whether he or she experiences it directly or observes it happening with a sibling. Most likely, the first child has learned that sexuality is an unacceptable topic for discussion, and the second child has learned that sexuality is something that can be talked about like other topics.

These areas of assessment permit further examination of modeling behavior and may suggest behavior patterns which deserve more detailed analysis. In addition, however, other areas of interest should be investigated. This part of the assessment would be reserved for the identification of specific adaptive and maladaptive behaviors or patterns of behavior that each person under consideration has exhibited. What are the significant behavioral excesses, deficits, or assets of those targeted? Which behaviors are open to observation by the child? What are some of the behavior characteristics of the prospective caretakers? Do they work hard? Do they keep themselves and their environment neat? Do they have a good sense of humor? Do they exhibit an optimistic attitude toward life? Do they drink to excess or use drugs? Have they openly committed adultery or had uncontrollable fits of anger or depression? Have they even been arrested? What for? How have they behaved toward each other? Are they organized and persistent? How do they respond to stressful situations? Are there any irrational fears or maladaptive habits? Are they assertive? In what situations? Do they like themselves and show it?

These questions and others like them can help to reveal a repertoire of behaviors which can then be operationalized and subjected to a functional analysis to determine the antecedent and consequent events which are associated with them. As such, statements can then be made about the likelihood of a particular child's imitating certain behaviors of a given individual in certain situations. Of course, any such statements would take into account all of the other data being gathered with respect to this child's acquisition, maintenance, inhibition, or disinhibition of behavior. For example, although a parent exhibits self-deprecating behavior, that does not necessarily mean that the child will learn this behavior. Other models and environmental contingencies may support behavior which demonstrates self-confidence and feelings of worth. The only way of knowing this with any degree of certainty would be to perform a complete functional analysis of the targeted behaviors. It may be discovered that although the child's mother is frequently putting herself down in front of the child, the child has a very important relationship with the third-grade teacher who exudes self-confidence. At the same time, she is consistently praising the child and rewarding her for positive self-statements. Under these conditions, the effects of the parental model may be overshadowed by the other individual.

The information gathered in this component of the evaluation is only one piece of data to be combined and evaluated with the rest. Regardless, the information is important and will assist in making the final decision on which placement best serves the child's interests. Which environment will be most beneficial to the child and increase the probabilities that patterns of behavior likely to result in effective life functioning will be acquired and maintained, while other patterns of behavior, ineffective and maladaptive, will be left unlearned or inhibited from occurring? Theoretically, the informational requirements discussed thus far for a thorough behavioral assessment should result in more realistic and efficacious custody decisions than do traditional procedures. This approach takes full account of the person–situation interaction, emphasizes the importance of empirically established principles, and eschews the need of underlying predispositions and personality constructs.

CHAPTER 7

Assessment of the Prospective Postdivorce Environments and Self-Ratings

THE FINAL LINKS IN THE PROCESS OF PREDICTION

The proposed model for assessment presented in this volume has reflected the theoretical assumptions underlying behavioral assessment and is consistent with the research in the areas of interactionism, classical and operant conditioning, and observational learning. Thus far, however, attention has been given only to identifying the behavioral repertoires of the children and of the prospective caretakers and their interactions in the past and current environments. Emphasis has been placed on the acquisition, maintenance, inhibition, and disinhibition of behavior and the identification of specific competencies and skill deficits. Although we are most concerned with making predictions, we have yet to address this topic directly. Of the many potential environments and alternative living arrangements available for a child, which has the greatest probability of resulting in good future adjustment? The important groundwork needed to answer this question has been laid in the previous chapters on parental competence, the functional analysis of the child's behavioral repertoire, and observational learning. In this chapter, two areas will be examined: the necessity of assessing each of the proposed alternative environments and the importance of self-ratings in predicting future behavior.

THE PROSPECTIVE POSTDIVORCE ENVIRONMENT

Given the overwhelming importance of environmental events in the control of behavior, any assessment effort aimed at the prediction of behavior in a criterion environment must determine not only the salient aspects of the current environment but also those of the criterion environment. In other words, it is not enough to know that specific child behaviors have been under the control of particular environmental antecedent and consequent events. Although this information is a necessary condition for the successful prediction of behavior because it identifies the relationship which exists between the selected behaviors and environmental events (i.e., those stimuli which set the occasion for responding or nonresponding), unless an assessment can be made of the criterion environment (the environment to which prediction is desired), accurate prediction is not likely. It would be necessary to assess the criterion environment and establish the availability, or lack thereof, of stimulus conditions already identified as necessary factors in the maintenance of targeted behaviors. Social learning theory predicts that the more similar one situation is to another, the more likely one behavior will occur in both situations. Similarly, the more dissimilar the environments, the more likely it is that behavior will change across situations. If the purpose of completing a child custody evaluation is to predict which of the alternative postdivorce environments is most appropriate and will result in the most suitable placement in terms of teaching and maintaining an effective behavioral repertoire, then an assessment of each of these environments is crucial. As Mischel (1968) indicates, "The assessor who tries to predict the future without detailed information about the exact environmental conditions influencing the individual's criterion behavior may be more engaged in the process of hoping than of predicting" (p. 140).

The Criterion Environment

Fairweather and his associates (Fairweather, 1964, 1967; Fairweather, Sanders, Maynard, & Cressler, 1969; Forsyth & Fairweather, 1961) have done extensive research in the area of posthospitalization adjustment of mental patients. Their research is important because it documents the significance of environmental variables in the prediction of behavior. Posthospitalization adjustment was found to correlate most highly with relevant aspects of the posthospitalization environment (Fairweather, 1964). Mental patients who remained outside of the hospital the longest were those who had supportive living environments (e.g., halfway house, lodge) and employment available to them upon discharge. This study found that no in-hospital behavior correlated significantly with posthospitalization adjustment. In other words, the behavior displayed by the patients during their hospitalization did not predict how well they would do once discharged. Appropriate behavior, that is, behavior which would result in discharge, had no relevance without a supportive environment to which the patients could be discharged.

A striking investigation by Wolf (1966) underscored the importance of social learning and environmental variables in the area of intellectual development and academic achievement. Among other things, the author investigated the relationship between a child's home environment with respect to verbal development, and intellectual development and academic achievement. Four variables were measured in the home environment: (1) the quality of language models; (2) opportunities available for enlarging the vocabulary; (3) the extent of feedback to the child about the proper use of language; and (4) the opportunity available to the child to practice verbal skills across situations. Each of these variables was considered important for the child's intellectual development. The results of this study were quite impressive. The correlation between the total environmental ratings and general intelligence was .69! This is quite significant considering the .20 to .50 correlations typically found in the area of personality research (Hunt, 1965). Furthermore, ratings of the home and its support for academic achievement correlated .80 with actual achievement based on an achievement battery test score. And finally, when the authors combined the ratings of academic support in the environment with the child's general intelligence and correlated them together with the total achievement test battery, the correlations increased even more ($r = .87$)! This combination of factors accounted for 76% of the overall variance in academic achievement scores. Without the addition of environmental factors, the correlation was .76 and accounted for only 58% of the variance, indicating the importance of the ignored situational determinants. Both of these lines of research underscore the importance of environmental events in the prediction of behavior. From the Wolf study one should be able to predict how well a child will progress academically if one has a knowledge of the environmental contingencies with respect to intellectual development (i.e., appropriate models and positive reinforcement for intellectual behaviors). Similarly, if one wished to predict the acquisition, maintenance, and so on of intellectual behaviors in a future environment, then the degree of accuracy would be expected to increase with a knowledge of the relevant aspects of the particular environment. This was demonstrated in the research by Fairweather (e.g., 1964) on posthospitalization adjustment, and one might expect to find similar results in the prediction of other behavior, although this awaits further study.

A supplementary area of research has regularly documented that the best predictor of future behavior is past behavior in similar circumstances (e.g., Fairweather, Simon, Gehard, Weingarten, Holland, Sanders, Stone, & Reahl, 1960; Fulkerson & Barry, 1961). The bulk of this research has also been with mental patients and the prediction of posthospitalization adjustment. For example, a number of studies (Fairweather et al., 1960; Fulkerson & Barry, 1961; Lorei, 1967; Zigler & Phillips, 1961a, 1961b, 1962) have assessed premorbid adjustment and investigated its relationship to various outcome ratings (e.g., rehospitalization, and success in the community after release). In the series of studies by Zigler and Phillips the degree of social competence achieved before hospitalization was compared with current patterns of behavior problems. Previous adjustment indices included such items as the level of education, IQ, occupational skill, stability of previous employment, occurrence and maintenance of marriage, and age reached before onset of the problem behavior. As in the other studies mentioned, these authors found that persons with high levels of premorbid adjustment had a better prognosis than those with troublesome past histories. A quite dramatic representation of the importance of past adjustment in predicting adjustment in the future is the findings of Lasky, Hover, Smith, Bostian, Duffendack, and Nord (1959) who found correlations from .31 to .62 between the weight of the patient's file and the problems experienced after discharge. The average correlation was .52, and the highest correlation (.61) was found between the weight of the folder and rehospitalization.

Similar results have been found in the prediction of grades (Kelly, 1966; Mischel & Bentler, 1965). The best predictor of future grades was the individual's past grade-point average. Also Farberow and McEvoy (1966) investigated the relationship between various behavioral indices of suicide and found that relevant past behavior, such as previous attempts, verbalizations of suicide, threats of suicide, and models in the family who have committed suicide, is predictive of future suicidal behavior. Lemerond (1978) found similar results.

There appears to be considerable support for the use of relevant past behavior in predicting future behavior. As previously noted, the greatest accuracy one can expect when predicting behavior occurs only after a detailed assessment of the contingencies that will be operating in the criterion environment. However, this may not always be possible, as Mischel (1968) notes:

> If there is no choice, however, and the assessor is faced unavoidably with the task of trying to predict outcomes from current or past indices with no information about the future conditions governing criterion behavior, his best predictions are likely to come from measures of directly relevant behavior. Predictions should be most accurate when the past situations in which the predictor behavior was sampled are most similar to the situations at which predictions about future behavior are aimed. Antisocial parole behavior should be best predicted by past antisocial behavior, future job success should be best predicted by prior job success, future academic achievement should be best predicted by past academic achievement, and assessments of future adaptive behavior should be best predicted by prior social acceptance and social adjustment history. (p. 140)

Implications

The importance of the information provided in this section for the child custody evaluation is clear. A detailed assessment of the various postdivorce environments in which a child could be placed must be completed. From the earlier components in this assessment procedure, a basic understanding has been obtained of the contingency relationships which exist between various parent and child behaviors and the environment. The identification and assessment of the models available to the child from which he or she will learn has also been completed. Prediction now requires a determination of the degree to which the same relationships in the assessment environment will exist in the criterion environment. The presence and/or absence of various stimulus conditions is significant information. For example, if placement in one environment results in the loss of potent models of intellectual behaviors, without their replacement, then the probability of this child's acquiring or maintaining similar patterns of behavior has been diminished. Similarly, one of the prospective environments may inhibit inappropriate behaviors that have previously been modeled and supported in the predivorce environment.

Mnookin (1975) has addressed the issue of prediction and the problem confronting the presiding judge. Essentially, the judge must compare the expected benefits for the child in each of the available placements. Mnookin identifies four kinds of information the judge must have in order to make an appropriate decision. Although much more information is needed, Mnookin's list is offered for two reasons. First, it highlights the kind of information to which the assessor must attend, and second, it notes the sophistication of some individuals in the legal community with the problems of prediction, as well as the general sense of hopelessness inherent in the area. The four areas with which the judge would be concerned are: (1) how each prospective caretaker has behaved in the past and how this has affected the child and the child's present condition; (2) the future behavior and circumstances of each prospective caretaker if the child were to remain with that person and gauging the effects of this behavior and these circumstances on the child; (3) the behavior of each person if the child were to live with the *other* person and how that might affect the child; and (4) if placement with one of the prospective caretakers required removing the child from his present circumstances, school, friends, familiar surroundings, how would this affect the child?

As Mnookin (1975) suggests:

> These predictions would necessarily involve estimates of not only the child's mutual relationships with the custodial parent, but also his future contact with the other parent and siblings, the probable number of visits by the noncustodial spouse, the probable financial circumstances of each of the spouses, and a myriad of other factors. (p. 257)

Undoubtedly, the task at hand is a difficult one. However, I do not share Mnookin's pessimism with respect to predicting outcomes. He says, "But even where a judge has substantial information about a child's past home life and the present alternatives, present-day knowledge of human behavior provides no basis for the kind of individualized predictions required by the best-interests standard" (p. 258). If Mnookin is interpreting the best interests standard to mean what is best for the child forever, I am not so naive as to disagree with him. However, more reasonable predictions of immediate postdivorce adjustment or three to five years into the future would seem possible, especially if one takes into consideration recent research on the effects of divorce on children (see, e.g., Wallerstein & Kelly, 1974, 1975, 1976, 1980a,b). However, the answer to this question will come only with more research.

Many questions need answering in this part of the overall assessment procedure. As Mnookin (1975) has suggested, it is necessary to determine not only how each placement would affect the child but also the individual responses of each of the involved parties should the living arrangement they desire not be sanctioned by the court. The expected response to a loss of custody must be evaluated, for it will undoubtedly have a major impact on the custodian–noncustodian–child system. Which of the prospective caretakers will effectively cope with the situation should the child not be placed with him or her under the desired arrangement? Can one of the parents be expected to hold a grudge or use the child as a weapon if he or she does not get his or her way? How well will the child be able to cope with the dissatisfied party? Is the age of the child relevant in these circumstances? These are but a few questions pertaining to the postdivorce environment that must be assessed.

Given the fact that behavior appears to remain stable across situations as long as the stimulus cues remain the same, the divorce alone would be expected to alter the child's environment. Therefore, one might expect the behavior of both the child and prospective caretakers to change simply as a result of the divorce and custody adjudication. The question becomes one of determining what will change and how much (see Hetherington, Cox, & Cox, 1979a, 1979b; Wallerstein & Kelly, 1974, 1975, 1976, 1980a,b). One might expect that the larger the degree of change in environmental conditions, the more pronounced will be the change in behavior. For example, if the child remains in the same home, school, and neighborhood and keeps the same friends and activities, his subsequent behavior should be expected to remain more stable than if he were removed from those familiar surroundings which act to elicit and reinforce long-term patterns of behavior. Changes are most likely to be reflected in the areas of the child's life wherein the departed parent has been most influential.

The effects of environmental change on a child's behavior may seem highly supportive of maintaining a *status quo* placement, that is, the child remains where she has always been and therefore there is no further disruption in the controlling antecedent and consequent conditions in her environment. However, what happens if the present environment has been supporting numerous maladaptive habits and patterns of behavior (e.g., there is a group of "undesirables" in the neighborhood whom the child emulates)? The preliminary assessment should be able to identify these circumstances, and a decision to remove a child from the *status quo* environment might be seriously considered. Regardless, the importance of the temporary custody orders is enlarged considerably with the understanding of the effects of environmental contingencies on behavior. It would appear that judges rarely modify their custody orders once a child has been placed, regardless of its supposed "temporary" status (Pearson, Munson, & Thoennes, 1982). Given the protracted battles which frequently characterize custody disputes, temporary orders can last for many months. This situation is of additional concern, especially in the assessment process, because the longer a child has been in one placement instead of another, the more accurate one would expect predictions to that environment to be. The child and caretaker have had the time to adjust to the new situation without the daily presence of the noncustodial party, making the assessment of that environment more reliable. In other words, the child has been placed in the care of this person, in this environment, for x number of weeks, months, or years. How has that child done in the environment? How has the caretaker done? How has the noncustodial parent been coping with the situation?

If the divorce and temporary custody orders have been relatively recent, then a reliable assessment of the situation is perhaps not possible, for none of the people involved has had the opportunity to adjust to the new set of circumstances. Therefore, the entire assessment will focus more closely on previous behavioral responses rather than on those which appear to have been elicited as a result of the divorce process (unless, of course, the behavior of those involved can be used as an appropriate sample of behavior in stressful circumstances).

Regardless of which living arrangement is selected, two factors should be kept under consideration. Although a child is removed from the predivorce environment (e.g., to a new state), this does not mean that the child's behavior will change entirely. The *temporal* consistency of behavior has been well documented and explained within a cognitive social learning model (Chapter 4; Mischel, 1973; Mischel & Peake, 1982; Staats, 1971, 1975). A person lives in a fairly stable environment especially with respect to cultural norms and expectations. Although the rural Midwest might differ from the industrial Northeast, both belong to the United States and maintain similar laws and so on. Also, most of our socialization is acquired through intermittent reinforcement under very complex combined schedules. Consequently, the behaviors are extremely durable and resistant to extinction. One might expect that the older the child, the more resistant to extinction will be certain socialization behaviors. Therefore, the older child's behavior, for better or worse, will not change as readily should a given decision find him or her in a completely unfamiliar environment.

In sum, although one might expect behavior to change as the stimulus properties of the environment change, there are certain environmental stimuli which remain fairly constant across time and place which would temper our prediction of change. Nonetheless, the most accurate predictions can be expected only in circumstances in which a detailed determination is made of the stimulus properties that can be expected in the criterion environment.

Given a lack of direct knowledge of the specific environmental conditions of a potential living arrangement, are there samples of similar conditions in the past? Although the exact circumstances are not likely to have occurred, samples of similar situations may be available. For instance, have there been marital separations in the past? Who remained with the children, and how did both the parent and child cope with this situation? How about the absent spouse? If there have been no previous marital separations, have there been any circumstances which have separated the parents? Business reasons? Illness? Vacation? If so, how did all those involved behave during the separation? Similar, but even less generalizable, is how each parent behaved in the presence of the child and in the absence of the other parent. For instance, what happens when mother is at work all day and father is left with the children? If grandparents wish to become the child's primary caretakers, what has happened in the past when the child has been left in their care for the summer, weekend, or overnight?

Each of these cases provides samples of relevant past behavior in similar circumstances. It should be noted, however, that the more dissimilar the situation (e.g., parent away for the weekend as opposed to being separated previously for four months), the less confidence one will be able to have in predictions based on this information. Other past behavior which may help in predicting to the postdivorce environment could include each person's responses to stressful situations or to being frustrated in attempts to accomplish or acquire something. For example, it may be very important to know that one of the child's parents has been very effective in coping with previous stressful events (e.g., loss of job, accident) or that he or she displays verbally and/or physically aggressive behaviors when thwarted in attempting to achieve desired goals. Such behavior can be helpful on two fronts: first, it gives a sample of how this person might react if not awarded custody; and second, their present behavior can provide a red flag of caution for the evaluation itself, that is, the investigators are alerted to evaluating the effects of the present behavior with respect to the entire assessment. In other words, is this a reliable assessment of this person's behavior or is it entirely, or in part, distorted due to stress? The assessment of the potential postdivorce environments, together with relevant past behavior, should provide ample information valuable for the prediction of child and caretaker behavior in that environment.

SELF-ASSESSMENT AND PREDICTION

The final area which deserves attention in this chapter is self-prediction, the person's own forecast of how he or she will behave in future circumstances. The research in this area strongly argues that an individual's own predictions, in the form of self-ratings and self-reports, are as accurate or more so than various personality tests, test batteries, or judgments by experienced clinicians (Hase & Goldberg, 1967; Holmes & Tyler, 1968; Lindzey & Tejessy, 1956; Melei & Hilgard, 1964; Mischel, 1965, 1977, 1981, 1983; Mischel & Bentler, 1965; Peterson, 1965; Wallace & Sechrest, 1963). Lindzey and Tejessey investigated the relationship between 10 TAT signs of aggression and various covert and overt dependent measures. They employed observer ratings, Rosenzweig Extrapunitive and Intrapunitive scores, diagnostic council ratings, and the subject's own self-ratings. Self-ratings generated the highest correlations with 7 of the 10 signs correlating significantly. The closest of the other measures was the Rosenzweig in which both the Extra- and Intrapunitive scores correlated significantly with only 3 of the 10 signs. This finding was rather unexpected and suggested the value of directly asking the subject to appraise his behavior rather than spending the time and money needed with the other measures.

Wallace and Sechrest (1963) used a multitrait–multimethod approach to the study of the frequency hypothesis of projective theory. They investigated 72 freshman nursing students on four traits (i.e., somatic concerns, hostility, achievement concern, and religiosity) with five methods (i.e., self-description, peer reputation, Rorschach content, Incomplete Sentences Blank, and TAT). Other measures included the number of visits to the health service, a medical symptom checklist, and scholastic average. None of the convergent and discriminant validity coefficients of any of the other measures was better than those for the self-descriptions. Together, all the peer reputation–self-description diagonals were highly significant.

Hase and Goldberg (1967) developed a series of personality- inventory scales using six different scale-construction strategies, each time pulling items from the 1957 version of the California Psychological Inventory. They were interested in the relationship between the way in which each peer rated each of the subjects and the six scales and subjects' self-ratings. The results clearly indicated that the best predictor of how peers rated subjects was the individual's own simple self-ratings. The strategy used to construct the scales had little effect. Self-ratings had validity scores which exceeded those produced by any of the individual scales or the best combination of scales. The results of this study provided further support for the relative success of self-ratings in the prediction of behavior over and above psychometrically sophisticated personality tests (see also Marks, Stauffacher, & Lyle, 1963).

Self-ratings and self-reports have also demonstrated greater predictive validity than indirect measures in the areas of academic achievement (Holmes & Tyler, 1968; Mischel & Bentler, 1965), hypnotizability (Melei & Hilgard, 1964), Peace Corps performance (Mischel, 1965), adjustment and introversion–extroversion (Peterson, 1965), and friendliness and conscientiousness (Bem & Allen, 1974).

Having thoroughly investigated the area of self-prediction, Mischel (1968, 1972, 1976, 1977) suggested:

> Useful information about a person may be obtained most directly by simply asking him. The predictions made in simple, direct self-ratings and self-reports generally have not been exceeded by those obtained from more psychometrically sophisticated personality tests, from combined test batteries, from indirect measures and clinical judges, and from complex statistical analyses.
> . . . These conclusions seem to hold for diverse areas as college achievement, job professional success, treatment outcome in psychotherapy, rehospitalization for psychiatric patients, and parole violations for delinquent children. (Mischel, 1976, pp. 262–263)

The implications of this line of research suggest that any effort aimed at predicting an individual's behavior or performance in some future time and environment should directly involve that individual. Mischel (1977) has suggested that the subject of assessment or study be considered an "expert and colleague." Furthermore, he asserts that the subjects are the best experts to participate in predictions about themselves and that if one wishes to get an accurate prediction from that individual it is vitally important that he or she be informed of the specific circumstances in which their behavior will be evaluated. The person's ability to predict his own future behavior better than personality tests or other people may be a function of the subject's familiarity with their own past behavior in similar circumstances.

These data further suggest that it can be important to ask each of the persons being assessed directly how they believe they will respond under various custody arrangements. Specific situations could be described to them reflecting possible postdivorce circumstances (e.g., having visitation canceled), and then they would be asked to indicate how they think they would respond given those conditions. Furthermore, the same kind of information can be obtained from the child. Although it does not seem appropriate to place a child in an untenable position by asking which parent or other person he would like to live with, it does seem feasible, even at younger ages, to present him with a problematic situation and ask him what he would do given the circumstances. Of course, the reliability of such a procedure would have to be investigated, as would the effects of any demand characteristics. However, the data seem to indicate that it may provide useful information.

Constant awareness must be given to the fact that the information generated from direct self-ratings and the like is not used in isolation. It constitutes only a small portion of the entire assessment procedure and can be expected to supplement previously presented information. The value of self-rating and self-reports for the prediction of behavior is proffered here and must not be overlooked for the same reason that one would not wish to discard any of the other information. All of it is closely tied to the theoretical assumptions presented earlier in this book, assumptions that have been supported by empirical evidence. Furthermore, each component of the evaluation model proposed here is either currently supported by research (e.g., observational learning and self-prediction) or amenable to empirical testing.

SUMMARY AND IMPLICATIONS

In Part II, I have addressed the question of what should be measured when one is completing an evaluation to determine the postdivorce living arrangements of children. Taking a behavioral perspective in the development of an assessment model and drawing from both the empirical literature directly supporting the theory upon which behavioral assessment is founded and other relevant empirical findings, I have proposed five different areas for assessment: (1) parental competence, (2) the child's behavioral repertoire, (3) the prospective caretaker as a model, (4) the potential postdivorce environment, and (5) the self-ratings and prediction of all significant persons. Although there is obvious overlap between the various areas targeted for assessment, each is considered distinct and important enough to warrant individual consideration. At no time, however, is it suggested that the assessment of any one of these areas can stand alone in achieving the goal of determining the optimal living arrangements for a child. It is hoped that each segment of the overall evaluation process will supplement the other components. The practice of combining several sources of data in a traditional test battery has not been able to improve clinicians' judgment or predictive accuracy (Golden, 1964; Kostlan, 1954; Sines, 1959; Wildman & Wildman, 1975), and as such one is cautioned against making similar assumptions with respect to behavioral assessment measures. Although the validity of such an assumption cannot be determined without research, it was suggested in Chapter 4 and elsewhere (e.g., Wiggins, 1973) that because behavioral assessment emphasizes direct sampling, focuses on the person–environment interaction, and carries with it relatively few assumptions involving little inference, the potential is substantial for greater predictive validity than has been found in studies using traditional approaches. Certainly the possibility of its being worse is remote.

The value of this model also lies with the fact that nowhere in the literature has anyone, to this author's knowledge, presented a model such as this for assisting the courts in deciding the living arrangements of children following their parents' divorce. Consequently, the utility of such procedures has never been investigated. Without some identification of the test responses needed to support a placement with any of the persons involved, the validity of the instruments used in an evaluation cannot be tested. This model provides the assessor with a sound theory of assessment, the important areas to be assessed, and a rationale for each. It is suggested that on the basis of this assessment process specific (as well as global) predictions can be made about how a child and caretaker will adjust to and cope with a given living arrangement. Consequently, the validity of these predictions is amenable to empirical testing. On a global level, one might compare how successful living arrangements have been depending on the manner in which the decision was made. For example, one could compare decisions which were made on the basis of a comprehensive behavioral assessment, a traditional battery of tests and interviews, an agreement between the contesting parties, or in court by the judge without the assistance of any mental health professional. Although an operational definition of *successful* would be required, this type of study would help answer the question concerning the relative merits of various assessment procedures. It might be discovered, however, that none of the procedures predicted success any better than did the court's decision alone. In such a case, useful information would have also been generated and everyone could hang up their Rorschach cards, coding systems, and interview formats and defer to the judge for judgment.

PART III

BEHAVIORAL ASSESSMENT STRATEGIES

HOW TO ASSESS

CHAPTER 8

The Behavioral Interview I

The interview is probably the most widely used behavioral assessment instrument (Hay, Hay, Angle, & Nelson, 1979; Haynes & Jensen, 1979; Keefe, Kopel, & Gorden, 1978; Linehan, 1977; Mash & Terdal, 1976). In fact, a recent survey of behavior therapists (Wade, Baker, & Hartmann, 1979) indicated that the behavioral interview is used with the greatest percentage of clients and that 76% of the sample of therapists used the interview more than any other assessment procedure. This becomes quite startling when one realizes that little research has been devoted to it (Atkeson & Forehand, 1981; Ciminero & Drabman, 1977; Linehan, 1977). Linehan made a frontal assault on the problem when she stated:

> The paucity of research on behavioral interviewing is truly amazing, especially when one considers that one of the strongest criticisms leveled at traditional assessment approaches by behaviorists is that they rely on unreliable methods of data collection and intuitive judgments in arriving at diagnostic and treatment decisions. (p. 49)

Certainly, this same criticism has been weighed against traditional approaches to assessment in the present volume, and its relevance to behavioral interviewing must not be dismissed without proper consideration. The interview will undoubtedly be an important component in the armamentarium of assessment procedures used to decide where a child will live after his or her parents divorce. The question is not whether to use the interview, because its use is practically unavoidable. The question is how reliable and valid is it for this purpose? What utility does it have for deciding the optimal living arrangements for a child? And what can be done in order to insure that the most reliable and valid data possible are obtained through the behavioral interview?

This chapter will be devoted to describing the behavioral interview, its similarities and differences with the traditional interview, and the available literature relevant to its reliability and validity. Finally, the behavioral interview will be evaluated in the light of this research, and the implications of this literature for evaluations completed within the context of divorce will be offered.

A COMPARISON BETWEEN THE BEHAVIORAL AND TRADITIONAL INTERVIEWS

Although there are a few points of similarity between the behavioral and traditional interview, for example, the importance of the client–therapist relationship (e.g., Rimm Masters, 1974), the role the interview plays as a major source of data collection, and the fact that both are subject to the same methodological and research considerations, the differences which exist between these two approaches are much more numerous and have been discussed in several places (Atkeson & Forehand, 1981; Ciminero & Drabman, 1977; Evans & Nelson, 1977; Keefe *et al.*,1978; Linehan, 1977; Mash & Terdal, 1976). One of the major points of departure concerns the importance of time and history. The behavioral interviewer spends a great amount of time in the present, investigating the current manifestations of the problem behaviors. In contrast, the past is more crucial to the traditional interviewer because it will reveal the roots of the individual's concern, which is exposing itself in the form of current symptoms. To the behavioral clinician, the past is important only if it helps to identify the current relationships between the person and the environment. The identification of the controlling variables—antecedent and consequent events—is the goal of assessment to which the interview is directed. For example, if a man enters therapy complaining of relationship problems at work, especially with his supervisors, the behavioral interviewer will complete a functional analysis of the current situation. What environmental stimuli appear to elicit the problem behaviors (i.e., thoughts, motor responses or physiological reactions)? What are the consequences of his responses? The interviewer may discover that the man has a conditioned emotional reaction (i.e., anxiety) in the presence of people whom he perceives to be better than he, which results in nonassertive behavior and subsequent feelings of worthlessness, negative self-statements, and increased interpersonal anxiety. It is the man's current interactions which identify for the behavioral interviewer how the problem behaviors are being main-tained. In contrast, a more traditional interviewer may request a large amount of information about the client's behavior in the past, as a child. In this case the interview may reveal that the client's relationship with his parents, especially his father, was based on fear. They frequently ridiculed him and punished him for talking back. Consequently, his problem is rooted in his past relationship with his parents, and it is this time in history and this relationship which is the subject of concern. This past history may be interesting to the behavioral interviewer for ob-taining some understanding of how the present problem behavior de-veloped, but it may be irrelevant to the goal of therapy.

A second significant way in which the two types of interviews differ is in the information required by each, that is, their language base. In the behavioral interview, the assessor attempts to obtain from the interviewee a clear description of the target behaviors. The focus is on operationally defining the behaviors using overt behavioral referents. For example, if a client states that she responded with anxiety, anger, and frustration to some problematic situation, it is important to know exactly what she means by these terms. The interviewer might ask such questions as, What do you mean by *anger* (*frustration* or *anxiety*)? De-scribe for me how you respond physically when you are anxious. What are your thoughts when you are frustrated? If I were present, but unnoticed, what would I observe you doing when you are angry, anx-ious, frustrated? With this line of questioning, the interviewer begins to identify the components of the target behavior with respect to the three modes of responses. The same kind of clearly described behavior is re-quired in identifying both antecedent and consequent events. Without this kind of information, the behavioral clinician would be hard-pressed to identify the important controlling variables in the environment. Cer-tainly, without this line of questioning the process of prediction is ham-pered. First, no clear understanding of the stimulus conditions which set the occasion for responding is obtained. And second, that which is being predicted is not clear. The only information that is available is that this person gets angry. Anger, however, may mean that she puts a fist through a windowpane or someone's jaw, or it may mean that she be-comes quiet and leaves the troublesome environment. Such information is vitally important in planning a therapeutic intervention or predicting her behavior in the future.

In the traditional interview, however, there is less of an emphasis on objective behavioral descriptions and more on the use of trait labels and dispositional terms (Mash & Terdal, 1976). The feelings and attitudes of the client are requested with little follow-up concerning exactly what is meant by those terms. Both the interviewer and interviewee are using a common language base, therefore, making the interview process less burdensome in that the client does not need to learn a new language. When the client says that he or she feels angry, depressed, or anxious these feelings are accepted at face value. The interviewer may respond to them in some fashion, possibly by acknowledging them and reflecting them back to the client, and this information can be added to other information (e.g., projective test results) and used to identify the individual's underlying personality structure.

Behavioral and traditional interviews are also dissimilar in the view they take of the behavior displayed during the interview itself. This difference is characterized by the dichotomy presented earlier in this volume, sign versus sample. For the behavioral clinician, the behavior displayed by the client during the interview is a sample of behavior in those specific circumstances, nothing more, nothing less (see Atkeson & Forehand, 1981, Ciminero & Drabman, 1977; Evans & Nelson, 1977; Keefe *et al.*, 1978; Linehan, 1977). The interviewer can obtain some information about how this particular individual responds to an unfamiliar person, in a presumably stressful situation. What social skills does this person appear to be capable of demonstrating? How assertive is he? Is he prompt? What is his level of cognitive functioning? A sample of these behaviors is available during the interview and can be important for generating hypotheses for future testing.

Consistent with the trait approach to assessment, the client's behavior during the interview can be considered an indirect sign of the underlying personality structure. As pointed out earlier in this volume, all of the assessee's actions and verbalizations are grist for the interpretive mill. Whatever the client's traits, needs, drives, or other predispositions, they will be revealed regardless of the situation, as long as the proper interpretations are made. Consequently, if the interviewee demonstrates visible signs of anxiety or discomfort during the interview, this may be a clue to an underlying problem and personality structure. Therefore, it must be taken note of, interpreted, and added to other similar signs. It may be indicative of an approach–avoidance conflict rooted in childhood oedipal fears, in which, as a child, the client was very much in love with his mother but shied from overt expression of this love for

fear of castration by his father. In the present, his anxiety with the female interviewer is a sign of this fear and must be interpreted as such.
This facet of the interview again highlights the importance of the past in
the traditional interview.

Although these are the major differences identified between the
two approaches to interviewing, others have been cited. For instance,
Keefe *et al.* (1978) noted that the behavioral interviewer is less ritualistic
about where and when the interview takes place. Interviews are frequently conducted in the home, at school, and over the phone, as well
as in the office. Others have suggested that behavioral interviewing is
more structured and educative (Haynes, 1978), as well as more
treatment- and goal-oriented (Haynes, 1978; Linehan, 1977). Furthermore, it would appear that the behavioral interview is less inferential,
therefore presenting a potential for greater reliability and validity.

RELIABILITY OF INTERVIEW DATA

Given the occasional overdependence on interview data in the
evaluative process, the importance of determining the accuracy and consistency of the information procured through this means should not be
underestimated. The absence of adequate research in the area of
behavioral interviewing, or interviewing in general, has already been
noted. The questions posed in this section with respect to reliability are
no less important than those briefly considered in Chapter 3 with reference to traditional testing methods. How consistant are the data obtained between interviews separated in time from the same person or
persons? If two individuals interview the same person, will they obtain
the same information? Will two different assessors, if presented with the
same interview data, agree about what it means? And, given the same
information, will the same decisions be made by different interviewers?
If interview data are not reliable (i.e., accurate and consistent) then their
value for making important judgments and decisions in general, and
specifically with respect to child's postdivorce living arrangements, can
be seriously questioned. The validity of the instrument can only be as
good as its reliability (Anastasi, 1976). Therefore, if it does not reach acceptable levels of accuracy and consistancy, it is unlikely that the instrument will be a particularly valid measure of whatever it is supposed to
be measuring.

Most of the questions posed above have not been answered di-

rectly, especially those concerning the decisions based on the information obtained. Indirect evidence, both supportive and nonsupportive, is
found mainly in the child development research, which bases much of
its theory and practice on information obtained from caretakers (mostly
mothers) with an anamnestic interview (e.g., Yarrow, Campbell, & Burton, 1970). Other sources come from the behavioral literature on self-
monitoring (e.g., Lipinski & Nelson, 1974), and only recently have investigators looked directly at the reliability of behavioral interview data
(Hay *et al.*, 1979; Iwata, Wong, Riordan, Dorsey, & Lau, 1982).

The data cited in the following pages and the conclusions and implications which arise therefrom apply equally to both behavioral interviewing and interviewing as a general procedure. Suggestions will be
made for how to increase the reliablilty of data generated from the interview, and it will be suggested as well that the behavioral interview, as a
result of its theoretical underpinnings and the type of information required for the functional analysis of behavior, is inherently a more reliable procedure. Of course, the true test of this presumption is empirical
validation.

The Evidence

Studies which address the accuracy of retrospective parental report
are important for several reasons. First, every interview requires historical information despite the fact that some solicit current history
(behavioral) and others, "ancient" history (psychodynamic). Second,
they provide some of the most relevant research in the area of parent
interviewing. Finally, the results of these studies provide both direct
and indirect support for the structure and procedure of the behavioral
interview.

The consensus among investigators who have examined the literature on the reliablilty of retrospective parental reports is that they are
basically inaccurate, inconsistent, and generally suspect when used by
themselves (e.g., Atkeson & Forehand, 1981; Ciminero & Drabman,
1977; Cox, 1975; Yarrow *et al.*, 1970). One of the earliest reports
investigating the accuracy of mothers' report (Pyles, Stolz, &
MacFarlane, 1935) compared medical and developmental data gathered
at birth and during the child's first year with the mother's recall of this
data at the time of the child's 11-month physical exam. The findings
showed that the mother's retrospective accounts of pregnancy and delivery were so unreliable they had to be discarded completely. McGraw

and Malloy (1941) came to essentially the same disappointing conclusion in their study comparing observational clinical record data with both the "usual" clinical interview and a more detailed interview for early physical and behavioral development. The anamnestic interview was seriously flawed in obtaining accurate information, with differences in some data being random in nature or reflecting directional biases. In a third study, Haggard, Brekstad, and Skard (1960) compared the accuracy of recall for 19 months on 27 different scales sampling three time intervals: prenatal, the child's first year, and the child's sixth year. Recall was tapped at two intervals: one to two years, and seven to eight years, to assess the possible effect of memory on reliability. The results demonstrated that the accuracy of parental reports when compared with their own reports six to eight years earlier is quite poor. For the total interview, correlations ranged from -.09 for the sixth year scale concerning whether the child was allowed to decide things for him or herself and the 8-year anamnesis, and .89 for the length of the child at birth for the first year scale and the 8-year anamnesis. The average correlation was .47. Furthermore, there was a considerable degree of variability from mother to mother in the consistency of reports. The range extended from .04 to .67, with an average of .47. Finally, on the important sixth year scales having to do with child rearing (e.g., agreement between parents in child care, attitude toward child's aggression to other children), the correlations, with few exceptions, were less than .40. The average was .24. These results present serious questions as to the usefulness of data gathered with the anamnestic interview.

Wenar and Coulter (1962) reinterviewed 25 mothers who had brought their children to a therapeutic nursery three to six years earlier. Again the material requested related to preganncy, delivery, early development, and various child-rearing and behavioral variables. Judges scored some 854 pairs of statements from the two interviews as the same (S) or different (D). Forty-three percent of the pairs were judged as different, and of these D statements, 40% represented extreme changes or complete reversals in the content of the "facts." Similarly striking discrepancies were found by Mednick and Shaffer (1963) when mother's memory of their child's health history was compared with the physician's medical records. One-third of the cases were descrepant, either denying illnesses that were in the records or claiming the child had had certain childhood diseases when he or she had not.

By far the most extensive investigation into the reliability and valid-

ity of the retrospective method has been completed by Yarrow *et al.*
(1970). In this longitudinal study which spanned anywhere from 3 to 30
years, 224 mothers were interviewed about their children (now 7 to 34
years of age) and asked to provide information on five basic classes of
variables: (1) infant characteristics, (2) maternal care in infancy, (3) the
developmental progress of the child, (4) familial environment and child
rearing of the first five years, and (5) personality characteristics of the
child in the preschool period. The baseline data to which the mothers'
reports were compared were obtained from nursery-school records and
consisted of observations, tests, ratings, and reports obtained at the
time of enrollment on the child, his family, and his experiences during
his years in the nursery school along with some parental reports of the
child's earlier development. Fifty variables were culled from these
sources for comparison between the two sets of data. Interviews
consisted of open-ended questions designed to obtain a reconstruction
of the information in the baseline records. The interview progressed
chronologically through the child's development up to the current period. Both the interview data, which were recorded, and baseline information were coded independently by two raters with the same procedure. All but 11 of the ratings had corrected reliability coefficients at or
above .80. Items failing to reach at least .70 were dropped from the
analysis.

A third set of data was obtained from the children of 190 of the original 224 families sampled three years after their mothers had been interviewed. The questionnaire used with these subjects was constructed to
obtain the same information secured from both the baseline data and the
mothers' interviews. The open-ended questions of the interviews with
the mothers were modified so that the questionnaire format would allow
"structured response alternatives" identical to the categories used in
coding the other two sets of data. The children were administered the
questionnaires in their homes or the nursery school and were informed
that the information was to be used for a study of recollections of childhood. They were not told of the other two sets of data.

On the basis of the information obtained from these three sources,
three comparisons were possible: the mothers' recall with the baseline
records (M–B); the children's recall with baseline (C–B); and the
mothers' recall with their childrens' recall (M–C). Although these three
comparisons reached significance on 90, 62, and 84 percent of the 50 variables, respectively, the authors point out that the magnitudes of associ-

ation were quite low. The correlations for all three sets of data ranged from .00 to .72, with means of .33 (M–B), .21 (C–B), and .29 (M–C). Again, the accuracy and utility of retrospective data had been challenged.

The available evidence overwhelmingly suggests that in a general way, retrospective reports from parents (usually mothers) are inaccurate and discrepant with earlier reports of the same data. Furthermore, the data suggest that there is a directional bias in these reports (e.g., Yarrow et al., 1970). Yarrow (1963) labeled mothers "ego-involved reporters," suggesting that they have a rather large investment in making their child and their relationship with their child more positive in hindsight than was originally reported. Several studies have supported this same conclusion (Chess, Thomas, Birch, & Hertzig, 1960; Graham & Rutter, 1968; Maccoby & Maccoby, 1954; MacFarlane, 1938; McCord & McCord, 1961; Mednick & Shaffer, 1963; Robbins, 1963; Wenar & Coulter, 1962; Yarrow et al., 1970). In the study by Yarrow et al. systematic and significant directional shifts were found in more than half of the 50 variables in all three sets of comparisons.

The authors reported:

> In reconstructing the infancy period, mothers recalled infancy generally as an easier, happier, healthier period than was the case in baseline reports, and credited themselves now with more handling of the infant and more sharing of his care with other adults. Similarly, the establishment of routines . . .was accomplished more smoothly in retrospect. Changes in ratings of the child's behavior almost always shifted toward recalling the past in a more favorable light: Childhood aggression, noncompliance, and problems of thumb-sucking and of stuttering were minimized, and the child's intelligence level and independence were elevated. (p. 37)

Directional biases have also been found with reference to developmental milestones such as walking (Robbins, 1963), completion of toilet training (Mednick & Shaffer, 1963; Robbins, 1963; Wenar & Coulter, 1962), age of weaning (Mednick & Shaffer, 1963; Robbins, 1963), and in judgments by the parents of their child's level of disordered behavior (Graham & Rutter, 1968). Mothers appear to make their children more precocious than they actually were (MacFarlane, 1938). Furthermore, it appears that to a large extent directional distortion is mediated by social stereotypes (McCord & McCord, 1961; Yarrow et al., 1970), popular theories for instance, sibling rivalry (Chess, Thomas, & Birch, 1966), and what Chess et al., (1960) refer to as "socially acquired concepts of functioning," that is, what the experts say should be expected at a certain age under normal or ideal conditions (Robbins, 1963; Yarrow *et al.*, 1970). One study (Robbins, 1963) reported that of the nine variables on which mothers tended to be inaccurate in their recall all of them erred in the direction of the recommendations clearly made in the child-rearing literature. For example, they report that of the 20 mothers who were inaccurate with respect to the mode of infant feeding, 65% shifted in the direction of more demand feeding and only 35% toward less. This and similar findings paralleled the recommendations put forth by Spock (1957). Although a cause-and-effect relationship cannot be drawn from such data, it is highly suggestive, especially in the light of later evidence of a similar kind (Yarrow *et al.*, 1970).

In sum, not only are retrospective reports generally inaccurate, but also there appears to be directional biases which place the presumed facts in a much more favorable light than was actually reported at the time of the initial compilation of the data. If the reports obtained from interviewees are distorted, inaccurate, and generally unreliable, then the decisions made on the basis of this information are generally suspect. Certainly, if the utility of the retrospective interview was to be evaluated with the present evidence only, then one would seem to have no other recourse but to conclude it to be worthless. However, if one looks at the data more closely, a different conclusion may be possible.

Thus far, the reliability of the retrospective interview has been examined as a whole, without regard to the variability in reliability coefficients. If one examines the different variables more closely, it becomes clear that the accuracy of retrospective reports is consistently greater with specific data than with attitudes, feelings, or other kinds of inferential data (Brown & Rutter, 1966; Haggard *et al.*, 1960; Herjanic, Herjanic, Brown, & Wheatt, 1975; Herjanic & Reich, 1982; Hodges, Kline, Stern, Cytryn, & McKnew, 1982; Lapouse & Monk, 1958; Rutter & Brown, 1966; Wenar & Coulter, 1962; Yarrow *et al.*, 1970). For example, two studies (Haggard *et al.*, 1960; Yarrow *et al.*, 1970) found the highest correlations with the recall of length and weight of the child, and the lowest with child-rearing variables and disciplinary practices. At the 8-year anamnesis, Haggard *et al.* (1960) found an average correlation of .80 for the following four scales: length, weight, normality of the child's birth time, and length of breast feeding. However, the 11 scales considered to encompass various child-rearing variables, had correlations which ranged from -.09 to .49, with an average correlation of .24, and the length of recall of these scales was only two years, whereas the other scales required recall of data gathered seven years earlier. Similarly, the Yarrow *et al.* (1970) study found quite similar results, although with lower values across the board. The average correlation for height and weight was .44 for mothers' recall and .49 for children's recall, and the lowest correlations across methods, ranging from .00 to .24 were those reported on disciplinary techniques.

Data from other research seem to reach the same conclusions: "hard-fact" data, that is, information requiring less inference on the part of the person providing the information, increases the amount of agreement and reliability. In an epidemiological study of behavior problems in normal children, Lapouse and Monk (1958) found that the more ill-defined the problem, the less reliable was the mothers' recall when reinterviewed. The agreement between first and second interviews was only 52% on overactivity of the child, and it increased incrementally from temper loss (65%), to nightmares (83%) to stuttering (98%). Similarly, when mothers' recall was compared with the child's recall of the same events, the lowest agreement was still with respect to overactivity (52%) and the highest to stuttering (76%). In a similar vein, Herjanic *et al.* (1975) compared children's responses with those of their parents and found that factual information (e.g., age and address) was more reliably reported than mental-status types of questions (84% versus 69%). Similarly, Herjanic and Reich (1982) reported that parents and children agree most frequently when responding to objective, concrete questions which ask for "simple, irrefutable facts." In contrast, they reported two factors which characterize areas questioned resulting in poor parent–child agreement: Questions which required judgment as to the presence, absence, or severity of a given symptom and questions which could easily be misunderstood or misinterpreted.

In a semi-structured interview, Graham and Rutter (1968) obtained parental reports of child behavior upon which they later made ratings on the degree of psychiatric disorder. They reported that the greatest level of test–retest reliability was found with items such as bed-wetting, stealing, and temper tantrums, and the items they found particularly unreliable fell into two main groups:

> those in which relationships of the child are concerned (e.g., peer relation-
> ships, sibling relationships, disobedience) and those in which, regardless of
> the intentions of obtaining only overt behavior, inferences often have to be
> drawn, e.g., miserable, stomach ache and biliousness. (p. 590)

They concluded that reliability is much more likely to be greater when there is no need to judge the quality of relationships or when the fewest number of inferences about what is going on inside the child's mind need to be made.

Other studies have also emphasized the importance of reducing the need for inference by focusing on specifics and actual frequencies rather than on feelings and attitudes (Brown & Rutter, 1966; Rutter & Brown, 1966; Rutter & Graham, 1968; Yarrow et al., 1970). Rutter and Brown developed a highly structured interview format with trained interviewers and used scales which (1) concentrated on a defined recent period of time (rather than asking about the "usual" pattern), (2) questioned about actual frequencies (rather than relying on answers of "often" or "sometimes"), and (3) used scores based on frequencies (rather than general ratings). They emphasized the importance of differentiating events and activities from emotions and attitudes about events and activities. During their interviews with various family members, alone and together, they found that the most salient feature in arriving at good across-interview agreement was a careful distinction between events and feelings about events, or between objective and subjective reports. This finding also received support in other studies (Haggard et al. 1960; Wenar & Coulter, 1962). Wenar and Coulter reported that the worst reliability coefficients were found in conjunction with highly emotional events, that is, parent *attitudes* toward the problem behavior for which their child had been referred three to six years earlier. It has been suggested that a blow-by-blow description of recent events can reduce difficulties in recalling events and emotional bias (Hoffmann, 1957; Rutter & Brown, 1968).

The data provide consistent evidence to suggest that the reliability of parental reports is intimately related to the degree of specificity of the individual items. The more ambiguous the information requested, as with reports of global feelings, attitudes, or dispositional labels, the more unreliable the information, and hence the less useful. The relevant issue concerns the degree of inference involved. Other research which supports the finding that reliability and validity decrease with the increasing need for inference was reported in Chapter 3 on projective tests and clinical judgment. As was pointed out by Allport and Postman (1947) and further amplified by Yarrow et al. (1970), inference is likely to flourish in situations wherein persons are confronted with ambiguous information, and the retrospective study (i.e., recall) is replete with ambiguities. "In general, recollection, by its very nature, collects and organizes ambiguities and hence is a ready medium for inference" (Yarrow *et al.*, 1970, p. 72). One can only conclude from the data, however, that the more objective and factual the information, the less inference needed and the more reliable and useful the resultant information.

Graham and Rutter (1968) state:

> It seems clear that those who rely on a nondirective approach in history-taking must expect a certain randomness in the responses their technique evokes, a randomness dictated, perhaps, by impermanent aspects of the mother–child relationship. A nondirective approach may well have a place in tapping maternal attitudes, and later on in therapy, but it would appear to be out of place if a reliable picture of how the child actually behaves is to be built up. (p. 591)

Similarly, Cox and Rutter (1977) concluded, "It is evident that systematic questioning is definitely superior to free reporting when it comes to obtaining full and detailed factual information" (p. 281).

The importance of the preceding evidence concerning the reliability of data obtained through interviews is obvious. If, as the evidence suggests, the most certain method of securing reliable information from interviewees is by focusing on specific, factual, or otherwise objective data or descriptions of behavior, then it would appear to follow that behavioral interviewing is likely to result in more reliable data than a more traditional, trait-oriented interview. This is especially clear when one considers that the theoretical foundations and functions of the behavioral interview and functional analysis of behavior requires the identification and specification of behavior so that it is either directly observable or reliably reported. It has been pointed out tirelessly throughout this volume that the behavioral approach to assessment is more direct, operational, specific, and less inferential and ambiguous than traditonal approaches. The fact that the data available on various kinds of interviews (although mainly retrospective) consistently call for and support the reliability of behavioral specificity, factual data, and a reduction in emphasis on attitudinal variables is not surprising. Therefore, it does not make sense to discard interviewing procedures as a whole when it appears that only certain kinds of information are unreliable. These data would appear to suggest that a behavioral interview would be more reliable than a traditional interview. Of course, direct support for this contention is not available at this time, and a comparison study would have to be completed to answer directly the question of comparative reliability.

However, it would also appear to be extremely important to keep as close to the data as possible in completing child custody interviews. Reliance on descriptions of attitudes, ambiguous dispositional concepts (e.g., dependency, hostility), and various emotional labels without reference to factual information, events, and behavior appears to have little utility and may in fact hinder the completion of a valid assessment. Consequently, decisions will be based on inaccurate information and probably result in less than optimum living arrangements for a child.

Behavioral interviews will focus on the current relationships between the environment and person. Antecedent and consequent events are solicited with an emphasis on specific conditions. The prediction of behavior requires knowledge of specific environmental conditions. It was noted earlier that even small changes in the stimulus environment can change behavior, therefore making it essential that the salient features of the environment (the controlling variables) be identified and specified. A few authors have suggested a blow-by-blow description of events in order to increase reliability and decrease the intrusion of emotional bias (Hoffman, 1957; Rutter & Brown, 1968). Certainly, this is what the trained behavioral interviewer will do (e.g., Iwata et al., (1982).

Given the increased reliability of such factual information, however, there will remain a number of very important reliability questions. If two interviewers interview the same individual at the same time, will they obtain the same information? What if the same interviewee is interviewed twice, either by the same person or by two different persons; will the same data be generated? Will the client's responses to the same questions across interviews be consistent? These questions are of vital importance. If a prospective caretaker is interviewed by two different evaluators and different data are generated, then it is suggested that different decisions, predictions, and so on will be made.

Several studies have been reported which present data with respect to interrater, across-interview, and across-interviewer reliabilities (Brown & Rutter, 1966; Douglas, Lawson, Cooper, & Cooper, 1968; Graham & Rutter, 1968; Hay et al., 1979; Herjanic & Reich, 1982; Perri, Richards, & Schultheis, 1977; Robbins, 1963; Rutter & Brown, 1966; Rutter & Graham, 1968; Weller & Luchterhand, 1969; Yarrow et al., 1970). Given the same interview data, are there means available which permit different assessors, raters, or coders to evaluate the material consistently? The question is one of *interrater* reliability. The answer to this question appears to be affirmative. Given proper training and a system for categorizing the information (e.g., specific codes, ratings on a Likert-type scale), the same data can be evaluated consistently. Rutter and Brown (1966) interviewed 20 families of which one parent was a newly admitted psychiatric patient. Two to three hours were spent interviewing the patient, three to four hours interviewing the patient's spouse, and one hour interviewing both. At each interview there were two investigators who made independent ratings of attitudes and emotions of independent members, family events and activities, and summary scales. The three different interviews with each family were conducted by different sets of raters, therefore, yielding six investigators and six sets of independent ratings. The interview was highly structured, especially with respect to events and activities. The interviewer was required to confine himself to specified events and activities and to cover all areas that had been listed. Frequency counts were most consistently obtained for these ratings. Emotions and attitudes were rated on a Likert scale and were based on specific operational definitions, not general ones. For example, "warmth" of the ratee was considered with respect to the way in which the interviewee spoke of a specified person and not whether they were warm in general. Extensive training, using special tape recordings and group discussions, was completed by all interviewers. Interrater reliabilities were high for both feelings and events based on the same interview data. "Irritability," a class of responses which included a number of specific scales (e.g., frequency of quarreling), obtained reliabilities of .79 when the informant was a patient and .85 when the informant was a nonpatient. A scale comparing the relative participation of the husband and wife in household tasks reached interrater reliability of .91 for the husband's participation and .87 for the wife's.

The scales on emotions were also found to be highly reliable. Ratings of warmth demonstrated by the informant when talking about the spouse was .79 with the patient, .75 for the nonpatient, an .85 for observed warmth in the joint interview. Critical comments made by the patients about or to their spouse reached .88, and for nonpatients, .92.

The assessment of the amounts of time which young children spend with different persons in their home in varying patterns of interaction was the subject of investigation in a study by Douglas et al. (1968). Detailed interviews were conducted to obtain information about the child's activities and interactions occurring in the preceding 24 hours. Mothers were questioned in a step-by-step fashion and led chronologically through the day's events. Analysis included (1) a variety of activities grouped into major categories (e.g., sleep, play, basic care and going out), (2) the child's interaction with other persons, and (3) overall attention given to the child. Each of these three categories included subclasses. Using four different samples, the authors examined a number of different reliability and validity questions, most of which will be reviewed later. In addition, the authors reported interrater reliabilities based on 25 interviews coded independently by two raters. The areas coded included the type of interaction and attention. "Concentrated" interaction, which involved physical contact and at least one of two other criteria, reached a correlation of .94. The other areas measured obtained correlations between .80 and .97. It seems clear that information obtained for the interview can be reliably categorized by independent investigators.

Other studies which have reported interrater reliabilities based on the same interview data also consistently demonstrate high agreement (e.g., Hay *et al.*, 1979; Herjanic & Reich, 1982; Yarrow *et al.*, 1970). The significance of this for the interview process is that assessors are able reliably to categorize information obtained by this method. If different individuals can agree on what the data are, then the first step has been taken in the process of assessment and making reliable and valid decisions. If two evaluators sit down independently with the same interview transcript but are unable to agree on how the information is to be culled, the likelihood of fair and objective decisions is remote. However, this tells us little of how consistent judgments would be if they were based on two different interviews, either by the same individual or two different individuals. If each time the interview is employed different data are generated, then it is most likely that different judgments will be made on the basis of that data. This causes obvious problems, especially if an evaluator decides to recommend a particular living arrangement for a child based on a series of interviews, when, if interviewed by a second evaluator, different information is elicited resulting in different judgments and recommendations. In other words, one could say that the interview is an unstable instrument of measurement. If it is being used for the same purpose, the interview must generate the same data, to be evaluated in the same fashion, if it is to be of any real value.

Several studies have reported inter-interviewer reliabilities (Douglas *et al.*, 1968; Graham & Rutter, 1968; Hay *et al.*, 1979; Rutter & Graham, 1968) with inconsistent results. In two of the investigations (Graham & Rutter, 1968; Rutter & Graham, 1968), interviews were conducted with children's parents or with the child, and the presence or absence of various symptoms was rated on a 4-point scale. When only the absence of symptoms was considered, the percentage of agreement between interviewers across interviews was excellent (i.e., all but one in the mid-80s to 100). However, when finer discriminations were required in the assignment of a degree of abnormality, agreement was much more variable and ranged from 0 to 100. Consistent with previously cited data, the higher percentages of agreement were associated with more specific items (e.g., bed-wetting, stealing).

Douglas *et al.* (1968), in the study reported above, had 10 families interviewed on six different weekdays within five weeks. Four interviewers were used and each carried out three of the total six interviews with each family. Comparisons between interviewers for "average time awake", in "play," and in "basic care" yielded average correlations of .89, .79, and .80, respectively.

An important investigation concerning the reliability of the behavioral interview was reported by Hay *et al.* (1979). Its importance is derived from the fact that it is designed specifically to evaluate the behavioral interview. The purpose for undertaking this study was two-fold. First, the authors wished to examine the reliability of the identification of problem behaviors in the behavioral interview. Second, they hoped to examine the influence of three factors on the reliability of specific problem identification. Two sources of variance rest with the interviewer and what he or she puts into the interview and what he or she takes out of it in terms of recording and dictation of client responses. The third factor involves the consistency of client response to the same questions. Hay *et al.* (1979) hypothesized that all three of these factors contribute to the overall variance present in the interview process.

Four interviewers, all advanced graduate students with at least 1,000 hours of clinical experience and advanced training in behavioral interviewing, interviewed the same four clients. They were given as much time as necessary to complete "comprehensive" behavioral interviews and were informed that the goal of the interview was to identify as many client problems as possble. Each interview was audiotaped and transcribed in order to obtain a verbatim account of what transpired during the interview. Immediately following each interview, the interviewer dictated a summary of the problems identified for the client. Subsequently, both the interview transcript and the dictated summary for each case were independently coded by two raters for problem areas and specific problem items and the areas and items questioned. There were a number of important findings.

Statistical analyses were carried out on the number of problem areas identified by each interviewer for each client on both the transcripts and dictations. Interviewers did not differ significantly from each other in the number of areas identified. However, these data are somewhat trivial because, although the number of areas identified was the same, it is possible that entirely different areas were identified by each interviewer. Further analyses computed inter-interviewer agreements between pairs of interviewers for specific areas identified and for problem items within specific areas (e.g., an area might be employment and an item within this area tardiness). Inter-interviewer agreement for the identification of problem areas in the transcript ranged from .25 to .76 with a mean of .55. For the subclasses of more specific items, the agreements range from .10 to 1.00, with an average of .40. General area identification on the dictations ranged between .22 and .80 with a mean of .48. None of these levels of agreement are very satisfactory. Therefore, although the *number* of problems can be reliably identified, exactly what the areas are is considerably less reliable.

To determine whether any of the three factors hypothesized to affect the reliability of interview data were in fact operating in this study, further data analysis was conducted. Investigating the impact of the input factor on reliability, the authors analyzed the number of areas in which the interviewers asked the client at least one question. The coded interview transcription was used for this purpose. They found that the interviewers differed with respect to the number of areas questioned. In addition, they examined whether interviewers asked questions in the same areas and if so whether the questions concerned the same problem items within that area. Agreement scores for specific areas questioned ranged from .33 to .87 with a mean of .62. Agreement for items questioned within an area ranged between 0.0 and .74 with a mean agreement of .29. The interviewers varied with respect to all areas of input: number of areas questioned and specific areas and items questioned.

These results are important because they suggest that unless some form of structured interview format is used in which specific areas are questioned information which can be directly compared across two interviews will not be available. If two interviewers have different theoretical orientations or believe that certain factors are important for determining the suitability of a potential caretaker, then different questions will be asked in different areas (i.e., different input (see chapter 2). Historically, diagnostic accuracy has suffered for similar reasons, although within the past six or seven years researchers in this area have made great strides. They have been developing interview formats which are highly structured and elicit information which is evaluated with respect to categories with operationally defined criteria of exclusion and inclusion (see Matarazzo, 1983, for a review). As such, the reliability of diagnostic systems has increased to levels not before available.

Hay *et al.* (1979) also examined the consistency of client responses by comparing their responses on the transcripts to questions which were asked by more than one interviewer. Agreement scores ranged between .67 and 1.00 with the mean agreement per pair of interviewers across clients was .86. These data suggest that given the same input, clients will give the same responses. Unfortunately, the exact interval between interviews is not clearly identified, therefore weakening the usefulness of this finding. The implication of this finding is that as long as the same questions are asked, who does the asking is not necessarily important. The client is likely to give the same response consistently across interviews and interviewers. This conclusion is somewhat weakened because of the circumstances surrounding these interviews. The clients knew the purpose of the study and knew that their responses were being recorded; inflated reliability is therefore possible. However, as will be suggested later, the use of similar conditions (e.g., cross-checking interview responses with client's knowledge) may be included in the assessment procedure for the purpose of increasing the reliability of the client's responses. This would appear to be especially important within the context of a custody evaluation.

The third factor given attention by Hay *et al.* (1979) is data output. How did the data obtained from dictations compare to the verbatim transcripts of each interview? Any discrepancy between the two can be attributed to incomplete or inaccurate recording of client responses by the interviewer. To determine the extent to which information was lost as a result of output error, the number of areas identified in both the verbatim transcripts and dictated summaries was compared to the total number of problem areas actually identified in the transcript. The percentage of problem areas noted during the interview but not commented on in the dictation ranged from 0.0 to 55% per interview, with an average of 28%. For whatever reason, interviewers lost over one-fourth of the information generated during the interview. Certainly, this is not a good record. At the other end, between 0.0 and 33% of the areas identified as problem areas in the dictation were not mentioned at all in the transcript. This means that some of the problems were "invented." The average percentage of such areas per interview was 5%, which the authors report as minimal compared to the 25% figure found in earlier studies.

Despite the fact that interview summaries were dictated immediately after each session, large portions of data were lost. The question arises of how much more would be lost with increasing intervals of time. These results also support, as the authors point out, the importance of audiotaping sessions. This would appear to be especially important when an objective evaluation of the data is going to follow, or in matters of considerable importance, such as a child custody evaluation, in which continuous contact with the client across time (especially in a therapeutic situation) is not typical. Also, one questions the extent to which evaluators are presently relying on their memories to evaluate individual interviews or various combinations of family interviews, either separated in time or held in close succession. Certainly, these data would make such practices, without audiotaping, seriously suspect as an assessment procedure.

The study by Hay *et al.* (1979) was important for its investigation of the interview. However, it is only the beginning of what must be done. The identification and specification of problems is certainly an important function of the interview. What about the controlling, antecedent, and consequent conditions? If the interview is to be a useful procedure in either treatment or prediction, it must be able to identify the controlling variables, as well as other factors, reliably. If problem identification is unreliable, then how reliable can the identification of variables associated with these problems be expected to be? It would seem that the reliable identification of problem areas and items in this study could have been substantially increased if a structured interview format had been used as well as audiotaping. The same might be expected with other factors important to the functional analyses. This research needs to be done.

In the meantime, however, the reliability of the behavioral interview, although it has been investigated directly only occasionally, seems to have considerable potential and gains indirect support from the literature presented above. Below is a list of factors which have been shown to increase the reliability of interview data and which have direct relevance to the theoretical foundations of the behavioral interview. The interview should include:

1. *A structured interview format* (Brown & Rutter, 1966; Graham & Rutter, 1968; Hay *et al.*, 1975; Linehan, 1977; Matarazzo, 1983; Spitzer, Endicott, Fleiss, & Cohen, 1970; Spitzer, Fleiss, Endicott, & Cohen, 1967). The use of a structured interview helps insure that the same input data will be used, therefore exposing each client to the same stimulus. This allows one to compare data across different individuals, with the same individuals across interviews; or with the same individuals across time. As the level of inference is reduced through such a method, the reliability of the data should increase.

2. *An objective coding system* for evaluating interview responses (Brown & Rutter, 1966; Douglas *et al.*, 1968; Graham & Rutter, 1968; Hay *et al.*, 1979; Perri *et al.*, 1977; Robbins, 1963; Rutter & Brown, 1966; Rutter & Graham, 1968; Weller & Luchterhand, 1969; Yarrow *et al.*, 1970). Unless there is an objective procedure for categorizing the information derived from an interview, the possiblilty of subjectively evaluating the data and making idiosyncratic clinical judgments increases. Again, the probability of interview data being reliably evaluated diminishes with increasing subjectivity. As such, the same individual interviewed by two different clinicians at different times is likely to receive varying evaluations. If this occurs the value of the instrument is questionable.

3. *Questioning for specific, factual information* (Brown & Rutter, 1966; Ciminero & Drabman, 1977; Douglas *et al.*, 1968; Evans & Nelson, 1977; Haggard *et al.*, 1960; Hay *et al.*, 1979; Herjanic *et al.*, 1975; Hoffman, 1957; Lapouse & Monk, 1958; McGraw & Molloy, 1941; Wenar & Coulter, 1962; Yarrow *et al.*, 1970). During the process of interviewing, if the interviewer formulates questions to generate objective descriptions of behavior, factual information, and/or actual frequencies and specifics by using and requesting precise statements, the reliability of the data increases. This is in contrast to generating attitudes, emotions, or dispositional labels without clear and objective behavioral referents.

4. *Audiotaping interviews* (Douglas *et al.*, 1968; Guest, 1947; Haggard *et al.*, 1960; Hay *et al.*, 1979; Payne, 1949; Perri *et al.*, 1977; Robbins, 1963; Rutter & Brown, 1966; Yarrow *et al.*, 1970). The taping of interviews will insure that none of the data are lost from the client's response to output. In addition, no "invented" data will be generated. Taking detailed notes, even immediately after an interview, can result in a loss of information which may be important in the overall evaluation. The inter-

viewer must be concentrating on a number of things during the interview and is likely to miss informaion if he or she has to take notes. Recording also results in accurate information for subsequent coding and evaluation.

5. *Reliability checks* (Hay *et al.*, 1979; Kohn & Carroll, 1960; Linehan, 1977; Lipinski & Nelson, 1974; Lytton, 1971; Nelson, Lipinski, & Black, 1975; Reid, 1970; Robbins, 1963). Interrater reliability and interviewee response consistency will increase across interviews if the interviewees are aware that the accuracy of their reports is being checked. Reliability checks for raters and coders of interview data may occur every nth interval or at random, and interviewee responses can be checked for accuracy by (a) telling the client that they will by taped, (b) interviewing other individuals for the same information; or (c) asking the same questions in different ways during the interview or across a series of interviews. If interviewees believe the accuracy of their information is to be checked in some fashion, it is more likely to be reliable.

6. *Training and periodic recalibration* of coders and interviewers (Goldfried & Sprafkin, 1974; Haynes, 1978; Johnson & Bolstad, 1973; Kent & Foster, 1977; Patterson, Reid, & Maerov, 1978). Individuals who are responsible for completing the interviews or coding interview data must be trained to a certain acceptable level to insure proper use of the instrument. Because there is a tendency for instrument decay to occur, interviewers and coders should receive retraining (or recalibration) periodically to determine that the instrument is still being used properly.

Although it is impossible definitely to attest to the level of reliability possible if the above six factors are combined without being properly researched, it is important to stick as close as possible to the data in developing and conducting interviews. If reliable information is to result from interviews conducted in child custody evaluations (or for any other purpose) and therefore provide the best possible data upon which determinations are to be made, then it is not only important but also imperative to use whatever methods have proved to be the most reliable. The use of anything less casts considerable doubt on the decisions being proffered and may present important ethical questions. It is apparent that at this point the interview is not the most reliable method available to us. However, since it will undoubtedly continue to be used, full application of the most effecacious procedures is certainly essential, as is a clear understanding of the limitations inherent in this kind of data.

CHAPTER 9

The Behavioral Interview II

VALIDITY OF INTERVIEW DATA

High reliability of data generated during a behavioral interview increases the probability that the instrument (i.e., the interview) will be valid. Put in a slightly different way, if the instrument is not reliable, it is not likely to be valid measure (Anastasi, 1976). However, the validity of the measure must be investigated independently to determine its usefulness for the purpose for which it was developed. There are a number of different kinds of validity, most of which have not been investigated with the behavioral interview or with interviews in general.

How well can the data obtained from the behavioral interview differentiate between naturally occurring groups (e.g., abusive and nonabusive parents, suitable and unsuitable caretakers)? This is a question concerning the discriminate validity of the instrument. It should be able to identify members of contrasted groups. How well does the interview agree with data generated with other instruments (i.e., convergent or criterion-related validity)? In other words, does the behavioral interview measure the same thing that some other instrument has already been shown to measure? For behavioral assessment, the most important measure with which the interview should correlate, the higher the better, is naturalistic observations of the same behavior. If the behavioral interview is conducted to identify and specify the controlling variables associated with a child's noncompliant behavior, then the variables identified should agree with those observed in the natural environment. As has been suggested, one of the important differences between behavioral and traditional approaches to assessment is that behavioral approaches have fewer levels of inference (see Goldfried & Kent, 1972).

Greater significance is placed on sampling behavior directly. Therefore, a direct sample of behavior is an important criterion for evaluating the validity of a measure, in this case, the behavioral interview.

The predictive validity of the interview method has not been investigated. It would be defined as the ability to predict some future behavior or pattern of bahavior on the basis of present performance on the measuring device. In this case, how well can the evaluator predict adjustment of a particular child within a particular living situation on the basis of information obtained during the interview?

The final type of validity that requires close attention is content validity. How well does the behavioral interview sample the relevant aspects of the responses or response classes being investigated? Content validity would include the three response modes where applicable and questions guided by the S-O-R-K-C model. Again, earlier portions of this volume emphasized the superior content validity in a behavioral approach to assessment, especially when compared with traditional devices which are not so concerned with the specific content of the test items.

Most of the research which has investigated the validity of information generated from traditional interviews or behavioral interviews has primarily examined criterion-related validity and occasionally discriminate validity. The findings of this line of investigation will be presented below, along with some discussion of its applicability to and implications for, an evaluation to determine a child's living arrangements after his parents' divorce. However, congruent with everything else that has been presented thus far, none of the available research has looked directly at the issure of validity in the context of a child custody evaluation. Extrapolation from the data is necessary in order to address the issue of validity in the present context. Without instruments already developed for this purpose, it is possible only to examine how valid interview data have been in other types of investigations and with other populations.

The Evidence

Although the breadth of investigation for interview validation is not substantial, several studies have been cited by Schwitzgebel and Kolb (1975) which examine the degree of accuracy between survey responses and some external criteria. In 1944, Hyman interviewed individuals about their United States War Savings Bonds. Seventeen percent of those questioned denied having redeemed their bonds when the records indicated they had. Pinneau and Milton (1958) found disagreement 22% of the time between men and their observer wives with respect to whether the husbands took cream and sugar in their coffee. Parry and Crossley (1950) found distortion in responses which ranged from 2% to 40% for questions on registration and voting; Community Chest contributions; possession of a valid library card, driver's license, and telephone; and ownership of an automobile and a home. In a more recent investigation (Walsh, 1967), randomly selected college students were asked for information regarding their academic performance. Their responses were checked against the actual school records. Their accuracy ranged from 49% in response to a question of their overall cumulative average, to 100% for the number of courses failed. The majority of responses were 70 to 80% accurate. In a study reported earlier, Haggard *et al.* (1960) investigated the accuracy of parental recall over a period of two to eight years on 27 different scales. Although most of the recall items were construed as investigating a reliability question, recall on four of the scales was considered to answer a validity question because they had an "objective external criteria with which to be compared." The four scales were length of the child at birth, weight of the child at birth, whether or not the child was born at normal term, and the length of breast feeding. The authors report correlations of .91, .77, .91, and .96 respectively, with an average of .91 for the six-month anamnesis, and .89, .71, .81, and .71, with an average of .80 for the eight-year anamnesis. These coefficients are fairly good and demonstrate considerable stability over time. It should be noted that these four scales are factual and specific, factors previously identified as important for increasing data reliability. As for the other studies reported above, the present author is unaware if the subjects in those studies knew that their responses were going to be checked. Previously cited research has indicated that if people know their reports will be checked their responses increase in accuracy (e.g., Hay *et al.*, 1979; Reid, 1970).

    In addition to the studies cited above in which verbal interview responses were compared with some objective external criteria, a few studies have been reported which made direct comparisons between interview and observational data (Antonovsky, 1959; Douglas *et al.*, 1968; Smith, 1958; Weller & Luchterhand, 1969). In the earliest of these studies, Smith (1958) observed and interviewed 30 mothers of nursery-school children and compared their responses to the two methods. The observation session was 45 minutes in duration and required the mother to interact with the child during the last 15 minutes "in order to provide an experimental measure of her behavior toward the child's dependency solicitations when she was busy." The observed behavior was coded with a 16-category scoring system (e.g., asking verbal help, teaching, comply, giving reward).

The interview, which was conducted two to four weeks after the observation session, consisted of 36 open-ended questions on infant care and training, present demands made upon the child, and other such variables. The interviews were recorded and responses rated on several 5-point scales (e.g., separation from the child, use of "do" and "don't," feelings of mother for the child, restrictions placed upon the child). The primary objective of the author was to compare various maternal behaviors and child dependency. As such, the bulk of the reported results examined the relationship between various interview or observation antecedents (e.g., rejection, punishment, overprotection) and total dependency scored from the interview or observation. Direct comparisons between reported maternal behavior and observed behavior in similar circumstances were minimally reported and were confined to ratings on the techniques preferred by the mothers. The reports by mothers of their behavior when they were busy were compared to their actual behavior during the last 15 minutes of the observation. No significant differences between the two sets of data were found. Smith (1958) reports that 70% of the mothers reported using techniques which were also observed to be used. The results of this study led the author to conclude that controlled observation and interviews are equally valid in obtaining measures of mother behavior and therefore interviewing is preferable "because it permits study of a wider range of behavior in a shorter time" (p. 282).

Although the results of this study could be considered promising, I am unable to agree with the author's conclusions. The important comparisons, that is, those which examine the direct relationship between what is reported to occur in certain circumstances and what actually occurs, have not been adequately reported. The fact that 70% of the mothers were observed using the same techniques they had reported using does not permit a determination of accuracy with respect to the specific circumstances in which the techniques are used.

Antonovsky (1959) examined the relationship between four mother behavior variables (affectional contact, expectation or level of demands, restrictiveness, and punishment) and three child behavior variables (dependency, aggression, and initiative), and examined the direct relationship between ratings of these variables obtained from three data sources: structured and unstructured interviews and observation. Each mother was given a rating on a 7-point scale on each of the four maternal behaviors for each set of data. The structured interview lasted approximately one hour and consisted of predetermined topic areas in which the mothers were asked about their attitudes, value, and practices with reference to various areas of child rearing. The unstructured interview was also an hour long and permitted the mother to discuss anything she wished. The observation session consisted of a half-hour session in which the mother and child were observed interacting in a playroom setting. The intercorrelations among the three sets of data for the various maternal behaviors were quite inconsistent and generally low. For example, the unstructured interview correlated .64 with observational data on affectional contact. However, the correlation for demands and restrictiveness were low (.30) and negative (-.08), respectively. The relationship between ratings based on observation and those from structured interviews, which might be expected to be better, were worse, with coefficients of .35, .42, and -.02 for affectional contact, demands, and restrictiveness, respectively.

The results of this study do not provide much hope for the validity of interview data. However, this investigation is subject to the same criticism weighed against Smith (1958). Global labels are being investigated and not specific responses to specific situations. A rating is made on how much of a certain variable a mother reports having used or appears to use, and it is then compared with a similar rating based on a different method. The global nature of these ratings weakens the results of this study with respect to the validity of a behavioral interview. Furthermore, in one set of interviews, supposedly structured, only the topics were determined; the information to be derived was not. Mothers were simply asked their "attitudes, values, and practices." The other set of interviews was even less useful, for they were unstructured, permitting the mothers to decide the topic and content.

In a previously reported study, Douglas et al. (1968) had observers record in 5-minute intervals the activities and interactions of the elder child of 10 two-child families for four hours in the morning. That afternoon, a second individual interviewed the mother about the morning's events in a stepwise, chronological fashion. The two sets of data were independently coded and then compared. The results indicated that the total amounts of time spent in basic care and play were remembered very well. Although they were frequently inaccurate about when things had occured, they always mentioned helping, reading, painting, messy play, and stories when they had also been noted by the observers. At no time did they indicate types of play that had not been observed. Finally, when the assessment of interaction was examined, close agreement was found. In comparing the amount of attention received by the child from all persons in all activities derived from observations with interviews, a correlation of .90 was obtained. In this case, the correspondence between interviews and observations was quite good. It should be noted that the comparisons were made very close in time and the interviews emphasized detailed factual information, not attitudes and values. This may help account for the high agreement and lend further support to the use of behavioral interviews which attempt to identify *detailed* information about *current* relationships. However, the relationship between interview and observational data on such variables as antecedent and consequent events has not gained any real clarity from the present investigation, although a detailed, factual interview appears to yield data comparable to that derived from observations.

The studies which have examined the validity of the interview by comparing its data with data generated through direct observations have been rare and equivocal in their results. Although Smith (1958) and Douglas *et al.* (1968) seem to support the validity of the interview, and Antonovsky (1959) and Weller and Luchterhand (1969) seriously questioned it, I am not pleased with the strength of any of the findings. None of the studies directly examines specific behavior–environment relationships.

In questioning the tendency of child development research to compare inferences based on interviews with inferences derived from direct observations, Yarrow (1963) warns:

> If one is interested in comparing the information on child-rearing which comes from interviews with that of observations, it is necessary to design studies which involve more than a line-up of (a) interview responses in which the mother has summarized her usual performance in the life of the child with (b) observations of mother–child interactions in a 5- to 30- minute play session in front of a one-way screen. Ideally, the study should be designed so that observed mother-child interactions and mothers' reports of interaction refer to the same or nearly the same samples of behavior. (p. 220)

More recent research has been cited by Haynes and Jensen (1979) that bolsters the validity of data obtained from the interview. With some target populations, the interview has been found to be a valid measure. Kleinmann, Goldman, Snow, and Korol (1977) interviewed hypertensive patients and compared their responses about life stressors with blood pressure levels. They found a significant relationship between the amount of stress reported by these patients and their blood pressure level. In a previously cited study, Herjanic et al. (1975) reported an average agreement of 80% between children's responses to several questions and their parents' responses to the same questions. Vogler, Weissback, and Compton (1977) found that initial interview data from alcoholics was positively correlated with their later response to treatment. Beiman, O'Neil, Wachtel, Fuge, Johnson, and Feuerstein (1978) reported that self-reported avoidance behavior was significantly related to other criterion measures of fear. Women's responses to a questionnaire measuring arousability correlated with their reports of sexual arousal (Wincze, Hoon, & Hoon, 1978). Perri et al. (1977) interviewed 48 college students, half of whom had been successful and half unsuccessful in self-initiated smoking reduction. They found that their structured interview procedure was able to differentiate between the two groups in a number of areas and time periods. The interview revealed differences between the two known groups which were significant at various confidence levels for all variables. Using the Child Assessment Schedule, a highly structured diagnostic interview format used with children, Hodges et al. (1982) were able to classify successfully behaviorally disordered outpatients, behaviorally disordered inpatients, and controls. There were significant differences between these three groups for total score, nine of eleven content areas (e.g., school, friends, and family), and eight of nine symptom complexes (e.g., depression, undersocialized conduct-aggressive).

The combined impact of these studies and others reviewed by Haynes and Jensen (1979) led them to the following conclusion:

> Data derived from interviews *can be* highly correlated with data from other assessment instruments (criterion-related validity); can covary with subjects' classifications in naturally occurring dimensions (discriminant validity); and can be sensitive to manipulations of conditions before or during interviews. It was also noted that the content validity and reliability of interviews can be indicative of the overall validity of the interview, although these have infre-

quently been investigated or reported. In view of the. . . findings supporting
the applicability, utility and validity of some interview formats, it is difficult
to account for the highly informal use of interviews in behavioral assessment.
(pp. 102–103)

Informality in interviewing appears to be unacceptable if reliable
and valid data are to be generated. Although the research presently
available is far from answering the question of validity for the behavioral
interview, it all appears to be pointing in the same direction; the more
factual and specific the information, the more structured the interview
procedure, the more objectively adhered to, the less inference required,
and so on, the more reliable the data. The more reliable the data, the
better the chances for a valid measure. Foster and Cone (1980) have suggested that "as objective, topographic features of behavior are increasingly emphasized in self-report items, the correspondence between self-
report and direct observation data increases (e.g., Bandura & Adams,
1977; McReynolds & Stegman, 1976; Zuckerman, 1979)" (p. 325).

The evidence presented above would seem to imply that any evaluation which occurs in response to custody litigation should not rely
solely on data from informal clinical interviews. Without incorporating
the factors discussed earlier which have been shown to increase the reliability of interview data, it is clear that the information thus obtained
and from which decisions concerning a child's future are to be made, is
highly suspect. Although it appears imperative that the appropriate
steps be taken to increase reliability, one must not lose sight of the fact
that the validity of intervew data has yet to be adequately determined.
The potential exists if the appropriate steps are taken, but until the interview technique is validated through empirical investigation its usefulness is unknown. The only recourse, therefore, is to use other sources of
the same information. If at all possible, the behavioral interview should
not be used alone. This is the opinion of many researchers in the field
(Atkeson & Forehand, 1981; Ciminero & Drabman, 1977; Evans & Nelson, 1977; Haynes, 1978; Keefe et al., 1978; Linehan, 1977; Lytton, 1971).
In an article addressing the validity of interview procedures, Lytton
wrote:

With the modifications introduced recently which mean that the information
input is more strictly controlled, the interview has shown reasonable agreement with other data that are inaccessible to direct observation and for information about internal cues. Above all, verbal reports by parents will inspire
greater confidence in their veracity and validity if they are supplemented by,
and checked against, observational measures. (p. 677)

SITUATIONAL SOURCES OF BIAS AND ERROR

An examination of the reliability and validity of clinical interviewing, and more specifically behavioral interviewing, would not be complete without some mention of the sources of error and bias that can threaten them. Recently, this topic has been addressed in the literature frequently (e.g., Cannell & Kahn, 1968; Haynes, 1978; Haynes & Jensen, 1979; Linehan, 1977; Schwitzgebel & Kolb, 1975) and typically indentifies various interviewer, interviewee, or situational variables which may result in a distortion or inaccuracy in the data. For example, Haynes and Jensen (1979) offered the following list of "presumed sources of error in interviews," some which have already been noted within this volume:

1. Differences in race, sex, or social class between the interviewer and client (Abramowitz & Dokecki, 1977)
2. The retrospective nature of the interview process and error associated with retrospective data (Ciminero & Drabman, 1977; Yarrow et al., 1970)
3. Interviewer knowledge of hypotheses or classification of clients
4. The social sensitivity and type of information elicited (Ciminero & Drabman, 1977; Haynes, 1978)
5. The age of the client
6. The population being interviewed (e.g., college sophomores or herion addicts)
7. The content, format, and structure of the interview (Rosenthal, Hung, & Kelly, 1977)
8. Bias in the reports of mediator–clients (e.g., parents, psychiatric staff)
9. Bias presumed to be inherent in all self-report measures

In an extensive review of the various factors which may affect the reliability and validity of interview data, Cannell and Kahn (1968) underscored the importance of motivational variables as a source of invalidity. This source is significant in the context of child custody litigation because it would include such factors as the client's dislike of what he or she is being asked to reveal during the interview. The questions may be viewed as intrusive and the responses potentially embarrassing and self-incriminating. As such, the interviewee may distort or withhold information for fear of the consequences which may follow. The price a prospective caretaker may have to pay for revealing certain kinds of information may be an unfavorable custody decision. Certainly one can see how such consequences might undermine the accuracy of verbal reports during this kind of an evaluation. Although there is no data which sheds light on the question of the invalidity of verbal reports obtained from interviews as part of a child custody evaluation, deliberate distortions and inaccuracies would appear to be unavoidable and pose a considerable threat under these circumstances.

The potency on motivational variables finds considerable support in the research on social desirability, demand characteristics (Orne, 1969), evaluation apprehension (Rosenthal, 1969), evaluation apprehension (Rosenthal, 1969), and impression management (e.g., Braginsky & Braginsky, 1967; Sherman, Trief, & Sprafkin, 1975). The literature presented earlier on the accuracy of retrospective data consistently found that if parents (i.e., mothers), distort reports of their own or their child's behavior, they do so in the direction of social desirability (e.g., Chess *et al.*,1960; McCord & McCord, 1961; Yarrow *et al.*, 1970). Inaccurate reporting tends to place the informant in a positive light, show precocious childhood development, and be in line with socially accepted childrearing practices (Evans & Nelson, 1977). For example, Graham and Rutter (1968) report that one-third of their sample of children who had been labeled with a "definite" psychiatric disorder by two independent psychiatrists were regarded by their parents as having no problems or as having problems of no more than average severity for a child at this age. McCord and McCord (1961) found the validity of their interviews to be questionable because of parents' tendency to make their family life conform to cultural stereotypes. The "ideal" family was viewed as one in which "the parents loved their children (and vise versa), the father directed family affairs, and the father was a 'decent' person who treated his son with kindness" (p. 185).

Survey research has identified the same phenomenon. Parry and Crossley (1950) concluded that questions most likely to lead to inaccurate answers were those which raised guilt feelings. Asking factual questions, they found the least amount of distortion from a question concerning the possession of a telephone (2%) and the greatest percent of distortion with respect to Community Chest contributions (40%). Walsh (1968) asked college students a series of questions about their academic performance with the incentive of the future participation in a pleasant, well-paying project. Their employment was dependent on their answers. It was found that only 36% of the males interviewed reported their grade point average correctly. Weiss and Davis (1960) interviewed a group of counselors and job applicants and found that the level of distortion appeared to be positively related to the social desirability of the replies.

The third area of research which relates to the issue of motivational sources of invalidity of interivew data is impression management, a term first coined by Goffman (1959) and subsequently supported in the literature (e.g., Braginsky & Braginsky, 1967; Braginsky, Braginsky, & Ring, 1969; Sherman et al., 1975). Sherman et al. defined this term as "the presentation of an interpersonal facade designed to facilitate attainment of personally valued goals" (p. 867). In other words, the interviewee fakes his or her responses during the interview to increase the probability of a desired outcome. So far as the prospective caretaker is concerned, he or she will behave and respond in such a way as to be viewed as a suitable caretaker for the child in question. Of course, what it means to be a suitable caretaker is a matter of debate, and it is unlikely that each concerned party will properly carry off the facade, not knowing exactly what is expected. However, whatever their particular perception of the term, the research in the area suggests that the person will attempt to distort his or her behavior in order to gain custody.

Yarrow (1963) has given ample consideration to the problem of "ego-involved" reports by mothers on various child-rearing variables and presents succinctly some of the issues in relation to motivational sources of invalidity:

> Stripped of all elaborations, mothers' interview responses represent self-description by extremely ego-involved reporters. . . .How well then can we expect the mother to report interactions of which she is a part and on which the culture has placed distinct values? When we ask the mother, "what do you usually do when your child does something that pleases you? or . . .that you have forbidden him to do?" can we expect an accurate report, uncontaminated by the mothers' particular needs and defenses, her values about parental and child behaviors, her class identifications and the child-rearing mores attached to them? (p.217)

Even more so, these same questions and concerns must be kept at the forefront in the use of any type of interview used in a child custody evaluation. The potency of social desirability and impressions management as sources of invalidity for interviews conducted within the present context is likely to be even greater than has been suggested by Yarrow (1963) because a prospective caretaker has the chance of losing a child bases on his or her reports, whereas in the research interview this possiblity does not exist. Of course, without proper empirical investigation the degree of influence this factor has on the evaluation will remain mere speculation.

Other sources, or potential sources, of error and bias which have been suggested include anxiety (Antonovsky, 1959; Haggard *et al.*, 1960; Smith, 1958), age (Riesman & Ehrilich, 1961), sex (Benney, Riesman, & Star, 1956), racial background of the interviewer (Athey, Coleman, Reitman, & Tang, 1960; Katz, 1942), interviewer attitude (Smith & Hyman, 1950), social class (Lenski & Leggitt, 1960), interviewer's interests (Raines & Rohrer, 1960), and mechanical error (Hay *et al.*, 1979; Guest, 1947; Payne, 1949).

FINAL REMARKS

There are many potential sources of error and bias in the interview process, although, as Haynes and Jensen (1979) suggest, the behavioral interview need not differ from any of the other myriad of assessment devices in the number and kind of variables that would need to be identified, explained, and controlled. They suggest, as have others (e.g., Linehan, 1977), that an empirical approach is required for the investigation of these threats to validity and reliability so that they can be controlled. Linehan notes that the impact of these variables does not condemn the use of the interview, but merely alerts us to factors which may help in deciding when interview data are likely to be accurate and when they are not.

The determination of a child's living arrangements after parental divorce will affect the lives of many people directly and indirectly for an extended period of time. A lot is at stake when the contesting parties and the children involved enter the fishbowl of evaluation. There is little doubt that each will be attempting to present their own side of the story and themselves in a positive light so that the decision will be favorable to each of their own interests. Their "interests" may or may not be what is most beneficial to the child (who also has his or her own interests and desires). The degree of influence that the various sources of error and bias noted above will have on interviews conducted in conjunction with the child custody evaluation is unknown. Research must be undertaken that will address these questions. One thing is certain: all forms of interviewing are subject to the same threats to reliability and validity. Neither traditional nor behavioral interviewing is exempt.

A reasonable objective would be to be cognizant of their possible impact on the interview data and go to whatever lengths necessary to control them, given that such methods of control are available and have been empirically demonstrated. For example, numerous suggestions were made earlier of how to increase the reliability of interview data. Trained interviewers, reliable rating or coding systems, reliability checks, and structured interview formats may all help to control for situational sources of error and bias. Of course, it may not be possible to control for every source of invalidity, but the awareness of the sources and the lack of control of their influence can also be useful. Instead of making recommendations based on various interview data with a high degree of confidence, one's report should note the possible sources of error and make recommendations which are at best probabilistic. To present a high degree of confidence in data derived from interview procedures which are uncontrolled and ridden with inference is misleading and irresponsible. Too much depends on any custody decision to present recommendations to the court which are based on a highly questionable use of a given method, especially when the recommendations are highly sought after and given considerable weight. Unfortunately, experience suggests that many custody evaluations are based almost exclusively on interview data which are not collected in any structured format, not evaluated in any reliable manner, and not used consistently with each person involved (see Chapter 2). All of this information must also be considered in the light of research presented in Chapter 3 on clinical judgment. Without controlled methods of interviewing, evaluators are left with their own clinical judgment, the accuracy of which has not been shown to increase with training or experience.

Structured Behavioral Observations I

It would seem clear that although the behavioral interview has the potential for being a fairly reliable and valid assessment instrument (as long as certain conditions are met) it still falls short of acceptability. Linehan (1977) pointed out, "In the final analysis, there is no way to verify whether the client is deliberately distorting events or not" (p.45). Various concerns with interview data have resulted in frequent warnings against their isolated use in behavioral assessment and have stressed the importance of increasing confidence in the data by using other more reliable and valid methods of assessment (Atkeson & Forehand, 1981; Ciminero & Drabman, 1977; Haynes, 1978; Keefe *et al.*, 1978; Linehan, 1977). One strategy which can be used for buttressing information obtained from the behavioral interview and which will provide a new, potentially more reliable and valid source of data is direct behavioral observation. The concept of potentiality is again underscored in this chapter because, as is the case with the behavioral interview, certain conditions must be fulfilled before the reliability, validity, and utility of this assessment strategy can be in any way assumed.

As an assessment procedure, behavioral observations are second only to behavioral interviews in their use by behavior therapists with their clients (Wade *et al.*, 1979). Together, they are used with approximately 90% of all clients. These figures testify to the importance of these procedures to the behavioral assessor. Behavioral observations constitute an indispensable component of the functional analysis of behavior and are consistent with the assumptions underlying a behavioral construct system. Throughout this section of the volume, the behavioral approach to personality assessment has been identified by the direct sampling of behavior. The direct observation of criterion behaviors significantly reduces the need for inference which is characteristic of the traditional assessment model, which posits underlying personality constructs (see Goldfried & Kent, 1972).

Many writers have attested to the importance and acceptability of direct observation for the assessment of behavior (Atkeson & Forehand, 1981; Ciminero & Drabman, 1977; Cox, 1975; Foster & Cone, 1980; Lytton, 1971). Atkeson and Forehand (1981) called direct observation "the most accepted procedure for obtaining a reliable and valid description of current child–parent interactions and/or child–teacher interactions" (p. 202). Similarly, Foster and Cone (1980) describe it as the "most valuable assessment tool of behavioral researchers" (p. 332), and Cox (1975) believes the "direct observation methods give the best hope for teasing out detailed sequences in parent–child interactions" (p. 258). Finally, Lytton describes the signficance of direct observation in saying, "The closer the researcher gets to the actual behavior and events, the more faith he will have in the data, and this means essentially that observation should replace or supplement second-hand data" (p. 678).

In the pages that follow, a description and definition of structured behavioral observation will be presented along with an explanation of its advantages, especially when compared with naturalistic observation, and its potential place as an assessment strategy in the proposed behavioral assessment model for determining the optimal living arrangement for a child. In addition, various aspects of reliability and validity will be explored, as well as methodological problems and their potential solutions.

In reviewing the literature on direct behavioral observation, attention will be given only to studies which consider parent–child interactions, unless some other study is of particular relevance. Unlike the research on the behavioral interview, there are many studies which have either directly or indirectly evaluated the use of direct behavioral observations, although it must be emphasized once again that none of the literature directly addresses the application of this procedure to the child custody evaluation. (It is clear however, that observation is used in child custody cases, see Chapter 2.) Therefore, it is possible to evaluate behavioral observations only as a general strategy, generalizing where possible to the child custody situation. Finally, questions of reliability and validity, or criticisms of methodology, can be applied equally to observational procedures presently being used by individuals doing child custody evaluations. Wherever possible, attention will be given to this point.

A GENERAL DESCRIPTION

Direct observational procedures, whether structured or naturalistic, have attracted a great deal of attention over the years, with books, chapters, and review articles providing individual definitions and discussions of the general methodology (e.g., Heyns & Lippitt, 1954; Hutt & Hutt, 1970; Jones, Reid, & Patterson, 1975; Kent & Foster, 1977; Mash & Terdal, 1976; Weick, 1968; Wiggins, 1973; Wright, 1960). A particularly useful definition is provided by Mash and Terdal (1976):

> A direct observational procedure is . . .a method for obtaining samples of behaviors and settings determined to be clinically important . . . , in a naturalistic situation or analogue situation that is structured in such a way as to provide information about behaviors and settings comparable to what would have been obtained *in situ*. They . . .involve the recording of behavior at the time it occurs, not retrospectively, the use of trained and impartial observers following clearly specified rules and procedures for recording, and behavioral descriptions that require a minimal degree of inference. (p. 261)

There are four extremely important points in this definition which are characteristic of good direct observational procedures. Most importantly, this methodology requires a direct sampling of the behaviors of interest in the appropriate settings. As indicated earlier, the sampling of criterion behaviors in the situations to which prediction is aimed (or those similar) avoids the need for positing hypothetical constructs. Second, behavior is recorded as it occurs. A time lag between display of the behavior and its documentation does not exist. This controls for loss of information through such factors as forgetting, competing information, or distortion, problems which can also plague the behavioral interview. Immediate recordings of the data may involve observers who code the data as it occurs, or procedures which capture the behavior in a form which can permit coding at a later date (e.g., audio-and/or videotaping, Hughes & Haynes, 1978). The third important element in this definition is the utilization of impartial observers who have been extensively trained in the use of whatever coding or rating system is being employed. The observational system typically requires that the observers follow specific rules and procedures. Essentially, these requirements are intended to increase the reliability of the instrument by making certain that it is administered in a standard fashion by each person on each occasion. Similarly, the persons who function as observers must remain impartial; otherwise the possibility of generating biased data is increased (see Chapter 11 on methodological considerations). This, of course, then reduces the reliability and validity of this particular assessment instrument. Finally, the level of inference needed to record behavior should be kept to a minimum. In order to achieve this requirement, each behavior tagged for measurement should be described with specific behavioral referents. The more specific the better. This tactic will also affect the reliability and validity of the instrument. Two independent observers should be able to identify the same behavior at the same time. If they are unable to do this with a high degree of consistency, the usefulness of the procedure must be questioned. For example, the level of inference required to identify when a person is "angry" is much higher than it is to identify when the person is "hitting." This is the crux of the last point in the Mash and Terdal definition; the behaviors of interest should be described with enough specificity so that two independent observers can identify it with a high rate of agreement and accuracy. The importance of all these factors will become increasingly clear in the present chapter and the next when attention will be given to reliablilty, validity, and an array of methodological considerations.

Numerous studies have been reported which employed observational systems either in a naturalistic or structured setting which fulfilled either some or all of the requirements put forth in the above definition. Although space limitations make it impossible to review even a small percentage of those studies here, a number of good reviews are available (e.g., Bell, 1964; Haynes, 1978; Hughes & Haynes, 1978; Lytton, 1971). Although obvious differences exist when using this strategy in a naturalistic setting or some contrived setting, the procedure itself remains essentially the same, and for the purpose of explanation it will be so described.

Each system of observation develops a highly specific coding format to be used to record behavior as it occurs. Each behavior is given an individual code. Several different systems being used in naturalistic settings have been reported (e.g., O'Leary, Romanczyk, Kass, Dietz, & Santogrossi, 1971; Patterson, Ray, Shaw, & Cobb, 1969; Wahler, House, & Stambaugh, 1976), as well as in structured environments (e.g., Eyberg & Johnson, 1974; Forehand & Peed, 1979; Glogower & Sloop, 1976; Tavormina, 1975). The specific behaviors chosen to be given codes and recorded are usually selected for their particular relevance to the theory or construct under study (Hughes & Haynes, 1978), although many of the same behaviors are selected in different systems. The total number of behaviors coded from one system to another is quite variable. Some may emphasize only a few discrete behaviors (Forehand & Peed, 1979), or comprehensive systems may be employed which focus on a wide range of behaviors. For example, Patterson's group at the Oregon Social Learning Center is currently using a 29-category code system (Reid, 1978), while Kogan, Wimberger, and Bobbitt (1969) focused on 43 codes and Moustakas, Sigel, and Schalock (1956) attempted to code 132 child behaviors and 39 parent behaviors.

Although earlier observational systems utilized codes which were less than adequate in terms of their specificity and behavioral descriptions (e.g., Antonovsky, 1959; Merrill, 1946), the more recent uses of this strategy, especially those reported in the behavioral literature, have been exceptional. Not only are operational definitions of each code provided, but also rules for deciding when and when not to use the particular codes and examples (e.g., Forehand, Peed, Roberts, McMahon, Griest,& Humphrey, 1978; Patterson *et al.*, 1978; Wahler *et al.*, 1976).

Coding systems which are very specific, discrete, and behaviorally defined are important for insuring high levels of interrater and other forms of reliability. The more precise the behavioral descriptions, the greater the chances for replicability (Hughes & Haynes, 1978). However, despite the objective characteristics of the codes themselves, their accurate application cannot be assumed. Extensive training experiences are required before an observer is able reliably to apply the code with clinical populations beyond the training environment. Forehand, Griest, and Wells (1979) have reported that their observers receive at least 50 hours of training prior to the start of "real" observations and then, one-hour training sessions weekly throughout the time they are collecting observational data. Maerov, Brummett, Patterson, and Reid (1978) also report an extensive training procedure with their observers, including memorization of the 29 code abbreviations and their definitions; practice writing the abbreviations on the coding sheets, with and without the use of criterion videotapes; didactic discussions of rules and special coding situations; and 15 to 20 hours of practice with the videotapes. All of this occurs before the first trial run in the natural setting. The observer is not considered reliable until an interobserver agreement of 75% is attained on two consecutive observations.

Once the observers have a command of the observational system, with all its codes, rules, and procedures, they are then ready to administer the system in whatever setting is used. Typically, the system employs both time and behavior sampling (Hughes & Haynes, 1978). After the data is gathered, the various behavior categories are usually expressed in terms of their frequency, rate, duration, or percentage of total behavior (Hughes & Haynes, 1978). Such quantification allows for objective, noninferential evaluation of the data and provides the opportunity to observe concrete changes before and after intervention, and make inter- and intrasubject comparisons. Furthermore, these types of data will increase the probability of obtaining and maintaining greater levels of reliability.

Although both naturalistic and structured observational procedures rely on a similar format, the latter procedure is different from naturalistic observations in one very significant way (other than being conducted in the clinic or laboratory rather than the natural environment, e.g., home or school). In the structured environment, the investigator brings parent–child dyads into the clinic or playroom under specially arranged conditions. Although some investigators have observed parent–child dyads in free-play situations with virtually no instructions (e.g., Baumrind, 1967; Bishop, 1946), typically the parents are instructed to engage in specific tasks and are observed from behind a one-way mirror. From this vantage point, the behaviors of interest are observed and recorded by the trained observers. Most often, the specific tasks or special situations utilized in structured behavioral observations are selected in order to elicit the behavior or behaviors under study. The environment is set up in such a way as to provide cues, prompting, and eliciting stimuli which facilitate the occurrence of the target behaviors (Haynes, 1978). For example, Smith (1958) was interested in studying dependency behavior in children and their mothers' responses to this behavior. During the last 15 minutes of a 45-minute playroom observation session, she had mothers withdraw their attention from their children by asking them to complete a long demographic data questionnaire. She then observed the children's bids for their mothers' attention and how the mothers responded to them. After an initial session in which mothers were observed in free play with their children, Bishop (1946) told one-half of the mothers that, although she thought the child had done the best he or she could with respect to constructiveness, imaginativeness, and maturity during the first session, she (the author) considered the child capable of higher achievement and was hoping to observe this in the second session. This manipulation was used to investigate the effect of increased motivation on maternal dominance. Rosen and D'Andrade (1959) also wanted to investigate dependency and set up the following situation to do so. They arranged for children to be almost entirely dependent on their parents' help by blindfolding them and asking them to build a tower with only one hand using unusally shaped blocks. Santostefano (1968) used a method he called "miniature situations," which involved observing the parent and child in several different tasks. A few included the child guiding the parent through a maze, the child having the parent give him a drink from a cup, the parent coloring a drawing for the child, and the child having the parent comb her hair. Finally, Forehand (e.g., Forehand Cheney, & Yoder, 1974; Forehand & King, 1974), constructed structured situations to increase the probability that noncompliant behaviors would be elicited. Children and their mothers were observed for 20 minutes in a playroom situation. During the first ten minutes, in what they called the Child's Game, the children were allowed to play with anything they wished. The parents were instructed not to intrude in any manner to change the structure of the game. However, when the ten minutes were over, the mothers now had the opportunity to play whatever they wanted (i.e., the Parent's Game) and the child was required to follow. This second situation was one replete with commands and provided ample opportunity for the child to display noncompliant behaviors.

In sum, structured observational systems are characterized by the following factors and procedural variables. The variables include: (1) direct sampling of criterion behaviors (2) in the clinic or laboratory, under (3) specially arranged situations and/or specific task instructions (4) at the time the behavior occurs, using (5) well-trained and impartial observers, who (6) record behavior, usually with a coding system of some kind, using (7) clearly defined rules and procedures, and (8) operational definitions of target behaviors, requiring a minimal amount of inference, resulting in (9) quantified data, which allow (10) pre- and postintervention and intra- and interindividual comparisons.

Although many studies have reported direct observations of behavior, not all have necessarily included all of these variables. Obviously, some of the factors would have to be included if the system is to be considered a direct observational procedure. However, others may not be used or are used inadequately, and it would appear that the systems that employ a greater number of these factors are more likely to be adequate than those that do not. The reasons for this statement will be considered at length in the next chapter.

ADVANTAGES OF STRUCTURED BEHAVIORAL
OBSERVATIONS

Direct behavioral observation in the natural setting is probably the most desirable strategy for assessing behavior. Such a procedure assesses criterion behaviors in criterion environments. Despite methodological considerations which may threaten the validity of data obtained from naturalistic observations, the question of whether behavior observed in this situation is representative of behavior exhibited in the criterion environment is unnecessary. This setting *is* the criterion situation. Generalization is not a concern. Whenever possible, direct observations in the natural environment should be used. However, as many authors have noted (e.g., Atkeson & Forehand, 1981; Haynes, 1978; Hughes & Haynes, 1978; Mash & Terdal, 1976; Santostefano, 1968), such a strategy is often not possible (e.g., child abuse, sexual dysfunction, etc.), is inefficient, especially with low-rate behaviors (e.g., temper tantrums), and is very time-consuming and economically unfeasible. With low-frequency behaviors, there is no guarantee that the behavior of interest will occur during the observation period. Consequently, a large number of observation sessions may be needed in order to obtain the desired interaction. This heightens the cost in terms of money and manpower hours. Furthermore, Santostefano (1968) pointed out that only so many environments can be observed for any one subject. This is not necessarily a problem if the investigator is only interested in behavior exhibited in one particular environment. However, if more extensive observations are required across several natural situations, the problems of time consumption and financial cost are multiplied.

Observations made in structured environments have many advantages over observations made in natural environments (Atkeson & Forehand, 1981; Evans & Nelson, 1977; Haynes, 1978; Hughes & Haynes, 1978 Lytton, 1971; Mash & Terdal, 1976; Nay, 1977; Santostefano, 1968). The major advantage postulated, although not empirically tested, is the efficiency of the procedure. With the use of specially arranged situations or task instructions, structured observational procedures are able to elicit the behaviors of interest, even those which maintain a low frequency in the natural environment. Behaviors which might not be observed in the natural environment are facilitated. As a result, the time needed to observe target behaviors and the financial cost involved are substantially reduced and the ease of administration enhanced. Examining the relationship between the amount of information gained and the time required for assessment, Haynes (1978) concluded that the use of structured observations is a very efficient practice.

The second important advantage of this procedure is that it permits the clinician to make valid comparisons between and within individuals, at the same time or across time. The structured situation provides a high degree of standardization or stimulus consistency to which the same individual can be exposed on different occasions over time. Also, two or more different persons can be compared in the same stimulus situation. This is a valuable aspect of the structured procedure.

Implied in the advantage just discussed is that the effects of an event on an individual can be measured efficiently. The event could be an intervention program, evaluated for its effectiveness by the changes that occur in response to a standard stimulus measured by pre- and postintervention behavioral observation. For example. Forehand, (e.g., Forehand & King, 1974) observes parent–child interactions in two structured situations and measures the frequency, rate, and percentage of total behavior for a number of discrete behaviors. Because he is interested in the treatment of noncompliance, the behaviors under investigation are directly related to this notion. After the initial assessment, he then trains the parents to change their behavior in response to the child's behavior. After completing the intervention program, he again places the parents and child in the same stimulus situation and records the same target behaviors, noting any changes. The observational system is usually sensitive to the changes that have been made as a result of the intervention program. Similarly, the use of a standard stimulus situation could also be used to evaluate changes incurred as a result of some naturally occurring event (e.g., divorce, custody decision or change of custody, death of a spouse, parent). Although this latter possibility has not been reported in the professional literature, its utility seems obvious.

A fourth major advantage of behavioral observations occurring in a structured environment is that the variability of the observed behaviors is reduced. This is a direct result of the subject's being exposed to the same stimulus complex on repeated occasions. If the variability of behavior is reduced, then one would expect the stability of behavior over time to increase. In turn, it may decrease the proportion of error variance in the resultant data and enhance the relative sensitivity of the measurement process (Haynes, 1978).

Finally, with the increased elicitation of important behavior–behavior and behavior–environment interactions, less time is needed to derive behavior rate estimates and hypotheses about antecedent and consequent events.

Despite these many advantages, structured behavioral observations are potentially flawed by the lack of generality from the laboratory to the natural environment. As Haynes (1978) has suggested:

> If the behavior of subjects in structured assessment situations deviates significantly from their behavior in the natural environment, the validity of inferences about the rate and topography of behavior drawn from structured situations is suspect and considerations of efficiency are irrelevant. (p. 230)

The question raised here is one of validity and will be taken up in detail later.

STRUCTURED BEHAVIORAL OBSERVATIONS AND DETERMINING THE POSTDIVORCE LIVING ARRANGEMENTS OF CHILDREN

The advantages of direct behavioral observations in general and of structured parent–child interactions specifically are wholly relevant to the context of the child custody evaluation. The fact that this approach requires direct sampling of behavior is of major importance. Despite the value of direct observation, however, one must not assume that simply because an investigator observes parents and children interacting that a valid measurement has been made. As defined earlier, direct observational procedures require trained, impartial observers who will record the behavior of child and parent and their interaction according to specific rules and procedures. Informal observations will be inadequate. It will be noted in a later section that many factors can threaten the reliability and validily of observational data if the proper precautions are not taken. Informal observations are highly suspect, being prey to, among other things, reactivity. Furthermore, informal observations would appear to be evaluated in terms of each observer's own personal construct system, with a reliance on experience and clinical judgment. The problems inherent in the use of clinical judgment have already been discussed at length.

Utilizing highly specific behavioral definitions helps to insure the quality of observational data. More than one independent observer will observe the same behavioral interactions and record the same data. This does not seem possible with loosely constructed observational precedures. Furthermore, the quantification of data into concrete categories assists the clinician in evaluating the products of observation in a predetermined fashion.

One of the primary benefits of structured behavioral observations as described here is the ability to make within- and, especially, between-subject comparisons. In essence, the child custody evaluation is completed to assist the courts in deciding which of the available living environments is most suitable for the particular child. The implied question is concerned with making direct comparisons. If the natural parents are being considered, and usually they are, is the mother *or* the father the more appropriate physical custodian? For this very important reason, a vehicle must be available which permits direct interpersonal comparisons. If standard stimulus situations are not used, such comparisons are not possible, at least not reliable and valid ones. As such, the structured behavioral observation provides the best opportunity for making such comparisons.

Furthermore, naturalistic observations are not, as a rule, feasible in the circumstances in child custody. It was suggested earlier that a variety of situations must be evaluated in order to obtain an adequate sample of parent–child interaction. In addition, it would be necessary to evaluate each prospective caretaker with each of the children involved. The time and cost, as well as the logistics, involved in completing such an assessment in the natural environment seem overwhelming. Laboratory observations appear to be the logical alternative (assuming adequate levels of reliability and validity). In this context, perhaps more than in any other, the efficiency of structural behavioral observations (i.e., information obtained/assessment time) is apparent.

The functions of this assessment strategy in the overall behavioral assessment model being proposed in this volume are multiple. Primarily, it would serve as a vehicle for evaluating parental competence in a variety of the situations generated through the criterion analysis discussed previously. Those situations which can be structured in a clinic environment can be measured with this procedure. Second, each situation will allow the direct observation of parent and child behaviors and their interaction. This will provide samples of behavior from which to complete a functional analysis of various child behaviors selected for assessment. It should be possible to identify the controlling variables of many of the behaviors of interest. For example, with a coding system which included such parental responses as rewards and disapproval, it would be possible to identify which parent was reinforcing or criticizing which child behaviors. There would be room not only for interparental comparison but also for statements with respect to the current maintaining variables for the targeted behavior.

Each of the prospective caretakers could be evaluated as a model. Hypotheses could be generated from this parental behavior leading to further evaluation with other measures. On a very gross level, if an individual assessee was found to use a high percentage of critical statements during a 20-minute observation session and very few positive statements, one source of data would be available for evaluating the person as a model. Does he or she display a high percentage of critical statements in other situations? With other children? If this pattern of responses was observed across most of the stimulus situations and with the use of another measure, a rather strong statement could be made about what kind of behavior this person would display as a model.

Information obtained through observational assessment could function as a source of validation for other measures used in the overall evaluation. It was suggested in the chapters on the behavioral interview that, although it held a great deal of promise as a reliable and valid measure in itself, it is better that it not stand alone. It was suggested that some form of direct observation be employed, first, to check the validity of the interview data, and second, to act as a deterrent to interviewees who might intentionally distort or give inaccurate information if they knew the same information would be solicited from another source (Lytton, 1971).

Consistent with the primary function of behavioral assessment, structured observational strategies can provide the necessary information for planning and evaluating treatment programs should they be desired. The entire behavioral assessment model proposed in this volume is constructed to identify various behavioral excesses and deficits, as well as behaviors under inappropriate stimulus control. In addition, the functional analysis of each of these behaviors will reveal the controlling variables which are currently maintaining targeted behaviors. As such, it is entirely possible to plan intervention strategies to change or enhance any of these responses if one desires. For example, if a child is placed in the physical custody of his mother and it has been discovered through the analysis that this child is consistently noncompliant, then it would be possible not only to identify how this mother's behavior is helping to maintain her son's noncompliance but also to teach her the necessary skills to change this unwanted behavior. The observational procedure can then be used a second time at the end of the treatment program to assess its effectiveness in reducing the child's noncompliant behavior. The same procedure could be followed with other behaviors as well.

THE RELIABILITY OF OBSERVATIONAL DATA

Interobserver Agreement

The degree of agreement between two or more independent observers in the clinical setting constitutes interobserver reliability and is widely recognized as an important requirement for any behavioral observation procedure (Johnson & Bolstad, 1973). According to Hughes and Haynes (1978), the level of interobserver agreement "sets the upper limit to the validity of inferences derived from the observation situation" (p. 439). If two observers using the same instrument (i.e., coding systems) are unable to obtain the same information from observing the same interactions, the usefulness of the instrument is seriously questioned. It has been suggested, however, that despite high levels of agreement between two or more independent observers, the accuracy of their observations may still be suspect (e.g., Johnson & Bolstad, 1973). Accuracy is measured by the level of agreement between the observer and some previously determined coding criterion based on an audio- or videotape. As will be pointed out later, it is entirely possible for two observers to reach high levels of agreement but be inaccurate with respect to the criterion.

Although one might question the appropriateness of referring to interobserver agreement as a form of reliability because it does not actually measure the consistency of the instrument over time in the traditional sense, the current belief, when viewed from the perspective of generalizability theory (Cronbach, Gleser, Nanda, & Rajaratnam, 1972), is that interobserver agreement can be considered a sort of alternate form reliablility with each observer functioning as a different form of the same measurement device (Cone, 1977; Johnson & Bolstad, 1973; Jones et al., 1975).

As far as identifying the minimally acceptable levels of interobserver agreement before discounting the data, Johnson and Bolstad (1973) make two suggestions. First, if percent of observer agreement is being used, the minimum requirement would be at least to show it was higher than would be expected by chance. With correlation calculations, it would be necessary at least to demonstrate that they were significant relationships. They further suggest that with very complex coding systems such as their own (see Johnson, Wahl, Martin, & Johansson, 1973; Johnson & Lobitz, 1974) and Patterson's (Patterson *et al.*, 1978) an overall agreement of 80% to 85%, using the traditional method of calculation

$$\frac{\text{number of agreements}}{\text{number of agreements plus disagreements}}$$

is the realistic upper limit.

In a comprehensive review of studies using structural laboratory observations of parent–child interactions, Hughes and Haynes (1978) reported interobserver reliabilities ranging from .62 to 1.00 with most falling between .80 to .90, well within the range of acceptability. This review examined 35 studies beginning in 1956 (Moustakas *et al.*, 1956) and ending in 1976 (Forehand, Doleys, Hobbs, Resnick, & Roberts, 1976). In two more recent studies by Zegiob (Zegiob & Forehand, 1978; Zegiob, Forehand, & Resick, 1979), interrater reliabilities were computed on maternal and/or child behavior categories (e.g., out of contact, playing interactively, direct commands, positive verbal). Interobserver agreement reached 85% or above and 90% or above in the two studies, respectively. Gordon (1976) reported average interrater reliabilities of .93, and Atkeson and Forehand (1978) cite a study by Jewett and Clark (1976), investigating the appropriate dinner-time conversation of preschoolers, which reported interobserver reliability of 97% accuracy.

It appears clear from this data that it is possible to obtain very high levels of interobserver agreement in the structured behavioral observation of parent–child interactions. This finding also suggests that such a strategy is capable of achieving valid information. Of course, a high level of interobserver agreement is only the first of many steps leading to a conclusion that behavioral observations are a valid method of assessment.

Stability or Consistency of Observational Behavior

Hughes and Haynes (1978) suggest that the stability of an observational system is "inferred from the serial correlation or variance between consecutive administrations or from comparisons of portions of one administration; it is also another indication of the upper limit of confidence which may be placed in any one administration of the instrument" (p. 440). In other words, if the stability of behavior across several occasions is ample, then it may be possible to secure similar information from a single adminstration of the instrument. Given that structured behavioral observations provide the assessees with the same or nearly the same stimulus conditions on consecutive observations, the stability of the observed behavior should be enhanced. Furthermore, when inconsistencies are identified across different sessions, they are the result of either natural variations in the behavior under observation or a function of error in the instrument (e.g., observer drift or reactivity—Hughes & Haynes, 1978; Lytton, 1971).

Studies reporting stability coefficients based on structured observational data are not in great abundance. Smith (1958) measured the maternal behavior of 30 mothers during a 45-minute play session with their children. Correlations were computed for the occurrence of seven of the categories between the first and second 15-minute segments and the first and third 15-minute segments. The correlations between the first and second 15-minute ranged from .15 to .72 with an average of .47. Four of these correlations were significant, and it appeared that some behavioral categories (e.g., structurize and noncomply) were more consistent than others (e.g., giving positive and negative directions). Prior to the last 15 minutes of interaction, the mothers were given a long questionnaire to complete, thereby changing the stimulus conditions of the session. On the basis of the changing condition, the degree of correlation between the first 15 minutes and the last 15 minutes would be expected to be lower than between the first and second, which were essentially the same stimulus condition. This is exactly what was found. The correlations for the second set of data ranged from -.02 to .38, with an average of .25. Eyberg and Johnson (1974) observed children and their parents in six separate 5-minute situations designed to require the child to engage in independent activity, to respond to standard parental commands, to tolerate separation from parents, and to interact appropriately with each parent. Using the average number of deviant behaviors per situation as the dependent measure, they found a .80 correlation for the entire sample between the pretreatment and posttreatment scores. This result demonstrates the extreme stability of some behavior, especially in the light of the 12-week intervention program which occurred between the two assessment sessions.

Merrill (1946) examined intersession correlations of approximately one week for 11 categories of behavior and found a range between .32 to .93, with an average of .71. Gordon (1976) also compared maternal behavior on two separate occasions separated by one week. Recording five general classes of maternal verbal behavior in the form of frequency counts and the child's noncompliance during a 20-minute free play session, he found a correlation of .71 between the maternal behaviors on the two occasions across all subjects and categories. The separate categories correlated as follows: describing, .72; praise, .36; questions, .94; directive, .97; and criticism, .52. The means for each of these categories were not significantly different between the two occasions. In a second experiment cited in the same report, the author examined the consistency of the same behaviors, but this time each of the two sessions was completed with a sibling. Therefore, the mothers' consistency of response was examined across two of her children. The average correlation across all subjects and categories was .73 and, by category they were describing, .77; praise, .71; questions, .60; directive, .82; and criticism, .57. Again, there were no significant differences between the means of any of these categories. Finally, when the two siblings observed were both six years of age or younger, the stability of maternal behavior was higher (.78) than when both were six or older (.65). It would appear that maternal behavior can be consistent across time with the same and different children. Some kinds of behavior appear to be more stable than others.

Hughes and Haynes (1978) reported two other studies that provide further evidence for the stability of behavior across sessions. Wahler, Winkel, Peterson, and Morrison (1965) observed the behavior of children in several different structured observation sessions. They presented the cumulative records of their behavior, and Hughes and Haynes (1978) noted that their slopes were almost identical, thus indicating that the behavior rates emitted across the sessions were similar. Scarboro and Forehand (1975) presented the average behavior rate of a control group across three baseline, three intervention, and three follow-up sessions. The rates were 2.8, 2.4, and 2.1, respectively, suggesting considerable consistency over time. On the basis of this data, Haynes (1978) suggested that three sessions may provide a reliable estimate of behavior rate under structure imposed by the authors.

Consistent with the study by Smith (1958) in which lower correlations were found between the beginning 15-minute segment and the last

15-minute segment of a 45-minute observation session due to a change in the stimulus conditions, Hatfield, Ferguson, and Alpert (1967) found low correlations (.30 to .40) for behaviors emitted in two different situations (a role-playing telephone game and a fishing game), and Leon (1971) discovered considerable variation in mother and child behavior across four different structured situations all presented during one large session.

Finally, three additional studies (Hatfield *et al.*, 1967; Herbert, Pinkston, Hayden, Sajwaj, Pinkston, Cordua, & Jackson, 1973; Johnson & Brown, 1969) provide different levels of consistency across time. For example, Hatfield *et al.* (1967) found the between-session correlations of 28 child and 28 mother behavior categories to range from -.14 to .78, with the modal range falling from .30 to .50.

Although, to my knowledge, split-half reliabiltiy data have not been reported for structured behavioral observations in the clinic, one study undertaken in the natural environment (cited in Johnson & Bolstad, 1973) reported a split-half reliability of .72 for "total deviant behavior score" in a sample of 33 normal children. In order to calculate this statistic, they took the total deviant behavior score for the first, third, and fourth days and the second half of the fifth day. They found a corrected reliability of .83 for the entire 5-day period after applying the Spearman-Brown correction formula.

On the basis of their review of literature concerning the stability of structured behavioral observations as a measurement instrument, Hughes and Haynes (1978) made the following inferences: (1) structured laboratory observation can result in parent–child interactions which are consistent across assessment sessions; (2) consistency varies with different target behaviors; (3) consistency varies with different structured situations; (4) empirical research on the degree and determinants of consistency is lacking (p. 441).

It would appear that, basically, structured behavioral observations can provide a reliable measure of behavior, although one is cautioned against assuming that the specific behaviors under observation are always stable. To be safe, several observation sessions would be an appropriate control for the possible lack of stability across sessions (Lytton, 1971). The implication of these findings is that, barring other methodological problems (e.g., reactivity), behavioral observations can provide the evaluator with a reliable sample of the individual's behavior. The information obtained during the structured observational assessment will

assist in the derivation of a functional analysis of the behaviors of interest. In addition, a reliable assessment can be made of each individual's
behavior with respect to modeling concerns. Although the reliability
data presented above set the upper limits to the instrument's validity,
that validity cannot be assumed.

THE VALIDITY OF OBSERVATIONAL DATA

Historically, not unlike the notion of classical reliability, the role of
validity in behavioral assessment has been generally overlooked, or at
least not given the attention it requires (Goldfried & Linehan, 1977;
Johnson & Bolstad, 1973). The point of contention involves the generally
agreed-upon fact that the most valid measure of behavior is the assessment of that behavior in the criterion environment. If behavior is directly observed in the criterion environment, then where is a suitable
criterion against which the direct assessment instrument can be validated? As far as criterion-related validity is concerned, there is not an
available criterion, or at least that is the argument often presented.
However, such a line of reasoning would seem to make sense only in
cases in which the behavior is measured in the natural environment
(and even there, there are internal threats to the validity of the measure), and only where criterion-related validity is being questioned and
not other forms of validity (e.g., sensitivity and discriminate validity).
Every other strategy stored within the behavioral assessment armamentarium, from the behavioral interview to enactment analogues (Nay,
1977, i.e., structured behavioral observations), can and should be validated against other measures of the same phenomenon. The most appropriate way to validate these measures is with other measures which
in a stepwise fashion get closer and closer to direct observation of the
criterion behaviors. The final step in this process, and the procedure of
assessment which is the closest to the criterion behaviors, is direct observation in the natural environment. Although some authors (e.g.,
Wiggins, 1973) would lead one to believe that behavioral assessors have
thrown away traditional psychometric theory along with the traditional
state–trait approach to personality assessment, the trend in the
behavioral literature is toward increasing the study of reliability and validity issues (Goldfried & Linehan, 1977).

The validation of structured behavioral observations basically encompasses three areas. First, a valid observational system should be

sensitive to changes that take place as a result of some treatment program or other relevant intervening variable. For example, if the coding system employed has been developed to measure various classes of aggressive behavior, and, after an initial session with the system, a treatment program is completed aimed at changing (i.e., decreasing) the amount of aggressive behavior displayed by the target subject, then the postintervention observation should reflect these changes in the rise and fall of various behavioral categories. If this does not occur, one might argue that the instrument was not sensitive to the changes that had taken place. This is an especially potent conclusion when other devices, also constructed to measure the same behaviors, indicate behavioral change. Second, criterion-related validity plays an important role in the development and acceptability of a structured behavioral observation system. Because these observations take place in the clinic under controlled conditions, it is extremely important that it be demonstrated that the behavior in the clinic is the same or similar to behavior in the natural environment under similar conditions. Without this demonstration, assessors would be unable to make strong statements about the generality of these behaviors beyond the controlled clinic environment. This lack of generality, however, does not necessarily reduce the data obtained in the contrived environment to a position of uselessness, as will be discussed later.

The final way in which the validity of this observational strategy can be tested is by investigating its ability to discriminate between two groups of individuals who already differ on some naturally occurring variable (e.g., clinic versus nonclinic population, abusive versus nonabusive parents). This form of validity, known as discriminate validity, tests the behavioral constructs which underlie the assessment instrument. For example, a hypothetical behavioral observation system constructed to evaluate persons involved in a child custody dispute would be developed to assess, among other things, a person's parental competence as defined earlier in this volume. As such, the instrument should be able to separate individuals into two groups on the basis of the results of the coding procedure, after already having been identified as two distinct groups prior to their assessment (e.g., those parents who have had a child removed from their custody because of abuse, neglect, etc., and those who are considered good parents by some other measurement). If the proposed system is unable to separate these people into two distinct groups with a high degree of accuracy, its validity is in question.

It is suggested that the most important form of validity for the purpose of assessment in the context of a child custody evaluation would be the instrument's ability to discriminate groups of people already separated by some other procedure. Discriminate validity holds a position of importance because discrimination is precisely the charge given to the evaluator; separate the suitable caretakers from the unsuitable. The idiographic nature of the child custody evaluation assumed, it is still essential for any assessment device to assist in making fine discriminations between persons.

The criterion-related validity of the structured observational procedure is also important. If little similarity exists between the behavior in a controlled clinic situation and the behavior in a similar natural situation (e.g., in the home), then the ability to predict behavior has been considerably weakened. Simply because an individual displays behavior X in the clinic, does not necessarily mean he or she will display that same behavior at home. Although the extent to which information obtained under such conditions can be utilized is restricted, the information need not be eliminated. If one views the structured environment as an opportunity to observe an individual's response capabilities (Wallace, 1966, 1967) rather than to make statements of generalization to the natural environment, the question of validity is less threatening. Nay (1977) states:

> If the assessor views the analogue as a probe or power test of the client's response repertoire and is not interested in making inferences about the natural setting, such validation becomes less meaningful. Thus an assessor may be interested only in determining a client's repertoire of positively reinforcing statements, facially expressive behaviors, or his ability to maintain eye contact. (p. 268)

The question becomes what response capabilities does this person have? Not will he or she use them in situation X? Obviously, the usefulness of this data is less than it is if generality has been demonstrated, especially with respect to predicting response performance in specific situations. However, an important finding may be simply that when pushed to their limits (e.g., by direct instructions to do their best) one individual has an enormous range of response capabilities whereas the other person has not.

Finally, the issue of sensitivity to treatment intervention or other change events does not appear to hold as much importance as do the other two forms of validity mentioned. The issue in child custody evaluations is not treatment or change, but prediction. Therefore, not having an instrument which is sensitive to change is not necessarily devastating to the overall usefulness of the device. However, as has been suggested throughout this volume, should intervention be desired, then the issue of sensitivity rises in importance. For example, if the court wishes to place a child in the physical custody of its mother, the only living parent, but the parent is deficient in specific parenting skills as assessed by the behavioral observations, and the court would first like to see that the mother has learned how to handle the child in the troublesome situations, then the sensitivity of the instrument to change is extremely valuable.

Sensitivity

An examination of outcome studies making use of structured behavioral observations in a clinic setting finds the preponderance demonstrating sensitivity to pre- and postintervention changes in the various targeted behaviors (Forehand & King, 1974, 1977; Forehand *et al.*, 1974; Herbert *et al.*, 1973; Johnson & Brown, 1969; Mash & Terdal, 1973; Peed, Roberts, & Forehand, 1977; Scarboro & Forehand, 1975; Seitz & Terdal, 1972; Tavormina, 1975; Wahler & Nordquist, 1973; Wahler *et al.*, 1965; Zegiob & Forehand, 1975; Zegiob, Arnold, & Forehand, 1975). Wahler *et al.* (1965) reported three single case studies in which they intervened in mother–child dyads by instructing each mother by means of a cuing system differentially to ignore or attend to their child's undesirable or incompatible behaviors. The subjects were all boys ranging in age from four to six years. By means of a microswitch system, the observers recorded the occurrence of two child behaviors (deviant and incompatible) and one mother behavior (her response to the child's behavior) every five seconds during each session. In each case, a reversal design was used whereby measurements were taken during baseline, and then with the mother using the new techniques, then returning to her old habits, and finally back to her newly learned responses. In each phase of the three cases, the observational procedure was sensitive to the changes taking place as measured by an examination of the slopes of the cumulative records. Johnson and Brown (1969) reported two cases, children aged 2 years and 9 months, and 6 years, one using a multiple intervention strategy and the other only a modeling procedure. Systematic observations were employed in both cases during baseline and treatment, with individually tailored four-category coding systems being used. In both cases changes in the behaviors which were the object of intervention were reflected in the appropriate changes in rate of the observational procedure.

In study of the relative effectiveness of behavioral and reflective group counseling with parents of mentally retarded children, Tavormina (1975) made use of, among other dependent measures, a behavioral coding system which measured three variables in each of two observation segments; unstructured free play and structured command play. The three variables were (1) total appropriate interaction (2) appropriate antecedent–response and (3) appropriate response–consequences. These variables were based on the principles of learning and were generated from data gathered by a sequential recording of each interaction during a 25-minute session. Antecedent, response, and consequent behaviors were coded for each interaction. Two baseline sessions were completed over a two-month interval before the beginning of an eight-week group training program. There were no significant changes in any of the measures from baseline one to baseline two, including all of the variables computed on the coding procedure. However, postintervention observations indicated significant changes in all the behavioral observation measures recorded during the structured command play.

Forehand and his co-workers have consistently demonstrated behavioral changes with their structured behavioral coding system as a function of a treatment program for noncompliant children (e.g., Forehand & King, 1974, 1977; Forehand et al., 1974; Peed et al., 1977; Scarboro & Forehand, 1975; Zegiob & Forehand, 1975; Zegiob et al., 1975). For example, Forehand and King (1974, 1977) found significant changes in specific mother and child behaviors from baseline to posttreatment as a result of a parent training program for noncompliance. In both of these studies, during the Child's Game, mothers significantly increased their use of rewards and significantly decreased their use of commands and questions. During the Parent's Game, maternal rewards also increased significantly as did child compliance. In each of these two studies, behavioral changes for both mothers and children were in the desired and predicted direction.

One study which did not report significant changes in behavior following modification training for parents was Eyberg and Johnson (1974). The frequency of deviant behaviors for the entire sample decreased by 21% from baseline to posttreatment and by 37% for a subsample of six children described as deviant. Although both of these were in the predicted direction and considered by the authors as "modestly supportive of the improvement evidenced by all other measures" (p. 605), neither of them was a significant reduction.

On the basis of the evidence cited above, it would appear that a verdict favorable to structured behavioral observations as a sensitive method for assessing the effects of intervention is warranted. However, it has been suggested elsewhere (Hughes & Haynes, 1978) that a blanket assumption of all structured observational situations being sensitive measures of change is not supported. Each system must be empirically tested before any such statement can be made with confidence.

Criterion-related and Discriminate Validity

The significance of criterion-related validity has been discussed previously. For structured observational procedures, a significant amount of covariation between target behaviors observed in the clinic and the same behaviors in the natural environment is required if the investigator is to have confidence in making predictive statements about behaviors in the natural environment based on observations of that behavior in a contrived setting. Without this kind of covariation, little confidence can be placed in specific predictions of behavior in settings other than the assessment setting. However, if the goals of the observational assessment is to "test the limits," that is, establish an individual's response repertoire or capabilities, and not necessarily the identification of which specific natural environmental stimuli will elicit these capabilities, then the importance of demonstrating covariation is substantially diminished.

The concordance of behavior between the two settings under discussion would not necessarily be expected, simply because the two environments are not the same (Ciminero & Drabman, 1977; Haynes, 1978; Hughes & Haynes, 1978; Lytton, 1971; Nay, 1977). Given the observed importance of situational specificity in the elicitation of behavior (e.g., Mischel, 1968), even slight stimulus inconsistencies may result in different behavior. However, the closer the contrived situation comes to reflecting the significant stimulus conditions of the natural environment, the greater the potential for generalization from the clinic to the natural environment (Haynes, 1978). This is consistent with the work of Mischel (1968) and others which has been presented throughout this manuscript. The work of Sobell and Schaefer (e.g., Schaefer, Sobell, & Mills, 1971) exemplifies an attempt to recreate as closely as possible the stimulus conditions controlling the target behavior in the natural environment within the structured setting. These authors were interested in studying the drinking behavior of alcoholics but were unable to control for the amount and percentage of alcohol in each drink and the subjects' drinking history prior to their observations if these observations took place in the natural environment (i.e., the bar). To control for these variables without significantly jeopardizing the generalizability of their results, they constructed an analogue bar setting, which included such natural stimuli as piped-in music, a half-moon bar, a mirror and bar stools, while controlling the variables mentioned above.

Extrapolating from this example, greater generalizability would be expected from the clinic setting to the natural environment the more closely the clinic setting resembled the natural setting. For example, if one wished to generalize the behavior of parents and children from the clinic to the home, one might construct a living room or dining room setting with all the environmental cues associated with those environments. Of course, such a setting is not the same as the natural one for each dyad, but it would be much closer than a clinic playroom or waiting room.

In reference to the criterion analysis proposed by Goldfried and Kent (1972, the same procedure advocated in the present model), Nay (1977) remarked:

> [It] . . . insures that items chosen are in fact representative of the natural settings, and provides the analogue constructor with sufficient information realistically to simulate each stimulus item on the analogue. This process greatly enhances the probability that behavior elicited by the clinical analogue will be consonant with behaviors elicited by the criterion stimuli. (p. 269)

The question of generalization is an important one; however, research investigating the concordance of laboratory and natural behavior is meager, unsystematic, and conflicting (Haynes, 1978; Mash & Terdal, 1976; Nay, 1977). An inspection of the research addressing this issue reveals that the majority of studies support the conclusion that there is an adequate level of concordance between the structured and natural environments (Baumrind, 1967; Forehand et al., 1974; Johnson & Brown, 1969; Martin, Dysart, & Gonzales, 1975; Mash, Terdal, & Anderson, 1973; Rapoport & Benoit, 1975; Schulman, Shoemaker, & Moelis, 1962; Wahler & Nordquist, 1973). However, other studies (Eyberg & Johnson, 1974; Moustakas et al., 1956) found discrepancies between comparative sets of data. It seems apparent that until more research is completed on this assessment strategy it will have to remain in the domain of a "*poten-*

tially valid method" (Hughes & Haynes, 1978, p. 444) as far as allowing
for specific predictions to the natural environment are concerned. As a
result of the great variation of observational procedures, target behaviors, and coding categories, it is difficult to partial out which behaviors
can be validly assessed in a structured setting and under what conditions. This type of information would be helpful in using such an instrument to its fullest potential.

The instrument's ability to discriminate between persons assigned
to different groups on the basis of some independent variable appears to
be much more entrenched. Several studies (Eyberg & Johnson, 1974;
Forehand *et al.*, 1974; Forehand & King, 1977; Forehand, Sturgis,
McMahon, Aguar, Green, Wells, & Breiner, 1979; Kogan *et al.*, 1969;
Peed *et al.*, 1977; Schuman *et al.*, 1962; Strans, 1967; Zegiob & Forehand,
1975, 1978) have demonstrated group discrimination on such dimensions as clinic-referred versus nonclinic and low socioeconomic versus
high socioeconomic status populations. These studies suggest that,
given a reliable observational procedure, structured assessment situations would be able to differentiate prospective caretakers on the basis of
their behavior in the clinic. This is significant because of the importance
of such a task in determining the postdivorce living arrangements for a
child.

In sum, structured behavioral observation appears to hold great
promise for use in the child custody evaluation. With respect to validity,
the data suggest that this strategy can be sensitive to the effects of intervention (and possible other naturally occurring change events including
divorce) and is able to distinguish between two groups of people who
have already been discriminated on the basis of some other independent
variable. Both of these forms of validity are very important in a child
custody evaluation. With respect to environmental concordance, the
data are not clear. Until further research is done, the confidence with
which one can predict behavior in the natural environment from clinic
behavior is weak. However, given greater concordance between the two
settings with respect to stimulus conditions, the more likely it is that
generalization can be expected. In the meantime, however, it would appear that the behavior displayed under structured conditions can be
evaluated with respect to an individual's response capabilities. A prospective caretaker who is able to exhibit appropriate behavior under

these conditions, either spontaneously or as a result of direct instructions, will be evaluated more positively than one who is unable to display such behavior even when asked to do so. Essentially, it might be said that one person has skills x, y, and z whereas another does not. This can be valuable information used in the overall determination of a child's future living arrangements.

CHAPTER 11

Structured Behavioral Observations II

METHODOLOGICAL CONSIDERATIONS

Not unlike other assessment devices, direct observational procedures have several methodological problems, which if left uncontrolled would seriously threaten the reliability and validity of the observational data. A number of good papers have provided reviews of this subject (Foster & Cone, 1980; Haynes & Horn, 1982; Johnson & Bolstad, 1973; Kent & Foster, 1977; Patterson *et al.*, 1978; Wasik & Loven, 1980; Wildman & Erickson, 1977). These problems have been identified with observational procedures used in either laboratory or naturalistic environments, although they may not evidence equal effects in both settings. Furthermore, given the fact that the most frequent purpose for using this procedure is to measure the effects of some treatment program, a few of the methodological issues will be relevant for direct observations associated with the effects identified within a research project (e.g., expectation bias). In some cases, these particular problems may not be relevant to observational procedures used in the context of a custody evaluation.

A few of the more significant problems associated with this form of assessment will be examined, drawing from research completed in either the laboratory or natural environment when it is relevant to both situations. Attention will be given not only to identifying the problem but also to the solutions which have been suggested in the literature.

Reactivity

If the subject of assessment changes as a function of that assessment, the strategy is said to be reactive. In the case of observational procedures, the instrument is labelled reactive if the behaviors targeted for observation are different when observed than when not observed. If the behaviors under investigation are reactive to observational assessment, then the strength of generalizing to other nonassessment situations is seriously undermined. However, the investigator could interpret clinic behavior as a sample of an individual's response capabilities without the support for making powerful predictive statements. Furthermore, although the exact rates of behavior may vary, the patterns or conditional probabilities may remain the same, therefore not jeopardizing all aspects of validity (Haynes & Horn, 1982).

An inspection of the various studies and reviews which have addressed this problem have provided a considerable degree of confusion as to whether reactivity is a significant problem in the use of observational procedures. Several papers (Bales, 1950; Behrens & Sherman, 1959; Bernal, Gibson, Williams, & Pesses, 1971; Bijou, Peterson, Harris, Allen, & Johnston, 1969; Dubey, Kent, O'Leary, Broderick, & O'Leary, 1977; Hagen, Craighead, & Paul, 1975; Harris, 1969; Heyns & Lippitt, 1954; Johnson & Bolstad, 1975; Kent, O'Leary, Dietz, & Diament, 1979; Moos, 1968; Nelson, Kapust, & Dorsey, 1978; Purcell & Brady, 1966; Soskin & John, 1963; Weinrott, Garrett, & Todd, 1978; Werry & Quay, 1969; Zegiob et al., 1979) provide evidence suggesting either negligible or no effects at all; several (Baum, Forehand, & Zegiob, 1979; Bishop, 1946; Johnson & Lobitz, 1974; Johnson, Christensen, & Bellamy, 1976; Lobitz & Johnson, 1975; Wells, McMahon, Forehand, & Griest, 1980; Zegiob et al., 1975; Zegiob & Forehand, 1978) have shown reactivity to the presence of an observer; and others (Martin, Gelfand, & Hartmann, 1971; Mercatoris & Craighead, 1974; White, 1973) provide mixed evidence with some variables exhibiting reactivity and others not.

Zegiob et al. (1979) examined the habituation effects of parental behavior in the presence of an observer over an average of eight sessions in three mother–child dyads. Observers of these dyads in a laboratory setting recorded three positive maternal behaviors (playing interactively, positive verbal comments, and helping) and one negative behavior (negative verbal comments). The mothers were told they would be observed from behind a one-way mirror and were free to do whatever they liked during the session. The frequency of all three positive behaviors decreased across sessions, while negative verbal comments evidenced a slight increase. However, upon the introduction of a new observer all three positive behaviors again increased, although not to the initial levels recorded with the first observer. For a second time, these behaviors decreased across repeated sessions. This study demonstrates that not only are some behaviors reactive, but given repeated observation there is also habituation. The authors argue for the use of a sufficient number of sessions in order to obtain a more valid level of behavior and for the use of the same observer across sessions in order to enhance habituation.

In a study cited by Patterson *et al.* (1978), Harris (1969) trained 15 mothers as observers and randomly assigned them to one of three conditions. In the first group, mothers served as observers in other families in all six sessions. In the second condition, the six sessions were divided in half, with the first three sessions being recorded by mothers for their own families and the second three by an outside observer. In the third group, mothers coded the entire six sessions in their own families. Father–child interactions were recorded for several desirable and deviant behaviors. Although it was predicted that there would be an increase in socially desirable behaviors with the presence of an outside observer, no significant main effects or interaction effects were found. An analysis of the total deviant child behavior produced nonsignificant results as well.

This study has been criticized (Patterson *et al.*, 1978) because of a failure to use reliability checks with the mother-observers and because of the small sample. In an attempt to rectify these problems, White (1972) used trained professional observers and had 25 subjects. The study took place in a large clinic room in which a living room environment was constructed. The subjects were informed that they would be observed for 30 minutes at a time, with 30-minute breaks during which the observer would leave to observe another family in an adjacent living room. In reality, no other family existed and the subjects were observed during these intervals from overhead. This design permitted the families to be observed during observer-present and observer-absent conditions. The results showed no significant effects for either the families' rates of social interaction or total deviancy. However, older children did reduce their level of deviant behavior under conditions of overt observation. Despite a successful attempt to replicate Harris (1969) by improving the study's design, the White (1972) study is also methodologically flawed. Kent and Foster (1977) have pointed out that the length of overt observation (two half-hour sessions) was not adequate, leaving little room for the occurrence of habituation effects which might have then provided evidence of initial reactivity.

On the basis of the two deception studies reported by Harris (1969) and White (1972), Patterson *et al.* (1978) wrote:

> Perhaps the best conclusion . . . is that if an observer presence effect exists, it is of small magnitude. It is most likely reflected in the relative absence of some of the more pathological behaviors found in family interactions. (p. 19)

In a 1971 study by Martin *et al.*, 100 children from five to seven years of age were observed in a free play situation following exposure to an aggressive model. There were five conditions into which equal numbers of boys and girls were placed: (1) observer absent, (2) female adult observer present, (3) male adult observer present, (4) female peer observer present, and (5) male peer observer present. The children's aggressive behavior was recorded under all conditions by observers placed behind a one-way mirror. When the amount of aggressive behavior displayed by the children without the presence of an observer was compared with the conditions of observer presence, no significant differences were found, thus providing further support for the notion that behavior is not reactive to observation. However, when the various observer-present conditions were compared with each other, some interesting findings resulted. When the observers were peers, the imitation of aggressive behaviors increased significantly when compared to adult observers, and with same-sex observers there was also more imitation. With respect to habituation, girls exhibited significant increases in aggressive behavior over time whereas the boys did not, indicating an initial reactivity on the part of the girl subjects.

The results of this study are important for a couple of reasons. First, it adds to the number of variables which must be considered when deciding if an observational system will be reactive or not. This study suggests that both the age and sex of the observers with respect to the observees are important. Second, as far as aggressive behaviors are concerned, it makes little difference whether an observer is present or absent. This is important because it implies the value of completing behavioral observations from a position of inconspicuousness, for example, from behind a one-way mirror. As such, it suggests the value of laboratory observations when compared with natural observations, considering the inability to be as inconspicuous in the natural environment. However, this assumes that the clinic observations are completed from a position of camouflage.

Recently, Baum *et al.* (1979) reviewed 17 studies from 1969 to 1979 which directly examined observer effects in adult–child interactions. They included studies undertaken in the home, classroom, or laboratory and further categorized them within one of three paradigms which have been used to study reactivity: habituation, conspicuousness, and awareness. The habituation paradigm assumes that behavior is initially reactive but levels out over time following the subject's adaptation to the observer's presence. Conspicuousness is investigated by varying the placement of the observer with respect to the parent–child dyads. For example, observations completed in the room with the subjects are more conspicuous than observations completed from behind a one-way mirror. These first two paradigms were initially described by Johnson and Bolstad (1973). The final paradigm manipulates the subject's awareness of being observed. Within the same investigation, one group of subjects is told they are going to be observed and a second group that they are not.

Although the authors do not report significance levels for behaviors shown to be reactive, as a whole, 73% of the investigations reported some form of reactivity. To break down the studies with respect to the paradigm used, 75% of the studies utilizing an habituation paradigm, 50% using the conspicuousness design, and 83% using the awareness manipulation reported reactivity. These figures are especially relevant when considering the interaction between the design and setting used. Ninety-one percent of the studies occurring in a laboratory environment reported some reactive behaviors, compared to 60% and 40% reported for home and classroom setting respectively. However, five of the eight studies completed in the laboratory utilized the awareness paradigm, the paradigm most likely to find reactivity, thus confounding the results with respect to setting effects.

The adult behaviors which demonstrated reactivity in the greatest number of studies were positive verbal and positive physical interactions and neutral verbal interactions. These behaviors tended to increase in the presence of an observer. The negative categories of behavior, physical and verbal, revealed the smallest degree of reactivity. The authors suggest that the increase of positive and neutral adult behaviors may be associated with an attempt to respond in a socially desirable fashion and appear to be "good caregiving agents."

Due to an inadequate sample of studies examining the reactivity of child behaviors, especially verbal behaviors, Baum *et al.* (1979) believe conclusions are unwarranted presently and that more research is needed to begin to answer this question. However, fewer studies reported behavioral reactivity in child behaviors than in adult behaviors when these behaviors were examined (66% versus 75%, respectively).

Zegiob *et al.* (1975) was one of the studies reviewed by Baum *et al.* (1979). The authors observed 12 mother–child pairs in a laboratory setting utilizing an awareness paradigm. Six categories of maternal behavior were observed and recorded: out of contact, playing interactively, positive verbal, negative verbal, structuring, and helping. The analysis showed significant differences for three of the six categories between the informed and uninformed conditions. When mothers knew they were being observed, they would play more with their children, use more positive verbalizations, and structure the child's play more frequently, giving commands and asking questions. Neither out-of-contact nor verbal negative behavior differed significantly under informed or uninformed conditions.

In a subsequent investigation (Zegiob & Forehand, 1978), a comparison was made of behaviors exhibited under informed versus uninformed conditions, with lower- and upper-middle-class mothers. The same maternal behaviors were recorded as in the previous study, although structuring was divided into three individual categories: questions and direct and indirect commands. In addition, three child-behavior categories were recorded (solitary play, compliance, and requests). The results were even more pronounced in this study than in the previous one, with seven out of the eight maternal behaviors changing significantly between the informed and uninformed conditions. Only the amount of negative verbal interaction did not differ significantly. Under the informed conditions, mothers were out of contact less with their children, played more with them, asked more questions, made more positive verbal comments, helped them more, and made more direct and indirect commands. Only one child behavior, solitary play, showed a significant difference, with the child playing alone more often during the uninformed condition.

It appears that mothers will increase the frequency of their behavior and maximize "good parent behavior" when they know they are being observed. It has been suggested (Zegiob *et al.*, 1975) that mothers attempt to bring out the best in their children by asking more questions and giving more commands, that is, structuring their performance. On the basis of informal observations, they found that under informed conditions mothers attempted to elicit certain child behaviors which could demonstrate the child's knowledge or skill to perform certain tasks. Similar results were reported by Merrill (1946) when suggesting to mothers prior to a second observation session that their children had not performed up to the level which the author thought they were capable of reaching.

The lack of reactivity for negative behaviors has also found consistent support (Mostakas *et al.*, 1956; Zegiob & Forehand, 1974; Zegiob *et al.*, 1975; Zegiob & Forehand, 1978; Zegiob *et al.*, 1979). Apparently negative behaviors rarely occur in parent–child investigations. Zegiob *et al.* (1975) have suggested that such behaviors are under such strict stimulus control that they are inhibited from occurring under experimental conditions.

On the basis of these studies, one might predict that similar behavioral reactivity would exist using behavioral observations in the context of a child custody evaluation. Prospective caretakers would maximize the output of good parent behavior while inhibiting negative, socially undesirable behaviors.

Johnson and Lobitz of the University of Oregon completed two very interesting studies which took a slightly different approach to the problem of reactivity. They posited that when a family enters treatment there are demand characteristics associated with the setting that would result in the inflation of problem behaviors during the initial assessment and deflation upon the termination of treatment. In a sense, the parent could justify the need for treatment by attempting to make the child look "bad," while attempting to make the child look better after treatment to justify the time and expense involved, please the therapist, or some other such motive. To test this notion, Johnson and Lobitz (1974) collected observational data on normal families in the home for six days. On three of these days, the parents were instructed to make their children look "bad and deviant," while on alternating days, the instruction was to make them look "good." Their findings showed that on bad days there were significant differences in child and parent behavior. Deviant child behavior, negative parent responses, and parental commands were all higher on bad days than on good days. The results supported their hypothesis that parents can manipulate their children's behavior to "fake bad."

In their second study, Lobitz and Johnson (1975) used 12 families with problem children and 12 families that were assumed to be problem-free. Three conditions were used: Two consecutive days of faking good, two of faking bad, and two of looking normal. The order in which families were observed in these conditions was varied, and each family was randomly assigned to one of the orders. The results replicated their earlier study with respect to faking bad. Both nonproblem (9 of 12) and deviant (10 of 12) families were able to increase deviant child behaviors significantly on the bad days when compared to the normal days. Consistent with their previous findings, this shift was characterized by significantly more frequent commands and parental punishment. In addition, there was a significant decrease in the frequency of positive consequences. However, attempts to fake good were not significant when compared with the normal days. Seven of the 12 no-problem families were successful in eliciting the change in behavior, and only four of the 12 deviant families could do so. Apparently, it is much easier to make one's child look bad than it is to make him or her look good. Furthermore, deviant families find it much harder to fake good than do no-problem families.

The results of these studies led Patterson *et al.* (1978) to suggest:

> Both parents and children find it difficult to "fake good" over extended periods of time. It seems possible that habitual modes of interacting provide powerful constraints for familial interaction patterns. Presumably, these constraints are more effective in controlling behavior than is set to look good. (p. 18)

If one assumes the existence of reactivity and faking in structural clinical observations, what are the implications of these studies for the child custody evaluation? Although parents and children are not being observed in the context of a treatment program, thus reducing the influence of a demand characteristic to increase deviant responding, the context of this evaluation, without a doubt, will have its own demand characteristics. It is suggested that the prospective caretaker will attempt to make himself or herself look good as well as the child with whom he or she is being observed. The stakes are high in this situation; therefore one might expect this response set. This question may be empirically investigated in a study similar to that of Johnson and Lobitz (1974), where instead of instructing the parent to "fake good" or "fake bad," they could be instructed to behave as if they were being evaluated as a potential caretaker for this child. An analogue such as this might begin to answer this question, although results similar to a "fake good" instruction are hypothesized.

An important consideration here is that subjects found it much more difficult to fake good, precisely the set one would expect in the custody evaluation. Furthermore, with repeated observation sessions there is a question of whether or not this positive response set would decrease from habituation. If habituation does occur, and there is some research to suggest that it does (e.g., Zegiob *et al.*, 1979), then all that may be required is a "period of acclimation" (Goldfried & Sprafkin, 1974) before serious consideration can be given to the observational data.

There is also the question of child behavior and the effects of observer presence on them. Although there is evidence that young children are not as reactive to observation as are older children or adults (e.g., White, 1972) and that they habituate quickly (Bijou *et al.*, 1969; Purcell & Brady, 1966; Werry & Quay, 1969), what role would children have in impression management during behavioral observations in the context of this evaluation? Will they intentionally change their own behavior, or respond in such a way as to bring out the best or worst of a prospective caretaker? What if the child wants to be placed with one parent instead of the other, to what extent can he or she deliberately structure behavior? What effect will the child's behavior have on the parent in these circumstances? These are important questions without answers at this time.

It would appear that behavior is reactive to being observed, although many variables must be taken into account in evaluating the effects of reactivity in any one observational procedure. Not only has it been shown that different behaviors have different levels of reactivity, but also that the environment in which the observation takes place and the placement of the observer influence the degree of reactivity. Furthermore, Johnson and Bolstad (1973) have suggested that, if it was reliably known that individuals increased their specific positive behaviors by 30% when observed, then it would be possible to adjust the resultant data to its appropriate level. Unfortunately, the magnitude of change which results when reactivity does occur has not been adequately reported. However, there does appear to be some consistency in the nature of behavioral change under observation. For example, it can be assumed that parents will increase their commands, questions, contact, and positive verbalizations to their children during initial observation sessions (Zegiob *et al.*, 1975; Zegiob & Forehand, 1978) and be inhibited from displaying negative behaviors. Perhaps the absence of such findings in an observational assessment should invite more concern than their presence.

Despite the apparent influence of observers on the behavior of persons being observed, these effects may not be a source of great concern in the context of a custody evaluation. Again, the difference between assessment for treatment and assessment for comparison and prediction enters into play. If the purpose of assessment is to obtain a reliable measure of target behaviors in order to demonstrate the effectiveness of a treatment program once completed, and the behaviors are highly reactive or the subjects are responding to the demand characteristics of the situation, then the effects of treatment are not easily partialled out from the changes due to habituation, posttreatment demands, or some other phenomenon. On the other hand, the child custody evaluation attempts to make comparisons between individuals and their environments on certain behaviors. The problem of reactivity is not so great in this context because it is assumed that each individual is equally reactive to the observation process and the demand characteristics of the situation. Therefore, although one might expect elevations and reductions in various categories of behavior, they can be expected from everyone being assessed. The variable of reactivity is held constant, thereby permitting an adequate comparison between individuals. In fact, it might be advantageous to maximize these effects by instructing each prospective caretaker to make himself or herself and the child look as good as possible. This increases the probability of receiving each person's response capabilities in the defined situations. Under these conditions, if a person is unable to attain some predetermined level of good behavioral responses, then behavioral deficits may be assumed.

Some authors have suggested that reactivity does not affect behavior across the board (Goldfried & Sprafkin, 1974; Jones et al., 1975; Patterson et al., 1978). It would appear that persons select specific behaviors and change them without having their behavior affected on a global level.

> To tell an individual his behavior is being observed would probably make him self-conscious, but it would provide little information as to what behaviors to be self-conscious about. Hence little behavior change would be expected. (Goldfried & Sprafkin, 1974, p. 7)

Patterson et al. (1978) similarly suggested that the effect of an observer's presence seems to be an increase in some specific task-oriented or socially oriented behaviors and not a global attempt to look good. "It seems people select one to two setting-appropriate behaviors and accelerate them when observed" (p. 16). It may be possible, therefore, to use a broad behavioral coding system and observe the effects of observation on only some of them. One would also expect that persons being evaluated with this method in order to be chosen as a child's primary caretaker would select behaviors which they thought were important in their cause. However, ambiguity in this context may leave the observee in a situation in which he or she is unable to decide which behaviors are appropriate to change and which are not. In this vein, Haynes (1978) has suggested the use of deception by telling the persons involved that certain behaviors are to be observed and then proceed in observing other behaviors, thereby deflecting the individuals' attention away from target behaviors. Although no empirical data accompanied this suggestion, it seems reasonable, but it would need to be tested.

In sum, despite the existence of studies which have demonstrated observer effects and others which have not, it appears from more recent investigations that reactivity is an issue which must be confronted if observational data are to be useful. The problem raised by the presence of these effects, however, is not a simple matter. There appears to be a complex interaction involving such things as where the observation takes place, the age of the persons being observed, the length of the observation, the intrusiveness of the observer, the behaviors observed, and the context in which the observations are set (see Haynes & Horn, 1982). Nonetheless, observational data can be useful within the context of the child custody evaluation, mainly because of the place of prominence given to assessing response capabilities and making interpersonal comparisons.

Expectation and Observer Bias

Rosenthal (1966) suggested that the possibility of experimental bias affecting the outcome of a research project is always present. With the employment of human observers for recording data, this source of invalidity may be even more relevant and take the form of systematic distortion of the data in the direction of the predicted outcomes. One of the earliest reports of this phenomenon in the area of observational procedures was a paper by Kass and O'Leary (1970). In this study, three groups of female undergraduate observers were used. Each group observed videotapes of two disruptive children in a simulated classroom. One group was told to expect the frequency of disruptive behavior to increase during the course of treatment, one was told to expect a decrease, and the third was told that the experimenters were unsure about what might happen. They used a nine-category code and recorded behavior for four baseline days and five treatment days. The results showed that, although all three groups evidenced a decrease in the frequency of disruptive behavior, the group told to expect such a decrease was significantly different from the others on seven of the nine categories, suggesting the presence of expectation bias. However, this study has been criticized (Johnson & Bolstad, 1973; Kent, O'Leary, Diament, & Dietz, 1974) because the observers were trained separately and computed reliabilities within their own groups only. This procedure has been shown to produce a "drift" phenomenon (see the section on consensual observer drift below) in which discussion of behavioral definitions within the group results in idiosyncratic interpretation. The effects discovered by Kass and O'Leary (1970) could simply be a function of this phenomenon.

In fact, subsequent research has not been able to replicate the findings of Kass and O'Leary (1970). Skindrud (1972) trained 28 women from the community as observers, employing only those who were able to reach a minimum of 70% accuracy after an intensive three-week training program. The women who remained were divided into three groups and given different explanations of what they would find (when the father was absent) in identical videotaped family interactions. The first group was led to believe that over a series of 12 sessions there would be a 30% increase in the child's disruptive behavior. A second group was given the bias to expect an equal decrease, and the third set of observers, who acted as controls, were not given any expectations. The results provided no evidence for an observer bias effect. There were no significant differences between any of the groups nor their interaction. In fact, even the trends were not in the expected direction.

In a second study, Kent et al. (1974) also attempted to replicate the findings of Kass and O'Leary (1970). They randomly assigned 10 well-trained observers to one of two groups. One group was told to expect a decrease in the target child's disruptive behavior, and the second group was told there would be no change. In reality, the series of videotapes from which they were to code behavior was selected for the stability of behavior across the tapes. A nine-category code was used to record behavior, and the observers were asked to fill out a questionnaire about the predicted direction of change. The results found no significant main effects for any of the nine categories. However, the biases in their global judgments about what had happened over the course of the videotaped sessions were striking. For example, 90% of the subjects who were told to expect the child's deviant behavior to increase reported an increase.

It would appear that when well-trained observers are using a specific behavioral coding system the magnitude of bias, if any, is minimal. However, the use of global judgments may allow substantial biasing of reports. This was also suggested by Shuller and McNamara (1976) who had four groups of observers record the behavior of the same child who had been assigned a different trait label for each group. No significant differences were found among the four groups using their behavioral coding system. However, they found significant differences among the groups when they were asked to rate the child's behavior using bipolar adjectives, thereby supporting the findings of Kent et al. (1974). If one construes the assignment of trait labels as background information which might affect the judgments of observers, then a study by King, Erhmann, and Johnson (1952) is relevant. They found that when one or both observers knew background information about the observees, their observer agreement decreased. This finding implies the need for uninformed observers in completing behavioral observations, lest they be biased.

Although it appears that observational data will not be biased simply by telling observers what to expect (as long as they are well trained), there are some data to suggest that feedback to the observers contingent on their recording can bias the data. O'Leary, Kent, and Kanowitz (1975) had four observers view videotapes of behavior and told them to expect two categories of behavior to decrease during the treatment phase and two others to remain the same. Subsequently, the experimenter reinforced the coder when their results reflected experimenter predictions and reprimanded the observers when they did not. The category changes which had been predicted and reinforced showed highly significant changes, and the two codes which were predicted to remain the same did so. The authors suggest that evaluative feedback be eliminated from observational studies because it is very possible that the observers will bias the data, thereby threatening the validity of the results.

Patterson et al. (1978) reviewed the studies concerning the effects of expectation and observer bias and concluded:

> As the findings now stand, it does not seem that experimenter or therapist expectancies ipso facto bias the data collected by *well* trained observers. Expectancies *can* affect observers' global judgments about what is going on. Experimenters could perhaps bias their coded data by using reinforcement contingencies but this is not likely to happen in most well run field studies. (p. 15)

Although these studies relate specifically to research projects which attempt to evaluate treatment effectiveness, there are equally important concerns which arise from this data in the context of an evaluation to determine the postdivorce living arrangements of children. Although one would not expect observers to be biased by knowing the stage of treatment or the investigator's hypotheses, for in actuality there is no treatment or experimental hypotheses, there is the potential of bias from knowing the prospective caretaker's background and social history. What would be the effects of an observer's knowing that one of the potential caretakers had a drinking problem, dated a lot of different men, or was a career army officer? What if the observer and the person who completes the history and functional analysis are one in the same? Of course, this is not known, although one might predict on the basis of some of the research presented above that as long as the observers are well trained in the use of a coding system with operationally defined categories no bias should result. However, if observers are not well trained, or if the observer and the principal investigator are the same, or global judgments are used instead of specific behavioral coding systems, then one might expect considerable bias. Haynes (1978) has suggested that the probability or degree of bias may be *maximized* under the following conditions: (1) the observers are informed of the experimental hypotheses; (2) the observers are informed of the status of the target subjects; (3) the observers are not instructed in the necessity of professional rigor in observing; (4) instructions are delivered to the observers in such a way as to lead them to expect certain events or behavior rates; and (5) behavioral definitions used are imprecise and lead to excessive inference by the observers.

One thing appears to be certain from reviewing this list: without a direct behavioral observation procedure as defined by Mash and Terdal (1976), all the conditions above are met, thereby maximizing the probability that the resultant data will be infiltrated by expectation or observer bias. Presently, this appears to be the predominant way of completing observations in the child custody evaluation (e.g., Cogan *et al.*, 1982; Jackson *et al.*, 1980; Levy, 1978). For whatever reason (e.g., money, time constraints), observations are done informally by the same clinician or group of clinicians who complete the entire evaluation. They are privy to all relevant background information and provide global judgments about the clients.

Reactivity of Observers to Reliability Assessment

There is considerable evidence to suggest that the reliability of observational data is adversely affected by the observer's knowledge that his or her reliability is being checked (Reid, 1970; Romnaczyk, Kent, Diament, & O'Leary, 1973; Taplin & Reid, 1973). Reliability checks are vital to the reliability and validity of an observational system because without them the question of whether observers are as accurate in later assessment sessions as initially trained remains unknown. It is therefore possible that there has been "instrument decay" over time (Campbell & Stanley, 1963). The instrument is no longer recording the same behaviors as accurately as was intended. Reliability checks are used to find out whether this decay has taken place. However, if observers are affected by knowing those checks are going to occur and become more diligent during these periods only, then the reliability of the instrument at other times is unknown. Reid (1970) trained observers up to eight days using videotaped material and a complex coding system. On alternate days during training, the observers were aware that their protocols were being checked against a criterion protocol. On four consecutive days after training, however, they were led to believe that they were scoring tapes that only they would see. They were told that the tapes would be erased so they could be reused immediately. In reality, criterion protocols had already been prepared for these tapes. In essence, the first set of protocols provided an overt assessment of observer reliability, and the second set, a covert assessment. The results demonstrated a drop in average agreement of approximately 25 percentage points from the last two days of training (75%) to the following four days (51%).

In a later study, Romancyzk *et al.* (1973) trained five observers in the use of a nine-category code for disruptive behavior, with which they later observed and recorded the behavior of eight first-grade children in a classroom setting. Their reliability was assessed by two assessors simultaneously throughout the study. Each of these assessors employed a unique version of the code in which four of the nine categories had different criteria. During overt assessment, although both observers were present and measured reliability, only one of them was identified to the observers as the assessor for that session. This procedure permitted the calculation of reliability with both an identified and unidentified assessor. During covert assessment, the observers did not know that reliability was still being measured. A comparison of occurrence reliabilities between the two conditions showed substantial differences (.77 with overt assessment, and .33 with covert assessment). Furthermore, knowledge of the assessor, despite the difference in criteria for the same code, resulted in average reliabilities of .77 with the identified assessor and .53 with the unidentified assessor. Finally, during covert assessment, observers recorded 25% less behavior. These results provided further support and clearly demonstrated the reactivity of observers to the knowledge that their reliability is being assessed. Not only will they be more diligent in their use of the code, but also they will tailor their interpretation of the categories to agreement with the assessor.

Finally, in a study by Taplin and Reid (1973), three groups of observers had their reliabilities checked under three different conditions. One group was told there would be no reliability checks, a second group that they would be checked without their awareness 20% of the time (random checks), and the third group that they would undergo spot checks but would be informed of them in advance. Immediately after training, there were significant drops in the reliability for all three groups. The spot check group yielded interesting results because each time their reliability was checked they obtained the highest level of agreement for that session. However, the remainder of their unchecked sessions fell below each of the other conditions. It was obvious that the observers were reactive to the assessment. Consistently, the most reliable condition was the random check condition, in which observers were told that their reliability would be checked 20% of the time but not when. Johnson and Bolstad (1973) suggest that "it is likely that the knowledge of a 'potential' assessment of accuracy will increase the observer's motivation and vigilance" (p. 20).

These data suggest that one cannot automatically assume observers will maintain the level of reliability attained during training, nor will simply completing reliability checks be sufficient to identify instrument decay should it occur. It would appear that the best way to obtain an accurate assessment of observer reliability is to make frequent overt reliability checks on a random basis without the observer's knowledge of when or by whom.

Consensual Observer Drift

Another way in which observational data can be the victim of instrument decay is observer drift. This phenomenon involves the distinction between observer agreement and observer accuracy. Although high levels of agreement may exist between two observers, they may not be

accurate with respect to some criterion. It has been pointed out that regardless of whether or not observers work alone or with a partner, there
is a tendency for them to develop idiosyncratic versions of various code
definitions and thereby "drift" from the original definition and record
unreliable data (Kazdin, 1977). In a study reported earlier, for example,
Kent et al. (1974) found that reliabilities computed within and between
pairs of observers differed significantly. The reliability of observers who
worked in pairs was nine percentage points higher on the average than
that of observers who did not. DeMaster, Reid, and Twentyman (1977)
trained 14 pairs of observers under three feedback conditions. In the "total feedback" condition, each protocol was scored and discussed using a
criterion protocol for comparison. The experimenter gave the observers
feedback concerning their accuracy. The second condition (pair agreement feedback) provided the observers feedback within their pairs but
not with criterion. In the final condition, reliabilities were not computed, nor were the records discussed between observers. The within-
pair reliability across groups was higher than scores computed against
the criterion or between observers in different pairs. There was a
significant main effect for the feedback condition, with the total feedback condition attaining the highest levels of reliability and the no feedback condition the worst. Similar results have also been reported by
Hawkins and Dobes (1977), Kent, Kanowitz, O'Leary, and Cheiken
(1977), and Wildman, Erickson, and Kent (1975).

In order to minimize the observer drift threat to reliability and validity, it has been suggested (Goldfried & Sprafkin, 1974; Haynes, 1978;
Johnson & Bolstad, 1973; Kent & Foster, 1977; Patterson et al., 1978) that
observers be periodically "recalibrated" to standard criterion protocols.
In this way, if they have begun to drift away from the appropriate
definitions and instructions, they will be given the opportunity to
reattain the proper levels of accuracy. It has also been suggested that
observers be rotated periodically between pairs, thereby not allowing idiosyncratic definitions within pairs to develop.

Cheating and Code Complexity

Several studies have introduced the possibility that cheating may
influence the reliability of observational data. For example, O'Leary and
Kent (1973) found that when the experimenter was in the room while
reliabilities were being computed the average was .55. However, when
he was absent it was .66. Similarly, the reliability was .66 when the ex-

perimenter was present but not closely monitoring the calculations and .58 when he calculated them himself. Kent *et al.* (1974) found similar results depending on whether the observer or experimenter calculated the scores, and Kent *et al.* (1977) reported an average increase of six points for reliabilities computed in the experimenter's absence. This may be explained by the observer's desire to win the experimenter's approval.

Code complexity has also been shown to affect the reliability of observational data (Dorsey, Nelson, & Hayes, 1979; Jones *et al.*, 1975; Mash & McElwee, 1974; Reid, Skindrud, Taplin, & Jones, 1973). Complexity is defined by the number of categories in the coding system or the number of discriminations required of the observer. In either case, there appears to be a negative correlation between complexity and observer agreement/accuracy. For example, Jones *et al.* (1975) reported negative correlations between -.52 and -.75 for the observer's percentage of agreement and code complexity. Dorsey *et al.* (1979) investigated the effects of three levels of code complexity on observer agreement/accuracy. Codes had either three, six, or nine categories, and the results demonstrated that with an increasing number of categories, agreement and accuracy decreased.

Combined Sources of Error

One comprehensive study (Kent *et al.*, 1977) investigated the cumulative effects of the following sources of bias: knowledge of reliability assessment, knowledge of the assessor, absence or presence of the experimenter during calculation, and within- versus between-group reliability. Their results demonstrated that knowledge of the assessor increased occurrence reliability by 10 points on the average (1 to 38) when compared to a group without this information. There was an average increase of 6 points in the reliability of individual categories when calculated during the experimenter's absence. Within-group reliabilities were 11 points higher (3 to 22) than between-group reliabilities on the average. Every experimental variable produced an increase in the reliability. When they combined all the factors shown to inflate reliability and compared them with all the variables that decrease reliability, they found an average increase of 28 points, from .50 to .78. This study provides ample reason to make every effort to control the various sources of bias. Otherwise, one cannot be sure if the data obtained with this instrument are a true representation of the target behaviors or the result of error.

Procedural Controls

Throughout this section various threats to the reliability and validity of observational data have been examined. The literature in this area has either directly stated or indirectly implied procedural modifications which can control for these threats and generate more reliable, valid, and useful data. The major sources on invalidity will be listed again below with procedural controls which have been suggested or implied.

1. Reactivity of the observees to the observation. The behavior of individuals when observed is different from their behavior when unobserved.
   a. Observations should be made from an inconspicuous position (e.g., behind a one-way mirror).
   b. If a one-way mirror is unavailable, the subjects should be instructed to "act naturally" and the observers should minimize their interaction with the subjects, including eye contact, etc. (Haynes, 1978).
   c. Deflect subjects away from target behaviors by informing them that other behaviors will be observed (Haynes, 1978).
   d. Repeat observations to permit possible habituation.
   e. Use telemetry, videocameras, or tape recorders (Haynes and Horn, 1982).
   f. Use participant observers (Haynes & Horn, 1982).
   g. Provide observees with a thorough rationale for being observed (Johnson & Bolstad, 1973).
2. Expectation and observer bias. Observers will systematically distort their data in accord with experimenter hypotheses, the status of the subject (e.g., treatment or control group; pre-, post-, or follow-up assessment) or knowledge of the subject's background.
   a. Observers should not be privy to information regarding the investigator's hypotheses or impressions about the client, the status of the target subjects, or the subject's background (e.g., Haynes, 1978; Johnson & Bolstad, 1973).
   b. The persons completing the observations should not be the same as those who gather the historical data or complete the behavioral interview.

      c. Observers should be instructed in the importance of professional rigor in completing their observations (Haynes, 1978).

      d. Precise behavioral definitions should be employed (e.g., Goldfried & Sprafkin, 1974; Haynes, 1978).

      e. Well-trained observers should be used (Patterson *et al.*, 1978).

3. Observer reactivity to reliability assessment. If observers know that their accuracy is to be checked, they appear to become more diligent and provide a more reliable use of the codes than when they do not know they are being assessed.

      a. Frequent overt reliability checks are necessary on a random basis without providing the observers with advance notice (Haynes, 1978; Johnson & Bolstad, 1973; Patterson *et al.*, 1978).

      b. Train observers to a high level of accuracy (.70 to .80) before allowing them to collect "real" data.

4. Consensual observer drift. Individual observers or observers working in teams will develop idiosyncratic definitions of behavioral codes and thereby "drift" in accuracy from the criterion.

      a. "Recalibrate" observers by periodically checking their accuracy with a criterion protocol and retrain if necessary.

      b. Rotate observers among themselves, thus diminishing the opportunity for within-pair idiosyncratic definitions to gain strength.

      c. Compute interobserver agreement frequently to check for proper code use.

5. Code complexity. The more complex the behavioral coding system with respect to either the number of individual codes or the number of discriminations required, the greater the potential for lowering the reliability.

      a. Use only the number of codes which are necessary to the purpose of observation.

      b. Train observers using videotapes with increasingly more complex interactions needing greater numbers of discrimination.

    c. Use teams of observers with large coding systems in which one observer records half of the codes and a second observer the other half.

6. Cheating. The calculation of observer reliabilities may be inflated when completed by the observers themselves.

    a. Closely supervise the computations.

    b. The investigator should perform the necessary calculations.

The use of these various procedures should control for the potential threats inherent in this assessment methodology. Without them, of course, extreme caution is probably necessary when interpreting the data.

CHAPTER 12

Concluding Comments

Determining the optimal postdivorce living arrangements for a child is an extremely complex multifaceted problem. Unfortunately, it must be solved under less-than optimal conditions. The effects of separation and divorce on all persons involved are far-reaching and well-documented. To say that divorcing spouses and their children are not at their best would undoubtedly be an understatement. However, for the most part, it is under these conditions that the mental health professional is instructed to make recommendations concerning custody and the best interests of the child which reach far into the future. Obviously, this is no small task. Unfortunately, it seems that the tools currently at the disposal of the mental health professional are often not very helpful. Many of them are old and would appear to have outlived their clinical usefulness. Others simply have not been developed to answer the kinds of questions raised in the context of a custody dispute. As such, the clinician is left with no alternative to doing the best evaluation possible with the tools available. Although it may be said that these clinicians make a valiant effort under entirely adverse conditions, it is not enough. The mental health professional has already assisted the courts in making custody decisions, but if current practice continues, the research would appear to suggest that the help they provide will probably have little to do with reliable and valid assessment methodologies. More importantly, the theory that underlies all traditional procedures has been seriously questioned.

The continued use of these procedures for determining the living arrangements of a child after divorce may be explained by the lack heretofore of any truly viable alternative (although even the introduction of an alternative does not insure the demise of its less useful predecessor).

It has been my intention to provide the groundwork for such an alternative and for the first time to address comprehensively the issues of what and how to measure in the context of custody litigation. Every attempt has been made to develop an assessment model which is inextricably bound to a theoretical perspective founded on empirically established principles (and testable hypotheses). It is imperative that the outcomes of our scientific investigations serve as a guide in deciding which procedures to use, how to use them, and why. It is clear from the data presented throughout Part 2 of this book that reliance upon informal procedures will not yield highly reliable or valid information. If the mental health professional relies on waiting-room or interview-session observations, various psychological tests and/or test batteries, and his or her own clinical judgment, then questions are immediately raised with respect to the validity of any conclusions and recommendations which may be based on these data. It appears crucial that an assessment model be consistent with the research demonstrating the major role of environmental variables in the understanding and prediction of behavior, substantially reduce the need for inference and subjective judgments, focus on the direct observation of criterion behaviors either in naturalistic or relevant analogue settings, and attempt to control the myriad of possible threats to an instrument's reliability and validity. A model which incorporates procedures that ignore the importance of these points is of questionable value.

The author is not suggesting that all the answers can be found within this volume, for only a small portion of the questions have been asked. It is suggested only that the professionals be guided by the available data which address the multitude of questions, that they continue to evaluate their procedures, and that they acknowledge the limitations of these procedures at any point in time. The data base is in a constant state of flux, and each evaluator must keep abreast of new developments and adjust practices accordingly. Otherwise, a severe disservice is being done to those who come to the mental health professional for assistance in making this extremely important decision.

The present volume is incomplete in that when considering what should be measured in developing the present model I selected areas which I felt would be most important in determining the living arrangements of a child after the parents' divorce. Certainly, there are other important areas to investigate, for example, the prospective caretaker's economic status and job security and health; many readers will suggest others. Furthermore, when considering how to measure, only two behavioral strategies were examined, albeit comprehensively, whereas others, such as checklists and self-report inventories, were ignored. Beyond these omissions, there is an entirely different literature base that was not considered but would be a serious oversight by the individual mental health professional charged with recommending custody arrangements. Research on the effects of marital discord and divorce on children is beginning to proffer some consistent findings which should be considered by every evaluator in this field. For example, individual studies and review articles have consistently reported that interparental conflict and hostility are primarily responsible for placing children at risk for adjustment and behavioral problems and not the separation and divorce per se (Anthony, 1974; Clingempeel & Reppucci, 1982; Emery, 1982; Hetherington, Cox, & Cox, 1976, 1979a; Jacobson, 1978; Kelly & Wallerstein, 1976; Westman, Cline, Swift & Kramer, 1970). Emery (1982) cites studies from five research areas which support this conclusion: (1) children from homes broken by death have fewer behavior problems than those by separation and divorce; (2) children from broken homes without conflict were less likely to have problems than those from intact but conflictual homes; (3) the responses of children to divorce and marital discord are similar in many ways; (4) children from divorced homes in which the conflict continues after divorce exhibit a larger number of adjustment problems than do those who come from conflict-free divorces; and (5) numerous behavior problems evident in children of divorce were present for a long time prior to their separation from a parent.

This information has important implications for any mental health professional involved in making recommendations concerning the postdivorce living arrangements of children. If the bulk of available research at any given point in time strongly suggests that interparental conflict is a major determinant in the future adjustment of children, then it would seem imperative that this variable be assessed and recommendations made accordingly. For example, how prudent would it be to recommend joint physical custody when the assessment has consistently indicated that in terms of past and current interactions these parents are extremely hostile toward each other? If the objective is to recommend living arrangements which will provide a child with an opportunity for optimal growth and development, and it is known that open, hostile interparental conflict places a child at risk for developing a variety of behavior problems, then barring other research to the contrary, the assessor's judgment might be questioned if he or she recommended a placement that would increase contact between openly hostile parents. This area of study would also seem to question the wisdom of any legislation which would presume the value of any one custody arrangement for all families. What is underscored here is the importance of family-by-family evaluation, incorporating all relevant information available to the assessor within the pertinent fields of scientific study.

A second area of research on the effects of divorce on children concerns the differential effects on boys and girls. In reviewing this literature Emery (1982) suggested that although the research seems to suggest that boys are effected more markedly by both marital discord and divorce, an important factor to consider in looking at sex differences is how boys and girls respond and to what degree. It appears that boys are more likely to respond with aggressive, disruptive types of behavior, whereas girls become more anxious, withdrawn, and possibly more well behaved. The behavior of boys, therefore, is more likely to come to the attention of adults who will bring them to clinics. Additionally, Santrock and Warshak (1979) have demonstrated that boys and girls have more behavior problems when in the custody of the opposite-sex parent. Therefore, boys will have a greater number of problems while in the custody of their mothers and girls, in the custody of their fathers. And, as Emery (1982) points out, if mothers obtain custody 90% of the time, then boys will have more problems after divorce. One may be tempted to suggest that, barring other significant data, boys should be placed with their fathers and girls with their mothers. However, in addition to desiring further replications of these findings, there are other studies that may help explain these sex differences and be important to consider when conducting an evaluation. It appears that children are disciplined more frequently by the same-sex parent (Baumrind, 1971) or, at least, boys are disciplined by both parents whereas girls are disciplined by their mothers (Margolin & Patterson, 1975). In either case, given the 90% maternal custody rate, it is more likely that boys will be allowed to express a full range of negative behaviors without consistent, effective discipline. If boys are more likely than girls to respond to a stress situation (i.e., divorce) with aggressive, aversive behaviors (Ross, 1980) and if through divorce they lose their primary effective disciplinarian, then their negative pattern of behavior is more likely to go unchecked and ineffectively disciplined. This may result in a pattern of coercive interactions between mothers and sons (see Patterson, 1982). From a social learning perspective, prior to divorce the boy was exhibiting some aggressive, hostile behavior. However, these behaviors were more frequently exhibited in the presence of his mother, who was unskilled in disciplining these behaviors and controlled her son by threatening the future discipline of his father. This threat would often manage the boy's disruptive behavior because Dad would consistently punish the boy's behavior. The disruptive behavior rarely occurred in father's presence. In essence, the boy had learned to behave differently in the presence of each of his parents. However, if the father leaves, taking with him his effective method of disciplining his son, all that remains is the boy's mother, who heretofore was the ineffective disciplinarian in whose presence the child had learned that he could misbehave without significant penalty.

How would this information be of value to the assessor? Most importantly, she would determine who was primarily responsible for disciplining the child prior to the divorce. She would assess how the child is responding to the separation and divorce and how the current caretaker has been able to manage him. If the father was the effective disciplinarian before divorce, then barring other significant factors, future adjustment of this child is more probable in the custody of his father. Similarly, although in general boys and girls seem to adjust better in the custody of the same-sex parent, perhaps in this particular family the mother has always been the primary disciplinarian and is able to manage her children's responses to separation and divorce effectively. Again, the research available guides us in our assessment and recommendations. At no time should an evaluator use the general conclusions of a single empirical investigation and apply them to every family assessed. The weight of the available evidence should alert the evaluator to important variables which must then be assessed. At all times, the nomothetic data of an individual investigation or group of studies should be interpreted in an idiographic manner. To what extent are the significant factors identified in this study relevant to this child–parent–family situation? How are they different? Are there other variables also relevant to this family situation which other investigations have suggested override the importance of the first set of variables? As the data accumulate, confirming the importance of one set of factors and the lesser weight of a second set, the assessment process should change. The assumptions held to tenaciously today may have to be put aside at some point in the future if not supported by the evidence. This is as it should be. At no time should a set of principles and procedures be maintained simply for tradition or for the sake of convenience. If the procedures used today are found to be unreliable and invalid then they should be replaced–in fact, must be.

Studies that give us important findings with respect to a child's adjustment in a variety of living arrangements are sadly lacking. When the results of future studies in this area become available, the assessment process will undoubtedly change. At that time, the mental health professional will begin to understand which children do best in which kind of post divorce living arrangements, and more importantly, why. What factors determine future adjustments can then be identified. With this information, the evaluator can then assess those factors in each child–parent–family situation and begin to offer predictions of future adjustment which can subsequently be tested over time. When this occurs, an important piece of information will become available that can assist all mental health professionals dedicated to helping the courts and families to determine the optimal post divorce living arrangements for children.

References

Abramowitz, C. V., & Dokecki, P. R. (1977). The politics of clinical judgment: Early empirical returns. *Psychological Bulletin, 84,* 460–476.

Adcock, C. J. (1965). In O. K. Buros, *Sixth mental measurements yearbook.* Highland Park, NJ: Gryphon Press.

Allport, G. W., & Postman, L. (1947). *The psychology of rumor.* New York: Holt.

Alpern, G. D. *Divorce: Rights of Passage.* (1982). Aspen, CO: Psychological Development Publication.

Alternatives to "parental right" in child custody disputes involving third parties. (1963). *Yale Law Journal, 73,* 151–70.

Anastasi, A. (1976) *Psychological testing* (4th ed.). New York: Macmillan.

Anthony, E. J. (1974). Children at risk from divorce: A review. In E. J. Anthony & C. Koupernik (Eds.), *The child in his family III.* New York: Wiley.

Antonovsky, H. F. (1959). A contribution to research in the area of mother–child relationship. *Child Development, 30,* 37–51.

Applezweig, D. G. (1954). Some determinants of behavioral rigidity. *Journal of Abnormal and Social Psychology, 49,* 224–228.

Argyle, M., & Little, B. R. (1972). Do personality traits apply to social behavior? *Journal for the Theory of Social Behaviour, 2,* 1–35.

Arkes, H. R. (1981). Impediments to accurate clinical judgment and possible ways to minimize their impact. *Journal of Consulting and Clinical Psychology, 49,* 323–330.

Arnoff, F. N. (1954). Some factors influencing the unreliability of clinical judgments. *Journal of Clinical Psychology, 10,* 272–275.

Athey, K. R., Coleman, J. E., Reitman, A. P., & Tang, J. (1960). Two experiments showing the effect of the interviewer's racial background on responses to questionnaire concerning racial issues. *Journal of Applied Psychology, 44,* 244–246.

Atkeson, B. M., & Forehand, R. (1978). Parent behavioral training for problem children: An examination of studies using multiple outcome measures. *Journal of Abnormal Child Psychology, 6,* 449–460.

Atkeson, B. M., & Forehand, R. (1981). Behavioral assessment of the conduct disordered child. In E. J. Mash & L. G. Terdal (Eds.), *Behavioral assessment of childhood disorders.* New York: Guilford Press.

Awad, G. A. (1978). Basic principles in custody assessment. *Canadian Psychiatric Association Journal*, 23, 441–447.

Bales, R. (1950) *Interaction process analysis*. Cambridge: Addison-Wesley.

Bandura, A. (1965). Vicarious processes: A case of no-trial learning. In L. Berkowitz (Ed.), *Advances in experimental social psychology*. (Vol. 2) New York: Academic Press.

Bandura, A. (1969). *Principles of behavior modification*. New York: Holt, Rinehart, & Winston.

Bandura, A. (1971a). *Social learning theory*. Morristown, NJ: General Learning Press.

Bandura, A. (1971b). Vicarious and self-reinforcement processes. In R. Glaser (Ed.), *The nature of reinforcement*. New York: Academic Press.

Bandura, A. (1973). *Aggression: A social learning analysis*. Englewood Cliffs, NJ: Prentice-Hall.

Bandura, A. (1977). *Social learning theory*. Englewood Cliffs, NJ: Prentice-Hall.

Bandura, A., & Adams, N. E. (1977). Analysis of self-efficacy theory of behavioral change. *Cognitive Therapy and Research*, 1, 287–310.

Bandura, A., & Huston, A. C. (1961). Identification as a process of incidental learning. *Journal of Abnormal and Social Psychology*, 63, 311–318.

Bandura, A., & Kupers, C. J. (1964). Transmission of patterns of self-reinforcement through modeling. *Journal of Abnormal and Social Psychology*, 69, 1–9.

Bandura, A., & Mischel, W. (1965). Modification of self-imposed delay of reward through exposure to live and symbolic models. *Journal of Personality and Social Psychology*, 2, 698–705.

Bandura, A., & Whalen, C. K. (1966). The influences of antecedent reinforcement and divergent modeling cues on patterns of self-reward. *Journal of Personality and Social Psychology*, 3, 373–382.

Bandura, A., Ross, D., & Ross, S. A. (1963a). Imitation of film mediated aggressive models. *Journal of Abnormal and Social Psychology*, 66, 3–11.

Bandura, A., Ross, D., & Ross, S. A. (1963b). A comparative test of status envy, social power, and secondary reinforcement theories of identificatory learning. *Journal of Abnormal and Social Psychology*, 67, 527–534.

Bandura, A., Grusec, J. E., & Menlove, F. L. (1967). Some social determinants of self-monitoring reinforcement systems. *Journal of Personality and Social Psychology*, 5, 449–455.

Barnard, C. P., & Jenson, G. (1984). *Child custody evaluation Manual: Precedents and practices*. Unpublished manuscript. Menomonie, Wisconsin: Midwest Custody Evaluation and Psychological Services.

Baum, C. G., Forehand, R., & Zegiob, L. E. (1979). A review of observer reactivity in adult–child interactions. *Journal of Behavioral Assessment*, 1, 167–178.

Baumrind, D. (1967). Child care practices anteceding three patterns of preschool behavior. *Genetic Psychology Monographs*, 75, 43–83.

Baumrind, D. (1971). Current patterns of parental authority. *Developmental Psychology Monograph*, 4, (1, pt.2).

Behrens, M. L., & Sherman, A. (1959). Observational research with emotionally disturbed children: Session I. *American Journal of Orthopsychiatry, 29,* 243–248.

Beiman, J., O'Neil, P., Wachtel, D., Fruge, E., Johnson, S., & Feuerstein, M. (1978). Validation of a self-report/behavioral subject selection procedure for analog fear research. *Behavior Therapy, 9,* 169–177.

Bell, R. Q. (1964). Structuring parent–child interaction situations for direct observation. *Child Development, 35,* 1009–1020.

Bem, D. J., & Allen, A. (1974). On predicting some of the people some of the time: The search for cross-situational consistencies in behavior. *Psychological Review, 81,* 506–520.

Bem, D. J., & Funder, D. C. (1978). Predicting more of the time: Assessing the personality of situations. *Psychological Review, 85,* 485–501.

Benedek, E. P., & Benedek, R. S. (1979). Joint custody: Solution or illusion? *American Journal of Psychiatry, 136,* 1540–1544.

Benny, M., Riesman, D., & Star, S. (1956). Age and sex in the interview. *American Journal of Sociology, 62,* 143–152.

Benton, A. A. (1967). Effects of the timing of negative response consequences on the observational learning of resistance to temptation in children. *Dissertation Absracts International, 27,* 2153–2154.

Bentovim, A., & Gilmour, L. (1981). A family therapy interactional approach to decision making in child care, access and custody cases. *Journal of Family Therapy, 3,* 65–77.

Berg, I. A. (1967). The deviation hypothesis: A broad statement of its assumptions and postulates. In I. A. Berg (Ed.) *Response set in personality assessment.* Chicago: Aldine.

Berger, S. M. (1962). Conditioning through vicarious instigation. *Pschological Review, 69,* 450–466.

Bernal, M. E., Gibson, D. M., Williams, D. E., & Pesses, D. I. (1971). A device for automatic audio tape recording. *Journal of Applied Behavior Analysis, 4,* 151–156.

Bernstein, L. (1956). The examiner as an inhibiting factor in clinical testing. *Journal of Consulting Psychology, 20,* 287–290.

Bespalec, D. A. (1978). The psychodiagnostic test battery: The effects of sequence of adminstration on Rorschach variables. *Dissertation Abstracts International, 38(12-B),* 6134–6135.

Bienenfeld, F. (1983). *Child custody mediation: Techniques for counselors, attorneys and parents.* Palo Alto, Calif: Science and Behavior Books.

Bijou, S. W., & Peterson, R. F. (1971). Functional analysis in the assessment of children. In P. McReynolds (Ed.), *Advances in psychological assessment* (Vol. 2) San Francisco: Jossey-Bass.

Bijou, S. W., Peterson, R. F., Harris, F. R., Allen, K. E., & Johnston, M. S. (1969). Methodology for experimental studies of young children in natural settings. *Psychological Record, 19,* 177–210.

Bishop, B. M. (1946). A measurement of mother–child interaction. *Journal of Abnormal and Social Psychology, 41,* 37–49.

Bishop, D. W., & Witt, P. A. (1970). Sources of behavioral variance during leisure time. *Journal of Personality and Social Psychology, 16,* 352–360.

Bishop, J. P. (1873). *Commentaries on the law of marriage and divorce, Vol. 2* (5th ed.). Boston: Little, Brown & Co..

Bohannon, P. (1970). *Divorce and after.* Garden City, NJ: Doubleday.

Bowers, K. S. (1973). Situationism in psychology: An analysis and a critique. *Psychological Review, 80,* 307–336.

Bradbrook, A. (1971). An empirical study of the attitudes of the judges of the Supreme Court of Ontario regarding the workings of the present child custody adjudication law. *Canadian Bar Review, 49,* 557–576.

Braginsky, B. M., & Braginsky, D. D. (1967). Schizophrenic patients in the psychiatric interview: An experimental study of their effectiveness at manipulation. *Journal of Consulting Psychology, 31,* 546–551.

Braginsky, B. M., Braginsky, D. D., & Ring, K. (1969). *Methods of madness: The mental hospital as a last resort.* New York: Holt, Rinehart & Winston.

Braginsky, B. M., Grosse, M., & Ring, K. (1966). Controlling outcomes through impression-management: An experimental study of the manipulative tactics of mental patients. *Journal of Consulting Psychology, 30,* 295–300.

Bremner, R. (1970). *Children and youth in America: A documentary history, 1600–1865.* Cambridge, MA: Harvard University Press.

Brown, G. M., & Rutter, M. L. (1966). The measurement of family activities and relationships: A methodological study. *Human Relations, 19,* 241–263.

Buros, O. K. (Ed.). (1978). *Eighth mental measurements yearbook.* Highland Park, NJ: Gryphon Press.

Burton, R. V. (1963). Generality of honesty reconsidered. *Psychological Review, 70,* 481–499.

Butcher, J. N., & Tellegen, A. (1978). Common methodological problems in MMPI research. *Journal of Consulting and Clinical Psychology, 46,* 620–628.

California Civil Code § 1600 and added section 1600.5, effective January 1, 1980.

California Assembly Committee Reports, 1963–1965. (1969). Cited by P. C. Ellsworth, & R. J. Levy, Legislative reform of child custody adjudication: An effort to rely on social science data in formulating legal policies. *Law & Society Review, 4,* 204–205.

Campbell, D., & Fiske, D. (1959). Convergent and discriminant validation by the multitrait–multimethod matrix. *Psychological Bulletin, 56,* 81–105.

Campbell, D. T., & Stanley, J. C. (1963). *Experimental and quasi-experimental designs for research.* Chicago: Rand McNally.

Cannell, C. F., & Kahn, R. L. (1968). Interviewing. In G. Lindzey & E. Aronson (Eds.), *The handbook of social psychology,* (2nd ed.). Reading, MA: Addison-Wesley.

Cantor, N., & Mischel, W. (1979). Prototypes in person perception. In L. Berkowitz (Ed.), *Advances in experimental social psychology* (Vol. 12). New York: Academic Press.

Charnas, J. F. (1981) Practice trends in divorce related to child custody. *Journal of Divorce, 4,* 57–67.

Chasin, R., & Grunebaum, H. (1981). A model for evaluation in child custody disputes. *The American Journal of Family Therapy, 9*, 43–49.

Chess, S., Thomas, A., Birch, H. G., & Hertzig, M. (1960). Implications of a longitudinal study of child development for child psychiatry. *American Journal of Psychiatry, 117*, 434–441.

Chess, S., Thomas, A., & Birch, H. G. (1966). Distortions in developmental reporting made by parents of behaviorally disturbed children. *Journal of the American Academy of Child Psychiatry, 5*, 226–231.

Child Custody Act of 1970, Public Act no, 91. *Michigan Compiled Laws Annotated* (sec. 7222.21–722.29). St. Paul, Minn. West Publishing Co.

Ciminero, A. R., & Drabman, R. S. (1977). Current developments in the behavioral assessment of children. In B. B. Lahey & A. E. Kazdin (Eds.), *Advances in clinical child psychology*, (Vol. 1). New York: Plenum Press.

Cleveland, S. E. (1976). Reflections on the rise and fall of psychodiagnosis. *Professional Psychology, 7*, 309–318.

Cline, V. B. (1955). Ability to judge personality assessed with a stress interview and sound-film technique. *Journal of Abnormal and Social Psychology, 50*, 183–187.

Clingempeel, W. G., & Reppucci, N. D. (1982). Joint custody after divorce: Major issues and goals for research. *Psychological Bulletin, 91*, 102–127.

Cogan, D. L., Gottlieb, B., Meitus, S. H., Uslan, S. E., & Wilson, G. G. (1982). The custody evaluation: Purpose, process and participants. In *Seventh Annual Child Custody Workshop. National Center for Continuing Legal Education.*

Cohen, R. (1976). Accuracy and confidence level in clinical inference as a function of cue validity, feedback, and specific practice. *Dissertation Abstracts International, 36*, (9-B), 4682.

Comments: Custody and control of children. (1936). *Fordham Law Review, 5*, 460–473.

Cone, J. D. (1977). The relevance of reliability and validity for behavioral assessment. *Behavior Therapy, 8*, 441–426.

Coogler, O. J. (1978). *Structured mediation in divorce settlement*. Lexington, MA: Lexington Books.

Cotroneo, M., Krasner, B. R., & Boszormenyi-Nagy, I. (1981). The contextual approach to child-custody decisions. In G. P. Sholevar (Ed.), *The handbook of marriage and marital therapy*. NY: Medical and Scientific Books.

Couch, A. S., & Keniston, K. (1960). Yea-sayers and nay-sayers: Agreeing response set as personality variable. *Journal of Abnormal and Social Psychology, 60*, 151–174.

Council of Representatives Report of the American Psychological Association. (1977, January). Minutes of the American Psychological Association Council of Representatives meeting, Washington, DC.

Cox, A. (1975). The assessment of parental behavior. *Journal of Child Psychology, Child Psychiatry and Allied Disciplines, 16*, 255–259.

Cox, A., & Rutter, M. (1977). Diagnostic appraisal and interviewing. In M. Rutter & L. Hersov (Eds.), *Child psychiatry: Modern approaches*. London: Blackwell Scientific Publications.

Cox, M. J. T., & Cease, L. (1978). Joint custody: What does it mean? How does it work? *Family Advocate*, Summer, 10–13.

Cronbach, L. J., Gleser, G. C., Nanda, H., & Rajaratnam, N. (1972). *The dependability of behavioral measures*. New York: Wiley.

Dahlstrom, W. G., Welsh, G. S., & Dahlstrom, L. E. (1975). *An MMPI handbook. Vol. II: Research applications* (Rev. ed.). Minneapolis: University of Minnesota Press.

Dana, R. H. (1972). In O. K. Buros *Seventh mental measurements yearbook*. Highland Park, NJ: Gryphon Press.

Dana, R. (1982). *A human science model for personality assessment with projective techniques*. Springfield, IL: Charles C Thomas.

Davids, A. (1973). Projective testing: Some issues facing academicians and practitioners. *Professional Psychology, 4,* 445–453.

Davis, K. (1943). A sociological and statistical analysis. *Law and Contemporary Problems*, 1943–1944, *10,* 700. Cited in A. Bradbrook, An empirical study of attitudes of the Supreme Court of Ontario regarding the workings of the parent child custody adjudication law. *Canadian Bar Review*, 1971, *49,* 557–576.

DeMaster, B., Reid, J. B., & Twentyman, C. (1977). Effects of different amounts of feedback on observer's reliability. *Behavior Therapy, 8,* 317–329.

DeMause, L. (1974). *The history of childhood*. New York: Harper & Row.

Derdeyn, A. P. (1975). Child custody consultation. *American Journal of Orthopsychiatry, 45,* 791–801.

Derdeyn, A. P. (1976). Child custody contests in historical perspective. *American Journal of Psychiatry, 133,* 1369–1376.

Devereux, E. C. (1970). The role of peer-group experience on moral development. In J. P. Hill (Ed.), *Minnesota Symposia on Child Psychology,* (Vol. 4). Minneapolis: University of Minnesota Press.

Dinoff, M. (1960). Subject awareness of examiner influence in a testing situation. *Journal of Consulting Psychology, 24,* 465.

Dorsey, B. L., Nelson, R. O., & Hayes, S. C. (1979, December). The effects of code complexity and behavior frequency on observer accuracy and interobserver agreement. Paper presented at the Association for Advancement of Behavior Therapy, San Francisco.

Douglas, J. W. B., Lawson, A., Cooper, J. E., & Cooper, E. (1968). Family interaction and the activities of young children. *Journal of Child Psychology, Child Psychiatry and Allied Disciplines, 9,* 157–171.

Doyle, P. & Caron, W. (1979). Contested custody interventions: An empirical assessment. In Olson *et al.* (Eds.) *Child custody: Literature review and alternative approaches*. Unpublished monograph, Minneapolis, MN.

Dubey, D. R., Kent, R. N., O'Leary, S. G., Broderick, J. E., & O'Leary, K. D. (1977). Reactions of children and teachers to classroom observers: A series of controlled investigations. *Behavior Therapy, 8,* 887–897.

Ebbesen, E. B. (1981). Cognitive processes in inferences about a person's personality. In E. T. Higgins, C. P. Herman, & M. P. Zanna (Eds.), *Social cogni-*

tion: The Ontario Symposium on Personality and Social Psychology. Hillsdale, NJ: Erlbaum.

Edwards, A. L. (1953). The relationship between the judged desirability of a trait and the probability that the trait will be endorsed. *Journal of Applied Psychology, 37,* 90–93.

Edwards, A. L. (1961). Social desirability or acquiescence in the MMPI? A case study with the SD scale. *Journal of Abnormal and Social Psychology, 63,* 351–359.

Ekehammar, B. (1974). Interactionism in personality from a historical perspective. *Psychological Bulletin, 81,* 1026–1048.

Ekehammar, B., & Magnusson, D. (1973). A method to study stressful situations. *Journal of Personality and Social Psychology, 27,* 176–179.

Ekehammar, B., Magnusson, D., & Richlander, L. (1974). An interactionist approach to the study of anxiety. *Scandinavian Journal of Psychology, 15,* 4–14.

Emery, R. E. (1982). Interparental conflict and the children of discord and divorce. *Psychological Bulletin, 92,* 310–330.

Endler, N. S. (1966). Estimating variance components from mean squares for random and mixed effects analysis of variance models. *Perceptual and Motor Skills, 22,* 559–570.

Endler, N. S. (1973). The person versus the situation—A pseudo issue? A response to Alker. *Journal of Personality, 41,* 287–303.

Endler, N. S. (1975a). The case for person–situation interactions. *Canadian Psychological Review, 16,* 12–21.

Endler, N. S. (1975b). A person–situation interaction model for anxiety. In C. D. Spielberger & I. G. Sarason (Eds.), *Stress and anxiety* (Vol. 1). Washington, DC: Hemisphere.

Endler, N. S., & Hoy, E. (1967). Conformity as related to reinforcement and social pressure. *Journal of Personality and Social Psychology, 7,* 197–202.

Endler, N. S., & Hunt, J. McV. (1966). Sources of behavioral variance as measured by the S–R Inventory of Anxiousness. *Psychological Bulletin, 65,* 336–346.

Endler, N. S., Hunt, J. McV. (1968). S–R inventories of hostility and comparisons of the proportions of variance from persons, responses and situations for hostility and anxiousness. *Journal of Personality and Social Psychology, 9,* 309–315.

Endler, N. S., & Hunt, J. McV. (1969). Generalizability of contributions from sources of variance in the S–R inventories of anxiousness. *Journal of Personality, 37,* 1–24.

Endler, N. S., & Magnusson, D. (1976). Toward an interactional psychology of personality. *Psychological Bulletin, 83,* 956–974.

Endler, N. S., & Okada, M. (1975). A multidimensional measure of trait anxiety: The S–R inventory of general trait anxiousness. *Journal of Consulting and Clinical Psychology, 43,* 319–329.

Endler, N. S., Hunt, J. McV., & Rosenstein, A. J. (1962). An S–R inventory of anxiousness. *Psychological Monographs, 76,* (Whole No. 536).

Endler, N. S., Wiesenthal, D. L., & Geller, S. H. (1972). The generalization of the effects of agreement and correctness on relative competence mediating conformity. *Canadian Journal of Behavioural Science, 4,* 322–329.

Epstein, R. (1966). Aggression toward outgroups as a function of authoritarianism and imitation of aggressive models. *Journal of Personality and Social Psychology, 3,* 574–579.

Epstein, S. (1979). The stability of behavior: I. On predicting most of the people much of the time. *Journal of Personality and Social Psychology, 37,* 1097–1126.

Epstein, S. (1980). The stability of behavior: II. Implications for psychological research. *American Psychologist, 35,* 790–806.

Epstein, S. (1983a). The stability of confusion: A reply to Mischel and Peake. *Psychological Review, 90,* 179–184.

Epstein, S. (1983b). Aggregation and beyond: Some basic issues on the predictions of behavior. *Journal of Personality, 51,* 360–392.

Erdberg, S. P. (1970). MMPI differences associated with sex, race, and residence in a southern sample. Unpublished doctoral dissertation. University of Alabama. *(Dissertations Abstract International, 1970, 30, 5236B).*

Eron, L. D. (1972). In O. K. Buros, (Ed.), *Seventh mental measurements Yearbook,* Highland Park, NJ: Gryphon Press.

Evans, I. M., & Nelson, R. O. (1977). Assessment of child behavior problems. In A. Ciminero, K. S. Calhoun, & H. Adams (Eds.), *Handbook of behavioral assessment.* New York: Wiley.

Everett, C. A., & Volgy, S. S. (1983). Family assessment in child custody disputes. *Journal of Marital and Family Therapy, 9,* 343–353.

Exner, J. E. (1974). *The Rorschach: A comprehensive system (Vol. 1).* New York: Wiley.

Exner, J. E. (1978) *The Rorschach: A comprehensive system. (Vol. 2) Current research and advanced interpretations* New York: Wiley.

Eyberg, S. M., & Johnson, S. M. (1974). Multiple assessment of behavior modification with families: Effects of contingency contracting and order of treated problems. *Journal of Consulting and Clinical Psychology, 42,* 594–606.

Eysenck, H. J. (1965). Extraversion and the acquisition of eyeblink and GSR conditions responses. *Psychological Bulletin, 83,* 258–270.

Fairweather, G. W. (Ed.) (1964). *Social psychology in treating mental illness: An experimental approach.* New York: Wiley.

Fairweather, G. W. (1967). *Methods in experimental social interaction.* New York: Wiley.

Fairweather, G. W., Simon, R., Gebhard, M. E., Weingarten, E., Holland, J. L., Sanders, R., Stone, G. B., & Reahl, J. E. (1960). Relative effectiveness of psychotherapeutic programs: A multicriteria comparison of four programs for three different patient groups. *Psychological Monographs, 74* (Whole No. 492).

Fairweather, G. W., Sanders, D. H., Maynard, H., & Cressler, D. L. (1969). *Treating mental illness in the community: An experiment in social innovation.* New York: Wiley.

Farberow, N. L., & McEvoy, T. L. (1966). Suicide among patients with diagnoses of anxiety reaction or depressive reaction in general medical and surgical hospitals. *Journal of Abnormal Psychology, 71,* 287–299.

Felner, R. D., & Farber, S. S (1980). Social policy for child custody: A multidisciplinary framework. *American Journal of Orthopsychiatry, 50,* 341–347.

Fero, D. D. (1976). A lens model analysis of the effects of amount of information and mechanical decision making aid on clinical judgment and confidence. *Dissertation Abstracts International, 36,* (11-B), 5788.

Ferster, C. B. (1965). Classification of behavioral pathology. In L. Krasner & L. P. Ullmann (Eds.), *Research in behavior modification.* NY: Holt, Rinehart and Winston.

Fisher, S. & Fisher, R. (1950). A test of certain assumptions regarding figure drawing analysis. *Journal of Abnormal and Social Psychology, 45,* 727.

Foote, C., Levy, R. J., & Sander, P. E. (1976). *Cases and materials on family law.* Boston: Little Brown.

Forehand, R., & King, H. E. (1974). Pre-school children's noncompliance: Effects of short-term behavior therapy. *Journal of Community Psychology, 2,* 42–44.

Forehand, R., & King, H. E. (1977). Noncompliant children: Effects of parent training on behavior and attitude change. *Behavior Modification, 1,* 93–108.

Forehand, R., & Peed, S. (1979). Training parents to modify the noncompliant behavior of their children. In A. J. Finch & P. C. Kendall (Eds.), *Treatment and research in child psychopathology.* New York: Spectrum.

Forehand, R., Cheney, T., & Yoder, P. (1974). Parent behavior training: Affects on the noncompliance of a deaf child. *Journal of Behavior Therapy and Experimental Psychiatry, 5,* 281–283.

Forehand, R., Doleys, D. W., Hobbs, S. A., Resnick, T. A., & Roberts, M. W. (1976). An examination of disciplinary procedures with children. *Journal of Experimental Child Psychology, 21,* 109–120.

Forehand, R., Peed, S., Roberts, M., McMahon, B., Griest, D., & Humphreys, L. (1978). Coding manual for scoring mother–child interactions (3rd ed.). Unpublished manuscript, University of Georgia.

Forehand, R., Griest, D. L., & Wells, K. C. (1979). Parent behavioral training: An analysis of the relationship among multiple outcome measures. *Journal of Abnormal Child Psychology, 7,* 229–242.

Forehand, R., Sturgis, E. T., McMahon, R. J., Aguar, D., Green, K., Wells, K. C., & Breiner, J. (1979). Parent behavioral training to modify noncompliance: Treatment generalization across time and from home to school. *Behavior Modification, 3,* 3–25.

Forsyth, R. P., & Fairweather, G. W. (1961). Psychotherapeutic and other hospital treatment criteria: The dilemma. *Journal of Abnormal and Social Psychology, 62,* 598–604.

Foster, H. H., Jr. (1972). Adoption and child custody: Best interests of the child. *Buffalo Law Review, 22,* 1–16.

Foster H. H. (1983). Child custody and divorce: A lawyer's view. *Journal of the American Academy of Child Psychiatry*, 22, 392–398.

Foster, H. H., Jr., & Freed, D. J. (1964). Child custody (Part I). *New York University Law Review*, 39, 423–443.

Foster, H. H., & Freed, D. J. (1980). Joint custody: Legislative reform. *Trial*, 16, 22–27.

Foster, H. H., & Freed, D. J. (1983). Child custody and the adversary process: Forum conveniens? *Family Law Quarterly*, 17, 133–150.

Foster, S. L., & Cone, J. D. (1980). Current issues to direct observation. *Behavioral Assessment*, 2, 313–338.

Fraser, B. G. (1976). The child and his parents: A delicate balance of rights. In R. E. Helfer & C. H. Kempe (Eds.), *Child abuse and neglect: The family and the community*. Cambridge, MA: Ballinger.

Freed, D. J., & Foster, H. H. (1979). Divorce in the fifty states–An overview as of 1978. *Family Law Quarterly*, 13, 105–141.

Fremouw, W. J., & Harmatz, M. G. (1975). A helper model for behavioral treatment of speech anxiety. *Journal of Consulting and Clinical Psychology*, 43, 652–660.

Fulkerson, S. C., & Barry, J. R. (1961). Methodology and research on the prognostic use of psychological tests. *Psychological Bulletin*, 58, 177–204.

Fulton, J. A. (1979). Parental reports of children's post-divorce adjustment. *Journal of Social Issues*, 35, 126–139.

Funder, D. C. (1983a). Three issues in predicting more of the people: A reply to Mischel and Peake. *Psychological Review*, 90, 283–289.

Funder, D. C. (1983b). The "consistency" controversy and the accuracy of personality judgments. *Journal of Personality*, 51, 346–359.

Gaddis, S. M. (1978). Joint custody of children: A divorce decision–making alternative. *Conciliation Courts Review*, 16, 17–22.

Gardner, R. A. (1982). *Family evaluation in child custody litigation*. Cresskill, NJ: Creative therapeutics.

Glick, P. C. (1979). Children of divorced parents in demographic perspective. *Journal of Social Issues*, 35, 170–182.

Glogower, F., & Sloop, E. W. (1976). Two strategies of group training of parents as effective behavior modifiers. *Behavior Therapy*, 7, 177–184.

Goffman, E. (1959). *The presentation of self in everyday life*. New York: Doubleday.

Goldberg, L. R. (1959). The effectiveness of clinician's judgments; The diagnosis of organic brain damage from the Bender-Gestalt Test. *Journal of Consulting Psychology*, 23, 25–33.

Goldberg, L. R. (1968). Simple models or simple processes? Some research on clinical judgments. *American Psychologist*, 23, 483–496.

Golden, M. (1964). Some effects of combining psychological tests on clinical inferences. *Journal of Consulting Psychology*, 28, 440– 446.

Goldfried, M. R. (1977). Behavioral assessment in perspective. In J. Cone & R. P. Hawkins (Eds.), *Behavioral Assessment: New directions in clinical psychology*. New York: Brunner/Mazel.

Goldfried, M. R., & D'Zurilla, T. J. (1969). A behavioral-analytic method for assessing competence. In C. D. Spielberger (Ed.), *Current topics in clinical and community psychology* (Vol. 1). New York: Academic Press.

Goldfried, M. R., & Kent, R. N. (1972). Traditional versus behavioral personality assessment: A comparison of methodological and theoretical assumptions. *Psychological Bulletin, 77,* 409–420.

Goldfried, M. R., & Linehan, M. M. (1977). Basic issues in behavioral assessment, In A. R. Ciminero, K. S. Calhoun, H. E. Adams (Eds.), *Handbook of behavioral assessment.* New York: Wiley.

Goldfried, M. R., & Sprafkin, J. N. (1974). *Behavioral personality assessment.* Morristown, NJ: General Learning Press.

Goldstein, J., Freud, A., & Solnit, A. J. (1973). *Beyond the best interests of the child.* New York: Free Press.

Goodenough, F. L. (1949). *Mental testing.* New York: Rinehart.

Gordon, D. A. (1976). Consistency of mothers' behavior in repeated play interactions with their children. *Journal of Genetic Psychology, 129,* 337–338.

Graham, P., & Rutter, M. (1968). The reliability and validity of the psychiatric assessment of the child: II. Interview with the parent. *British Journal of Psychiatry, 114,* 581–592.

Green, R. F. (1951). Does a selection situation induce testees to bias their answers on interest and temperament tests? *Educational and Psychological Measurement, 11,* 503–515.

Gross, L. R. (1959). Effects of verbal and nonverbal reinforcement in the Rorschach. *Journal of Consulting Psychology, 23,* 66–68.

Group for the Advancement of Psychiatry. (1981). *Divorce, child custody, and the family.* San Francisco: Jossey-Bass.

Grusec, J. (1966). Some antecedents of self-criticism. *Journal of Personality and Social Psychology, 4,* 244–252.

Grusec, J. E. (1971). Power and the internalization of self-denial. *Child Development, 42,* 93–105.

Grusec, J. E., & Skubiski, S. L. (1970). Model nurturance, demand characteristics of the modeling experiment and altruism. *Journal of Personality and Social Psychology, 14,* 352–359.

Guest, L. (1947). A study of interviewer competence. *International Journal of Opinion Attitude Research, 1,* 17–30.

Haase, W. (1972). Rorschach diagnosis, socio-economic class, and examiner bias. Unpublished doctoral dissertation. New York University, 1956. (University Microfilms, No. 16-758). Cited in R. H. Dana, *A human science model for personality assessment with projective techniques.* Springfield, IL: C. Thomas.

Hagen, R. L., Craighead, W. E., & Paul, G. L. (1975). Staff reactivity to evaluate behavioral observations. *Behavior Therapy, 6,* 201–205.

Haggard, E. A., Brekstad, A., & Skard, A. G. (1960). On the reliability of the anamnestic interview. *Journal of Abnormal and Social Psychology, 61,* 311–318.

Haller, L. H. (1981). Before the judge: The child-custody evaluation. *Adolescent Psychiatry, 9,* 142–164.

Harris, A. M. (1969). Observer effect on family interaction. Unpublished doctoral dissertation, University of Oregon. Cited by G. R. Patterson, J. B. Reid, & S. L. Maerov, (1978). Development of the family interaction coding system (FICS). In J. B. Reid (Ed.), *A social learning approach to family intervention. Vol. 2: Observation in home settings.* Eugene, Oregon: Castalia.

Harris, S. & Masling, J. (1970). Examiner sex, subject sex, and Rorschach productivity. *Journal of Consulting Psychology, 34,* 460–63.

Harrison, R. H. & Kass, E. H. (1967). Differences between Negro and white pregnant women on the MMPI. *Journal of Consulting Psychology, 31,* 454-463.

Hartmann, D. P., Roper, B. L., & Bradford, D. C. (1979). Some relationships between behavioral and traditional assessment. *Journal of Behavioral Assessment, 1,* 3–19.

Hartshorne, H. & May, M. A. (1928). *Studies in the nature of character. Vol. 1: Studies in deceit.* New York: Macmillan.

Hase, H. D., & Goldberg, L. R. (1967). Comparative validity of different strategies of constructing personality inventory scales. *Psychological Bulletin, 67,* 231–248.

Hatfield, J. S., Ferguson, L. R., & Alpert, R. (1967). Mother–child interaction and the socialization process. *Child Development, 38,* 356–414.

Hathaway, S. R., & McKinley, J. C. (1980). Construction of the schedule. In W. G. Dahlstrom & L. Dahlstrom (Eds.), *Basic readings on the MMPI: A new selection on personality measurement.* Minneapolis: University of Minnesota Press.

Hawkins, R. P., & Dobes, R. W. (1977). Behavioral definitions in applied behavior analysis: Explicit or implicit. In B. C. Etzel, J. M. LeBlanc, D. M. Baer (Eds.), *New developments in behavioral research: Theory, method, and application. In honor of Sidney W. Bijou.* Hillsdale, NJ: Lawrence Erlbaum Associates.

Hay, W. M., Hay, L. R., Angle, H. V., & Nelson, R. O. (1979). The reliability of problem identification in the behavioral interview. *Behavioral Assessment, 1,* 107–118.

Haynes, J. (1981). *Divorce mediation: A practical guide for therapists and counselors.* New York: Springer Publishing Company.

Haynes, S. N. (1978). *Principles of behavioral assessment.* New York: Gardner Press.

Haynes, S. N., & Horn, W. F. (1982). Reactivity in behavioral observation: A review. *Journal of Behavioral Assessment, 4,* 369–385.

Haynes, S. N., & Jensen, B. J. (1979). The interview as a behavioral assessment instrument. *Behavioral Assessment, 1,* 97–106.

Heaton, R. K., Smith, H. H., Lehman, R. A., and Vogt, A. T. (1978). Prospects for faking believable deficits on neuropsychological testing. *Journal of Consulting and Clinical Psychology, 46,* 892–900.

Heffler, B., & Magnusson, D. (1979). Generality of behavioral data: IV. Cross-situational invariance of objectively measured behavior. *Perceptual and Motor Skills, 48,* 471–477.

Helzer, J. E., Clayton, P. J., Pambakian, R., & Woodruff, R. A. (1978). Concurrent diagnostic validity of a structured psychiatric interview. *Archives of General Psychiatry, 35,* 849–853.

Herbert, E. W., Pinkston, E. M., Hayden, M. S., Sajwaj, T. E., Pinkston, S., Cordua, G., & Jackson, C. (1973). Adverse effects of differential parental attention. *Journal of Applied Behavioral Analysis, 6*, 15–30.

Herjanic, B., & Reich, W. (1982). Development of a structured psychiatric interview for children: Agreement between child and parent on individual symptoms. *Journal of Abnormal Child Psychology, 10*, 307–324.

Herjanic, B., Herjanic, M., Brown, F., & Wheatt, T. (1975). Are children reliable reporters? *Journal of Abnormal Child Psychology, 3*, 41–48.

Hersen, M. (1970). Sexual aspects of Rorschach administration. *Journal of Projective Techniques, 34*, 104–105.

Hersen, M., & Bellack, A. S. (1977). Assessment of social skills. In A. R. Ciminero, K. S. Calhoun & H. E. Adams (Eds.), *Handbook for behavioral assessment*. New York: Wiley.

Hersen, M., & Greaves, S. (1971). Rorschach productivity as related to verbal reinforcement. *Journal of Personality Assessment, 35*, 436–441.

Hetherington, E. M. (1965). A developmental study of the effects of sex of the dominant parent on sex-role preference, identification, and imitation in children. *Journal of Personality and Social Psychology, 2*, 188–194.

Hetherington, E. M., & Frankie, G. (1967). Effects of parental dominance, warmth, and conflict on imitation in children. *Journal of Personality and Social Psychology, 6*, 119–125.

Hetherington, E. M., Cox, M., & Cox, R. (1976). Divorced fathers. *Family Coordinator, 25*, 417–428.

Hetherington, E. M., Cox, M., & Cox, R. (1979a). Family interaction and the social, emotional, and cognitive development of children following divorce. In V. C. Vaughn & T. B. Brazelton (Eds.), *The family: Setting priorities*. New York: Science and Medicine Publishers.

Hetherington, E. M., Cox, M., & Cox, R. (1979b). Play and social interaction in children following divorce. *Journal of Social Issues, 35*, 26–49.

Heyns, R., & Lippitt, R. (1954). Systematic observational techniques. In G. Lindzey (Ed.), *Handbook of social psychology* (Vol. 1). Cambridge, MA: Addison-Wesley.

Hicks, D. J. (1965). Imitation and retention of film-mediated aggressive peer and adult models. *Journal of Personality and Social Psychology, 2*, 97–100.

Hiler, E. W., & Nesvig, D. (1965). An evaluation of criteria used by clinicians to infer pathology from figure drawings. *Journal of Consulting and Clinical Psychology, 29*, 520–529.

Hirsch, J. M. (1978). *The elementary school-age child of divorce: How to determine which parent should be given custody*. Unpublished Manuscript. University of Denver, School of Professional Psychology.

Hodges, K., Kline, J., Stern, L., Cytryn, L., & McKnew, D. (1982). The development of a child assessment interview for research and clinical use. *Journal of Abnormal Child Psychology, 10*, 173–189.

Hoffman, M. L. (1957). An interview method for obtaining descriptions of parent–child interaction. *Merrill-Palmer Quarterly, 4*, 76–83.

Hoffman, M. L. (1970). Moral development. In P. H. Mussen (Ed.), *Carmichael's handbook of child psychology* (Vol. 2). New York: Wiley.

Hoffman, M. L. (1979). Development of moral thought, feeling, and behavior. *American Psychologist, 34,* 958–966.

Holmes, D. S., & Tyler, J. D. (1968). Direct versus projective measurement of achievement motivation. *Journal of Consulting and Clinical Psychology, 32,* 712–717.

Holsopple, J. G., & Phelan, J. G. (1954). The skills of clinicians in analysis of projective tests. *Journal of Clinical Psychology, 10,* 307–320.

Horowitz, M. J. (1962). A study of clinicians' judgments from projective test protocols. *Journal of Consulting Psychology, 26,* 251–256.

Hughes, H. M., & Haynes, S. N. (1978). Structured laboratory observation in behavioral assessment of parent–child interactions: A methodological critique. *Behavior Therapy, 9,* 428–447.

Hunt, J. McV. (1965). Traditional personality theory in the light of recent evidence. *American Scientist, 53,* 80–96.

Hutt, S. J., & Hutt, C. (1970). *Direct observation and measurement of behavior.* Springfield, IL: Charles C. Thomas.

Hyman, H. (1944). Do they tell the truth? *Public Opinion Quarterly, 8,* 557–559.

Inker, M. L., & Perretta, C. A. (1971). A child's right to counsel in custody cases. *Family Law Quarterly, 5,* 108–120.

Irving, H. (1980). *Divorce mediation: The rational alternative.* Toronto: Personal Library Publishers.

Iwata, B. A., Wong, S. E., Riordan, M. M., Dorsey, M. F., & Lau, M. M. (1982). Assessment and training of clinical interviewing skills: Analogue, analysis, and field replication. *Journal of Applied Behavior Analysis, 15,* 191–203.

Jackson, A. M., Warner, N. S., Hornbein, R., Nelson, N., & Fortescue, E. (1980). Beyond the best interests of the child revisited: An approach to custody evaluation. *Journal of Divorce, 3,* 207–222.

Jackson, D. N. (1973). Structured personality assessment. In B. B. Wolman (Ed.), *Handbook of general psychology,* Englewood Cliffs, NJ: Prentice-Hall.

Jackson, D. N., & Messick, S. (1958). Content and style in personality assessment. *Psychological Bulletin, 55,* 243–252.

Jackson, D. N., & Messick, S. (1962). Response styles and the assessment of psychopathology. In S. Messick & J. Ross (Eds.), *Measurement in personality and cognition.* New York: Wiley.

Jacobs, A., & Barron, R. (1968). Falsification of the Guilford-Zimmerman Temperament Survey: II. Making a poor impression. *Psychological Reports, 23,* 1271–1277.

Jacobson, D. S. (1978). The impact of marital separation/divorce on children: II. Interparental hostility and child adjustment. *Journal of Divorce, 2,* 3–20.

Jakubczak, L. F., & Walters, R. H. (1959). Suggestibility as dependency behavior. *Journal of Abnormal and Social Psychology, 59,* 102–107.

Jensen, A. R. (1959). In O. K. Buros (Ed.), *Fifth mental measurements yearbook.* Highland Park, NJ: Gryphon Press.

Jensen, A. R. (1965). In O. K. Buros (Ed.), *Sixth mental measurement yearbook.* Highland Park, NJ: Gryphon Press.

Jewett, J., & Clark, H. B. (1976). Training preschoolers to use appropriate dinnertime conversation. An analysis of generalization from school to home. Unpublished manuscript, University of Kansas. Cited by B. M. Atkeson & R. Forehand. (1978). Parent behavioral training for problem children: An examination of studies using multiple outcome measures. *Journal of Abnormal Child Psychology, 6,* 449–460.

Johnson, S. M., & Bolstad, O. D. (1973). Methodological issues in naturalistic observation: Some problems and solutions for field research. In L. A. Hamerlynch, L. C. Handy, & E. J. Mash (Eds.), *Behavior change: Methodology, concepts, and practice.* Champaign, IL: Research Press.

Johnson, S. M., & Bolstad, O. D. (1975). Reactivity to home observation: A comparison of audio-recorded behavior with observers present or absent. *Journal of Applied Behavior Analysis, 8,* 181–185.

Johnson, S. M., & Brown, R. A. (1969). Producing behavior change in parents of disturbed children. *Journal of Child Psychology and Psychiatry, 10,* 107–121.

Johnson, S. M., & Lobitz, G. K. (1974). Parental manipulation of child behavior in home observations. *Journal of Applied Behavior Analysis, 7,* 23–32.

Johnson, S. M., Christensen, A., & Bellamy, G. T. (1976). Evaluation of family intervention through unobtrusive audio recordings: Experiences in bugging children. *Journal of Applied Behavior Analysis, 9,* 213–219.

Johnson, S. M., Wahl, G., Martin, S., & Johansson, S. (1973). How deviant is the normal child? A behavioral analysis of the preschool child and his family. In R. D. Rubin, J. P. Brady, & J. D. Henderson (Eds.), *Advances in behavior therapy,* (Vol. 4). New York: Academic Press.

Jones, R. R., Reid, J. B., & Patterson, G. R. (1975). Naturalistic observation in clinical assessment. In P. McReynolds (Ed.), *Advances in psychological assessment* (Vol. 3) San Francisco: Jossey-Bass.

Kanfer, F. H., & Saslow, G. (1969). Behavioral diagnosis. In C. M. Franks (Ed.), *Behavior therapy: Appraisal and status.* New York: McGraw-Hill.

Kass, R. E., & O'Leary, K. D. (1970). The effects of observer bias in field-experimental settings. Paper presented at symposium, Behavior Analysis in Education, University of Kansas, April, 1970. Cited by R. N. Kent & S. L. Foster. (1977). Direct observational procedures: Methodological issues in naturalistic settings. In A. Ciminero, K. S. Calhoun, & H. E. Adams (Eds.), *Handbook of behavioral assessment.* New York: Wiley, p. 282.

Katkin, D., Bullington, B., & Levine, M. (1974). Above and beyond the best interests of the child: An inquiry into the relationship between social science and social action. *Law and Society Review, 8,* 669–687.

Katz, D. (1942). Do interviewers bias poll results? *Public Opinion Quarterly, 6,* 248–268.

Kazdin, A. E. (1974a). Effects of covert modeling and model reinforcement on assertive behavior. *Journal of Abnormal Psychology, 83,* 240–252.

Kazdin, A. E. (1974b). Covert modeling, model similarity and reduction of avoidance behavior. *Behavior Therapy, 5,* 325–340.

Kazdin, A. E. (1977). Artifact, bias, and complexity of assessment: The ABC's of reliability. *Journal of Applied Behavioral Analysis, 10,* 141–150.

Keefe, F. J., Kopel, S. A., & Gordon, S. B. (1978). A practical guide to behavioral assessment. New York: Springer.

Kelly, E. L. (1966). Alternate criteria in medical education and their correlates. In A. Anastasi (Ed.), *Testing problems in perspective*. Washington, DC: American Council on Education.

Kelly, J. B. & Wallerstein, J. S. (1976). The effects of parental divorce: Experiences of the child in early latency. *American Journal of Orthopsychiatry, 46*, 20–32.

Kent, R. N., & Foster, S. L. (1977). Direct observational procedures: Methodological issues in naturalistic settings. In A. Ciminero, K. S. Calhoun, & H. E. Adams (Eds.), *Handbook of behavioral assessment*. New York: Wiley.

Kent, R. N., O'Leary, K. D., Diament, C., & Dietz, A. (1974). Expectation biases in observational evaluation of therapeutic change. *Journal of Consulting and Clinical Psychology, 42*, 774–780.

Kent, R. N., Kanowitz, J., O'Leary, K. D., & Cheiken, M. (1977). Observer reliability as a function of circumstances of assessment. *Journal of Applied Behavior Analysis, 10*, 317–324.

Kent, R. N., O'Leary, K. D., Dietz, A., and Diament, C. (1979). Comparison of observational recordings *in vivo*, via mirror, and via television. *Journal of Applied Behavior Analysis, 12*, 517–522.

King, G. F., Erhman, J. C., & Johnson, D. M. (1952). Experimental analysis of reliability of observations of social behavior. *Journal of Social Psychology, 35*, 151–160.

Kleinman, K. M., Goldman, H., Snow, M. Y., & Korol, B. (1977). Relationship between essential hypertension and cognitive functioning. II: Effects of biofeedback training generalized to nonlaboratory environment. *Psychophysiology, 14*, 192–197.

Klinger, E. (1966). Fantasy need achievement as a motivational construct. *Psychological Bulletin, 66*, 291–308.

Kogan, K. L., Wimberger, R. C., & Bobbitt, R. A. (1969). Analysis of mother–child interaction in young mental retardates. *Child Development, 40*, 799–812.

Kohn, M. L., & Carroll, E. E. (1960). Social class and the allocation of parental responsibilities. *Sociometry, 23*, 373–392.

Kornhaber, R. C., & Schroeder, H. E. (1975). Importance of model similarity on extinction of avoidance beahvior in children. *Journal of Consulting and Clinical Psychology, 43*, 601–607.

Koscherak, S., & Masling, J. (1972). Noblesse oblige effect: The interpretation of Rorschach responses as a function of ascribed social class. *Journal of Consulting and Clinical Psychology, 39*, 415–419.

Kostlan, A. (1954). A method for the empirical study of psychodiagnosis. *Journal of Consulting Psychology, 18*, 83–88.

Kram, S. W., & Frank, N. A. (1982). *The law of child custody: Development of the substantive law*. Lexington, MA: Lexington Books.

Lamb, M. E. (1976). Interactions between eight-month-old children and their fathers and mothers. In M. E. Lamb (Ed.), *The role of the father in child development*. New York: Wiley.

Lapouse, R., & Monk, M. A. (1958). An epidemiologic study of behavior characteristics in children. *American Journal of Public Health, 48,* 1134–1144.

Lasky, J. J., Hover, G. L., Smith, P. A., Bostian, D. W., Duffendack, S. C., & Nord, C. L. (1959). Post-hospital adjustment as predicted by psychiatric patients and by their staff. *Journal of Consulting Psychology, 23,* 213–218.

Lemerond, J. N. (1978). Suicide prediction for psychiatric patients: A comparison of the MMPI and clinical judgments. *Dissertation Abstracts International, 38(10-A),* 5926–5927.

Lenski, G. E., & Leggett, J. C. (1960). Caste, class and deference in the research interview. *American Journal of Sociology, 65,* 463–467.

Leon, G. R., (1971). Case report: The use of a structured mother–child interaction and projective material in studying parent influence on child behavior problems. *Journal of Clinical Psychology, 27,* 413–416.

Levy, A. M. (1978). Child custody determination: A proposed psychiatric methodology and its resultant case typology. *Journal of Psychiatry and Law, 6,* 189–214.

Levy, M. (1970). Issues in the personality assessment of lower-class patients. *Journal of Projective Techniques and Personality Assessment, 34,* 6–9.

Levy, M. & Kahn, M. (1970). Interpreter bias on the Rorschach test as a function of patient's socioeconomic status. *Journal of Projective Techniques and Personality Assessment, 34,* 106–112.

Levy, M. R., & Fox, H. M. (1975). Psychological testing is alive and well. *Professional Psychology, 6,* 420–424.

Lindzey, G., & Tejessy, C. (1956). Thematic Apperception Test: Indices of aggression in relation to measures of overt and covert behavior. *American Journal of Orthopsychiatry, 26,* 567–576.

Linehan, M. M. (1977). Issues in behavioral interviewing. In J. D. Cone, & R. P. Hawkins (Eds.), *Behavioral assessment: New directions in clinical psychology.* New York: Brunner/Mazel.

Lipinski, D., & Nelson, R. (1974). The reactivity and unreliability of self-recording. *Journal of Consulting and Clinical Psychology, 42,* 110–123.

Lobitz, W. C., & Johnson, S. M. (1975). Parental manipulation of the behavior of normal and deviant children. *Child Development, 46,* 719–726.

Lorei, T. W. (1967). Predictions of community stay and employment for released psychiatric patients. *Journal of Consulting Psychology, 31,* 349–357.

Lubin, B., Wallis, R. R., & Paine, C. (1971). Patterns of psychological test usage in the United States: 1935–1969. *Professional Psychology, 2,* 70–74.

Lytton, H. (1971). Observation studies of parent–child interaction: A methodological review. *Child Development, 42,* 651–684.

Maccoby, E. E., & Maccoby, N. (1954). The interview: A tool of social sciences. In G. Lindzey (Ed.), *Handbook of social psychology,* Reading, MA: Addison-Wesley.

Maccoby, E. E., & Wilson, W. C. (1957). Identification and observational learning from film. *Journal of Abnormal and Social Psychology, 55,* 76–87.

MacFarlane, J. W. (1938). Studies in child guidance. I. Methodology of data collection and organization. *Monographs of the Society for Research in Child Development, 3,* No. 6 (Serial No. 19).

Machover, K. (1949). *Personality projection in the drawing of the human figure: A method of personality investigation.* Springfield, IL: Charles C. Thomas.

Maddox, B. (1975). *The half parent.* New York: Signet.

Maerov, S. L., Brummett, B., Patterson, G. R., & Reid, J. B. (1978). Coding of family interactions. In J. B. Reid (Ed.), *A social learning approach to family intervention (Vol. 2). Observation in home settings.* Eugene, Oregon: Castalia.

Magnussen, M. G. (1960). Verbal and nonverbal reinforcers in the Rorschach situation. *Journal of Clinical Psychology, 16,* 167–169.

Magnussen, M. G. (1967). Effect of test order upon children's Rorschach animal content. *Journal of Projective Techniques and Personality Assessment, 31,* 41–43.

Magnusson, D. (1971). An analysis of situational dimensions. *Perceptual and Motor Skills, 32,* 851–867.

Magnusson, D. (1974). The individual in the situation: Some studies on individuals' perception of situations. *Studia Psychologica, 16,* 124–132.

Magnusson, D., & Ekehammar, B. (1973). An analysis of situational dimensions: A replication. *Multivariate Behavioral Research, 8,* 331–339.

Magnusson, D., & Ekehammar, B. (1975). Anxiety profiles based on both situational and response factors. *Multivariate Behavioral Research, 10,* 27–43.

Magnusson, D., & Heffler, B. (1969). The generality of behavioral data: III. Generalization as a function of the number of observational situations. *Multivariate Behavioral Research, 4,* 29–42.

Magnusson, D., Gerzén, M., & Nyman, B. (1968). The generality of behavioral data: I. Generalization from observation on one occasion. *Multivariate Behavioral Research, 3,* 295–320.

Magnusson, D., Heffler, B., & Nyman, B. (1968). The generality of behavioral data: II. Replication of an experiment on generalization from observation on one occasion. *Multivariate Behavioral Research, 3,* 415–422.

Marafiote, R. A. (1981). In the best interests of the child: Behavioral assessment and the child custody evaluation. Unpublished doctoral paper, University of Denver, School of Professional Psychology.

Margolin, G., & Patterson, G. R. (1975). Differential consequences provided by mothers and fathers for their sons and daughters. *Developmental Psychology, 11,* 537–538.

Marks, J., Stauffacher, J. C., & Lyle, C. (1963). Predicting outcome in schizophrenia. *Journal of Abnormal and Social Psychology, 66,* 117–127.

Martin, B. (1975). Parent–child relations. In F. D. Horowitz (Ed.), *Review of child development* (Vol. 4). Chicago: University of Chicago Press.

Martin, M. F., Gelfand, D. M., & Hartmann, D. P. (1971). Effects of adult and peer observers on boys' and girls' responses to an aggressive model. *Child Development, 42,* 1271–1275.

Martin, S., Dysart, R., & Gonzalez, J. (1975). A comparison of family interaction in clinic and in home settings. Unpublished manuscript, University of Houston. Cited by E. J. Mash & L. G. Terdal (Eds.). (1976). *Behavior therapy assessment: Diagnosis, design, and evaluation.* New York: Springer.

Marwit, S. J. (1971). Further notes on the effect of pretest expectancies on the psychological test report. *Journal of Personality Assessment, 35,* 303–306.

Marwit, S. J., & Strauss, M. E. (1975). Influences of instructions on expectancy effects in the Rorschach testing. *Journal of Personality Assessment, 39,* 13–18.

Mash, E. J., & McElwee, J. D. (1974). Situational effects on observer accuracy: Behavior predictability, prior experience, and complexity of coding categories. *Child Development, 45,* 367–377.

Mash, E. J., & Terdal, L. G. (Eds.). (1976). *Behavior therapy assessment: Diagnosis, design, and evaluation.* New York: Springer.

Mash, E. J., Terdal, L., & Anderson, K. (1973). The response-class matrix: A procedure for recording parent–child interactions. *Journal of Consulting and Clinical Psychology, 40,* 163–164.

Masling, J. (1960). The influence of situational and interpersonal variables in projective testing. *Psychological Bulletin, 57,* 65–85.

Masling, J., & Harris, S. (1969). Sexual aspects of TAT administration. *Journal of Consulting and Clinical Psychology, 33,* 166–169.

Mason, B., & Ammons, R. B. (1956). Note on social class and the TAT. *Perceptual & Motor Skills, 6,* 88.

Matarazzo, J. D. (1983). The reliability of psychiatric and psychological diagnosis. *Clinical Psychology Review, 3,* 103–145.

McArthur, C. (1955). Personality differences between middle and upper classes. *Journal of Abnormal and Social Psychology, 50,* 247–254.

McCall, R. J. (1959). In O. K. Buros (Ed.), *Fifth mental measurements yearbook.* Highland Park, NJ: Gryphon Press.

McCord, J., & McCord, W. (1961). Cultural stereotypes and the validity of interviews for research in child development. *Child Development, 32,* 171–185.

McDermott, J. F., Tseng, W. S., Char, W. F., & Fukunaga, C. S. (1978). Child custody decision making. The search for improvement. *American Academy of Child Psychiatry Journal, 17,* 104–116.

McDermott, P. A. (1980). Congruence and typology of diagnoses in school psychology: An empirical study. *Psychology in the Schools, 17,* 12–24.

McGraw, M., & Molloy, L. B. (1941). The pediatric anamnesis: Inaccuracies in eliciting developmental data. *Child Development, 12,* 255–265.

McReynolds, W. T., & Stegman, R. (1976). Sayer versus sign. *Behavior Therapy, 7,* 704–705.

Mednick, S. A., & Schaffer, J. B. P. (1963). Mothers' retrospective reports in child rearing research. *American Journal of Orthopsychiatry, 33,* 457–461.

Melei, J. P., & Hilgard, E. R. (1964). Attitudes towards hypnosis, self-predictions, and hypnotic susceptibility. *International Journal of Clinical and Experimental Hypnosis, 12,* 99–108.

Mercatoris, M., & Craighead, W. E. (1974). The effects of non-participant observation on teacher and pupil classroom behavior. *Journal of Experimental Psychology, 66,* 512–519.

Merrill, B. (1946). A measurement of mother–child interaction. *Journal of Abnormal and Social Psychology, 41,* 37–49.

Messick, S., & Jackson, D. N. (1961). Acquiesence and the factorial interpretation of the MMPI. *Psychological Bulletin, 58,* 299–304.

Messick, S. & Jackson, D. N. (1966). Response style and the factorial structure of the MMPI. In E. I. Megargee (Ed.), *Research in clinical assessment*. New York: Harper & Row.

Miller, D. J. (1979). Joint Custody. *Family Law Quarterly, 13, 345–412.*

Milne, A. (1978). Custody of children in a divorce process: A family self-determination model. *Conciliation Courts Review, 16,* 1–10.

Milner, J. S. (1975). Administrators' gender and sexual content in projective test protocols. *Journal of Clinical Psychology, 31,* 540–541.

Mischel, W. (1965). Predicting the success of Peace Corps volunteers in Nigeria. *Journal of Personality and Social Psychology, 1,* 510–517.

Mischel, W. (1968). *Personality and assessment.* New York: Wiley.

Mischel, W. (1969). Continuity and change in personality. *American Psychologist, 24,* 1012–1018.

Mischel, W. (1972). Direct versus indirect personality assessment: Evidence and implications. *Journal of Consulting and Clinical Psychology, 38,* 319–324.

Mischel, W. (1973). Toward a cognitive social learning reconceptualization of personality. *Psycological Review, 80,* 252–283.

Mischel, W. (1976). *Introduction to personality (2nd ed.).* New York: Holt, Rinehart & Winston.

Mischel, W. (1977). On the future of personality measurement. *American Psychologist, 32,* 246–264.

Mischel, W. (1981). A cognitive-social learning approach to assessment. In T. V. Merluzzi & M. Genest (Eds.), *Cognitive assessment.* New York: Guilford Press.

Mischel, W. (1983). Alternatives in the pursuit of the predictability and consistency of persons: Stable data that yields unstable interpretations. *Journal of Personality, 51,* 578–604.

Mischel, W., & Bentler, P. (1965). The ability of persons to predict their own behavior. Unpublished manuscript. Stanford University. Cited by W. Mischel. (1968). *Personality and assessment.* New York: Wiley.

Mischel, W., & Grusec, J. (1966). Determinants of the rehearsal and transmission of neutral and aversive behaviors. *Journal of Personality and Social Psychology, 3,* 197–205.

Mischel, W., & Grusec, J. E. (1967). Waiting for rewards and punishments— Effects of time and probability on choice. *Journal of Personality and Social Psychology, 5,* 24–31.

Mischel, W., & Liebert, R. M. (1966). Effects of discrepancies between observed and imposed reward criteria on their acquisition and transmission. *Journal of Personality and Social Psychology, 3,* 45–53.

Mischel, W., & Peake, P. K. (1982). Beyond déjà vu in the search for cross-situational consistency. *Psychological Review, 89,* 730–755.

Mnookin, R. H. (1975). Child-custody adjudication: Judicial functions in the face of indeterminacy. *Law and Contemporary Problems, 39,* 226–293.

Mnookin, R., & Kornhauser, L. (1979). Bargaining in the shadow of the law: The case of divorce. *Yale Law Journal, 88,* 950–997.

Moos, R. H. (1967). Differential effects of ward settings on psychiatric patients. *Journal of Nervous and Mental Disease, 145,* 272–283.

Moos, R. H. (1968). Behavioral effects of being observed: Reactions to a wireless radio transmitter. *Journal of Consulting and Clinical Psychology, 32,* 383–388.

Moos, R. H. (1969). Sources of variance in responses to questionnaires and in behavior. *Journal of Abnormal Psychology, 74,* 405–412.

Moos, R. H. (1979). Differential effects of psychiatric ward settings on patient charge. *Journal of Nervous and Mental Disease, 5,* 316–321.

Moos, R. H., & Clemes, S. (1967). Multivariate study of the patient–therapist system. *Journal of Consulting Psychology, 31,* 119–130.

Moos, R. H., & Daniels, D. (1967). Differential effects of ward settings on psychiatric staff. *Archives of General Psychiatry, 17,* 75–83.

Moustakas, C. E., Sigel, I. E., & Schalock, H. D. (1956). An objective method for the measurement and analysis of child–adult interaction. *Child Development, 27,* 109–134.

Mussen, P. H. (1953). Differences between the TAT responses of Negro and white boys. *Journal of Consulting Psychology, 17,* 373–376.

Mussen, P. H. (1961). Some antecedents and consequents of masculine sex-typing in adolescent boys. *Psychological Monographs, 75,* No. 2 (Whole, No. 506).

Mussen, P. H. & Scodel, A. (1955). The effects of sexual stimulation under varying conditions on TAT sexual responsiveness. *Journal of Consulting Psychology, 19,* 90.

Nay, W. R. (1977). Analogue measures. In A. R. Ciminero, K. S. Calhoun, & H. E. Adams (Eds.), *Handbook of behavioral assessment.* New York: Wiley.

Nelsen, E. A., Grinder, R. E., & Mutterer, M. L. (1969). Sources of variance in behavioral measures of honesty in temptation situations: Methodological analysis. *Developmental Psychology, 1,* 265–279.

Nelson, C. M., Worrell, J., & Polsgrove, L. (1973). Behaviorally disordered peers as contingency managers. *Behavior Therapy, 4,* 270–276.

Nelson, R. O., & Hayes, S. C. (1979). Some current dimensions of behavioral assessment. *Behavioral Assessment, 1,* 1–16.

Nelson, R. O., Lipinski, D. P., & Black, J. L. (1975). The effects of expectancy on the reactivity of self-recording. *Behavior Therapy, 6,* 337–349.

Nelson, R. O., Kapust, J. A., and Dorsey, B. L. (1978). Minimal reactivity to overt classroom observations on student and teacher behaviors. *Behavior Therapy, 9,* 659–702.

Newcomb, T. M. (1931). An experiment designed to test the validity of a rating technique. *Journal of Educational Psychology, 22,* 279–289.

O'Leary, K. D., & Kent, R. N. (1973). Behavior modification for social action: Research tactics and problems. In L. Hamerlynck, L. C. Handy, & E. J. Mash (Eds.), *Behavior change: Methodology, concepts and practice.* Champaign, IL: Research Press.

O'Leary, K. D., Kent, R. N., & Kanowitz, J. (1975). Shapping data collection congruent with experimental hypothesis. *Journal of Applied Behavior Analysis, 8,* 43–51.

O'Leary, K. D., Romanczyk, R. G., Kass, R. E., Dietz, A., & Santogrossi, E.

(1969). Procedures for classroom observations of teachers and children. Unpublished manuscript.

Olson, D. H., Cleveland, M., Doyle, P., Rochcastle, M. F., Robinson, B., Reimer, R., Minton, J., Caron, W., and Cohen, S. (1979). *Child custody: Literature review and alternative approaches.* unpublished monograph, Minneapolis, MN.

Orne, M. T. (1969). Demand characteristics and the concept of quasi-controls. In R. Rosenthal & R. Rosnow (Eds.), *Artifact in behavioral research.* New York: Academic Press.

Orthner, D. K., & Lewis, K. (1979). Evidence of single-father competence in child rearing. *Family Law Quarterly, 13,* 27–47.

Oskamp, S. (1962). The relationship of clinical experience and training methods to several criteria of clinical prediction. *Psychological Monographs, 76,* (28, Whole No. 547).

Oskamp, S. (1965). Overconfidence in case-study judgments. *Journal of Consulting Psychology, 29,* 261–265.

Oskamp, S. (1967). Clinical judgment from the MMPI: Simple or complex? *Journal of Clinical Psychology, 23,* 411–415.

Oster, A. M. (1965). Custody proceeding: A study of vague and indefinite standards. *Journal of Family Law, 5,* 21–38.

Parry, H. J., & Crossley, H. M. (1950). Validity of responses to survey questions. *Public Opinion Quarterly, 14,* 61–80.

Patterson, G. R. (1982). *A social learning approach to family intervention. Vol. 3: Coercive family process.* Eugene, OR: Castalia.

Patterson, G. R., Ray, R. S., Shaw, D. A., & Cobb, J. A. (1969). Manual for coding family interactions, sixth revision. Available from ASIS National Auxiliary Publications Service, in care of CCM Information Services, Inc., 909 Third Avenue, NY, NY 10022, Document 01234.

Patterson, G. R., Reid, J. B., & Maerov, S. L. (1978). Development of the Family Interaction Coding System (FICS). In J. B. Reid (Ed.), *A social learning approach to family intervention. Vol. 2: Observation in home settings.* Eugene, OR: Castalia.

Payne, S. L. (1949). Interviewer memory faults. *Public Opinion Quarterly, 13,* 684–685.

Pearson, J., & Thoennes, N. (1982). Mediation and divorce: The benefits outweigh the costs. *Family Advocate, 4,* 25–32.

Pearson, J., Munson, P., & Thoennes, N. (1982). Legal change and child custody awards. *Journal of Family Issues, 3,* 5–24.

Pearson, J., Thoennes, N., & Milne, A. (1982). *Directory of mediation services.* Denver, CO: The Divorce Mediation Research Project. The Association of Family Conciliation Courts.

Pearson, J., Thoennes, N., & Vanderkooi, L. (1982). The decision to mediate: Profiles of individuals who accept and reject the opportunity to mediate contested custody and visitation issues. *Journal of Divorce, 6,* 17–35.

Peed, S., Roberts, M., & Forehand, R. (1977). Evaluation of the effectiveness of a standardized parent-training program in altering the interaction of mothers and their noncompliant children. *Behavior Modification, 1,* 323–350.

Perri, M. G., Richards, C. S., & Schultheis, K. R. (1977). Behavioral self-control and smoking reduction: A study of self-initiated attempts to reduce smoking. *Behavior Therapy, 8,* 360–365.

Pervin, L. A. (1968). Performance and satisfaction as a function of individual–environment fix. *Psychological Bulletin, 69,* 56–68.

Peterson. D. R. (1965). Scope and generality of verbally defined personality factors. *Psychological Review, 72,* 48–59.

Peterson, D. R. (1968). *The clinical study of social behavior,* New York: Appleton-Century-Crofts.

Peterson, R. A. (1978). In O. K. Buros (Ed.), *Eighth mental measurements yearbook,* Highland Park, NJ: Gryphon Press.

Pinneau, S. R., & Milton, A. (1958). The ecological veracity of the self-report. *Journal of Genetic Psychology, 93,* 249–276.

Porro, C. R. (1968). Effects of the observation of a model's affective responses to her own transgression on resistance to temptation in children. *Dissertation Abstracts, 28,* 3064.

Purcell, K., & Brady, K. (1966). Adaptation to the invasion of privacy: Monitoring behavior with a miniature radio transmitter. *Merrill-Palmer Quarterly, 12,* 242–254.

Pyles, M. K., Stolz, H. R., & MacFarlane, J. W. (1935). The accuracy of mothers' reports on birth and developmental data. *Child Development, 6,* 165–176.

Radcliffe, J. A. (1966). A note on questionnaire faking with 16PFQ and MPI. *Australian Journal of Psychology, 18,* 154–157. Cited by A. Anastasi. (1976). *Psychological testing* (4th ed.). New York: Macmillan.

Radin, M. (1927). *Handbook of Roman law.* St. Paul, Minnesota: West Publishing.

Raines, G. N., & Rohrer, S. H. (1960). The operational matrix of psychiatric practice. II. Variability in psychiatric impressions and the projection hypothesis. *American Journal of Psychiatry, 117,* 133–139.

Rapoport, J. L., & Benoit, M. (1975). The relation of direct home observations to the clinic evaluation of hyperactive school age boys. *Journal of Child Psychology and Psychiatry, 16,* 141–147.

Raush, H. L. (1965). Interaction sequences. *Journal of Personality and Social Psychology, 2,* 487–499.

Raush, H. L. (1972). Process and change—A Markov model for interaction. *Family Process, 11,* 275–298.

Raush, H. L., Dittmann, A. T., and Taylor, T. J. (1959a). The interpersonal behavior of children in residential treatment. *Journal of Abnormal and Social Psychology, 58,* 9–26.

Raush, H. L., Dittmann, A. T., & Taylor, T. J. (1959b). Person, setting and change in social interaction. *Human Relations, 12,* 361–378.

Raush, H. L., Farbman, I., & Llewellyn, L. G. (1960). Person, setting and change in social interaction: II. A normal control study. *Human Relations, 13,* 305–333.

Reciprocity of rights and duties between parent and child. (1928). *Harvard Law Review, 42,* 112–115.

Reid, J. B. (1970). Reliability assessment of observation data: A possible methodological problem. *Child Development, 41,* 1143–1150.

Reid, J. B. (Ed.). (1978). *A social learning approach to family intervention. Vol. 2. Observation in home settings.* Eugene, OR: Castalia.

Reid, J. B., Skinrud, K. D., Taplin, P. S., & Jones, R. R. (1973). The role of complexity in the collection and evaluation of observation data. Paper presented at the American Psychological Association, Montreal. Cited by R. N. Kent & S. L. Foster. (1977). Direct observational procedures: Methodological issues in naturalistic settings. In A. Ciminero, K. S. Calhoun, & H. E. Adams (Eds.), *Handbook of behavioral assessment.* New York: Wiley.

Reznikoff, M. (1972). In O. K. Buros (Ed.), *Seventh mental measurements yearbook.* Highland Park, NJ: Gryphon Press.

Riesman, D., & Ehrlich, J. (1961). Age and authority in the interview. *Public Opinion Quarterly, 25,* 39–56.

Riesman, F., & Miller, S. M. (1958). Social class and projective techniques. *Journal of Projective Techniques, 22,* 432–439.

Rimm, D. C., & Masters, J. C. (1974). *Behavior therapy: Techniques and empirical findings.* New York: Academic Press.

Roback, H. B. (1968). Human figure drawings: Their utility in the clinical psychologist's armamentarium for personality assessment. *Psychological Bulletin, 70,* 1–19.

Robbins, L. C. (1963). The accuracy of parental recall of aspects of child development and of child rearing practices. *Journal of Abnormal and Social Psychology, 66,* 261–270.

Rodgers, D. A. (1972). In O. K. Buros (Ed.), *Seventh mental measurements yearbook.* Highland Park, NJ: Gryphon Press.

Rodgers, T. A. (1976). The crisis of custody: How a psychiatrist can be of help. *Bulletin of the American Academy of Psychiatry and Law, 4,* 114–119.

Romanczyk, R. G., Kent, R. N., Diament, C., & O'Leary, K. D. (1973). Measuring the reliability of observational data: A reactive process. *Journal of Applied Behavior Analysis, 6,* 175–184.

Rorer, L. G., & Goldberg, L. R. (1966). Acquiescence in the MMPI? In E. I. Megargee (Ed.) *Research in clinical assessment.* New York: Harper & Row.

Rosekrans, M. A. (1967). Imitation in children as a function of perceived similarity to a social model and vicarious reinforcement. *Journal of Personality and Social Psychology, 7,* 307–315.

Rosekrans, M. A., & Hartup, W. W. (1967). Imitative influences of consistent and inconsistent responses consequences to a model of aggressive behavior in children. *Journal of Personality and Social Psychology, 7,* 429–434.

Rosen, B. C., & D'Andrade, R. (1959). The psychosocial origins of achievement motivation. *Sociometry, 22,* 185–217.

Rosenblith, J. F. (1959). Learning by imitation in kindergarten children. *Child Development, 30,* 69–80.

Rosenblith, J. F. (1961). Imitative color choices in kindergarten children. *Child Development, 32,* 211–223.

Rosenhan, D., & White, G. M. (1967). Observation and rehearsal as determinants of prosocial behavior. *Journal of Personality and Social Psychology, 5,* 424–431.

Rosenthal, R. (1966). *Experimenter effects in behavioral research*. New York: Appleton-Century-Crofts.

Rosenthal, R. (1969). Interpersonal expectations effects of the experimenter's hypothesis. In R. Rosenthal & R. Rosnow (Eds.), *Artifact in behavioral research*. New York: Academic Press.

Rosenthal, T. L., Hung, J. H., & Kelly, J. E. (1977). Therapeutic social influence: Sternly strike while the iron is hot. *Behavior Research and Therapy, 15,* 253–259.

Ross, A. O. (1980). *Psychological disorders of children*. New York: McGraw-Hill.

Rushton, J. P. (1976). Socialization and the altruistic behavior of children. *Psychological Bulletin, 83,* 898–913.

Rutter, M. L., & Brown, G. W. (1966). The reliability and validity of measures of family life and relationships in families containing a psychiatric patient. *Social Psychiatry, 1,* 38–53.

Rutter, M., & Graham, P. (1968). The reliability and validity of psychiatric assessment of the child. I. Interview with the child. *British Journal of Psychiatry, 114,* 563–579.

Rychlak, J. F., & Boland, G. C. (1973). Socioeconomic status and the diagnostic significance of healthy and unhealthy group Rorschach content. *Journal of Personality Assessment, 37,* 411–419.

Salius, A., *et al.* (1978). The use of mediation in contested custody and visitation cases in the family relations court. Unpublished manuscript. Hartford, CN: Superior Court. Cited in Pearson, J., Thoennes, N., & Vanderkooi, L.(1982). The decision to mediate: Profiles of individuals who accept and reject the opportunity to mediate contested custody and visitation issues. *Journal of Divorce, 6,* 17–35.

Santostefano, S. (1968). Miniature situations and methodological problems in parent–child interaction research. *Merrill-Palmer Quarterly, 14,* 285–312.

Santrock, J. W., & Warshak, R. A. (1979). Father custody and social development in boys and girls. *Journal of Social Issues, 35,* 112–125.

Sarbin, T. R., Taft, R., & Bailey, D. E. (1960). *Clinical inference and cognitive theory*. New York: Holt, Rinehart & Winston.

Sayre, P. (1942). Awarding custody of children. *University of Chicago Law Review, 9,* 672–683.

Scarboro, M. E., & Forehand, R. (1975). Effects of two types of response-contingent time-out on compliance and oppositional behavior of children. *Journal of Experimental Child Psychology, 19,* 252–264.

Schaeffer, H. H., Sobell, M. B., & Mills, K. C. (1971). Baseline drinking behaviors in alcoholic and social drinkers: Kinds of sips and sip magnitude. *Behaviour Research and Therapy, 9,* 23–27.

Schaeffer, R. W. (1964). Clinical psychologists ability to use the Draw-A-Person test as an indicator of personality adjustment. *Journal of Consulting Psychology, 28,* 383.

Schinka, J. A., & Sines, J. O. (1974). Correlates of accuracy in personality assessment. *Journal of Clinical Psychology, 30,* 374–377.

Schulman, R. F., Shoemaker, D. J., & Moelis, I. (1962). Laboratory measurement of parental behavior. *Journal of Consulting Psychology, 26,* 109–114.

Schwitzgebel, R. K., & Kolb, D. A. (1975). *Changing human behavior: Principles of planned intervention.* New York: McGraw-Hill.

Seitz, S., & Terdal, L. A. (1972). A modeling approach to changing parent–child interactions. *Mental Retardation, 10,* 39–43.

Sherman, M., Trief, P., & Sprafkin, R. (1975). Impression management in the psychiatric interview: Quality, style, and individual differences. *Journal of Consulting and Clinical Psychology, 43,* 867–871.

Shuller, D. Y., & McNamara, J. R. (1976). Expectancy factors in behavioral observation. *Behavior Therapy, 7,* 519–527.

Shure, G. H., & Rogers, M. S. (1965). Note of caution on the factor analysis of the MMPI. *Psychological Bulletin, 63,* 14–18.

Silverberg, J. (1976). Theoretical models of clinical decision-making: The discrimination of significant parameters of the judgmental process. *Dissertation Abstracts International, 36(8-B),* 4180.

Siegel, A. I. (1954). An experimental evaluation of the sensitivity of the empathy test. *Journal of Applied Psychology, 38,* 222–223.

Silverman, L. H. (1959). A Q-sort of the validity of evaluations made from projective techniques. *Psychological Monographs, 73,* (7, Whole No. 477).

Simmons, W. L., & Christy, E. G. (1962). Verbal reinforcement of a TAT theme. *Journal of Projective Techniques, 26,* 337–341.

Sines, L. K. (1959). The relative contribution of four kinds of data to accuracy in personality assessment. *Journal of Consulting Psychology, 23,* 483–492.

Skindrud, K. (1972). An evaluation of observer bias in experimental field studies of social interaction. Unpublished doctoral dissertation, University of Oregon. Cited by B. G. Wildman & M. T. Erickson. (1977). Methodological problems in behavioral observations. In J. Cone & R. Hawkins (Eds.), *Behavioral assessment: New directions in clinical psychology.* New York: Brunner/Mazel.

Skinner, B. F. (1953). *Science and human behavior.* New York: Macmillan.

Slovenko, R. (1973). *Psychiatry and law.* Boston: Little, Brown.

Smith, H. (1958). A comparison of interview and observation measures of mother behavior. *Journal of Abnormal and Social Psychology, 57,* 278–282.

Smith, H. L. & Hyman, H. (1950). The biasing effect of interviewer expectations on survey results. *Public Opinion Quarterly, 14,* 491–506.

Snyder, M. (1981). "Seek and ye shall find..." In E. T. Higgins, C. P. Herman, & M. P. Zanna (Eds.), *Social cognition—The Ontario Symposium on Personality and Social Psychology.* Hillsdale, NJ: Erlbaum.

Soskin, W. F., & John, V. (1963). The study of spontaneous talk. In R. Barker (Ed.) *The stream of behavior.* New York: Appleton-Century-Crofts.

Spitzer, R. L., Fleiss, J. L., Endicott, J., & Cohen, J. (1967). Mental status schedule. *Archives of General Psychiatry, 16,* 479–493.

Spitzer, R. L., Endicott, J., Fleiss, J. L., & Cohen, J. (1970). The psychiatric status schedule. *Archives of General Psychiatry, 23,* 41–55.

Spock, B. (1957). *Baby and child care.* (rev. Ed.). New York: Pocket Books.

Staats, A. W. (1971). *Child learning, intelligence, and personality,* New York: Harper & Row.

Staats, A. W. (1975). *Social Behaviorism*. Homewood, IL: Dorsey.

Steiner, C. (1978). The effect of experience, training and cue-availability on clinical judgment. *Dissertation Abstracts International, 39(4-B)*, 1970.

Stewart, D. J., & Patterson, M. L. (1973). Eliciting effects of verbal and nonverbal cues on projective test responses. *Journal of Consulting and Clinical Psychology, 41*, 74–77.

Strans, M. A. (1967). The influence of sex of child and social class on instrumental and expressive family roles in a laboratory setting. *Sociology and Social Research, 52*, 7–21.

Strauss, M. E., Gynther, M. D., & Wallhermfechtel, J. (1974). Differential misdiagnosis of blacks and whites by the MMPI. *Journal of Personality Assessment, 38*, 55–60.

Stricker, G. (1967). Actuarial, naive clinical, and sophisticated clinical prediction of pathology from future drawings. *Journal of Consulting Psychology, 31*, 492–494.

Stricker, L. J. (1969). "Test-wiseness" on personality scales. *Journal of Applied Psychology Monographs, 53*, (3, Part 2). Cited by A. Anastasi. (1976). *Psychological testing* (4th ed.). New York: Macmillan, p. 515.

Stuart, R. B. (1970). *Trick or treatment: How and when psychotherapy fails*. Champaign, IL: Research Press.

Swensen, C. H., Jr. (1957). Empirical evaluations of human figure drawings. *Psychological Bulletin, 54*, 431–466.

Swensen, C. H. (1968). Empirical evaluations of human figure drawings: 1957–1966. *Psychological Bulletin, 70*, 20–44.

Taft, R. (1955). The ability to judge people. *Psychological Bulletin, 52*, 1–28.

Tannenbaum, P. H., & Gaer, E. P. (1965). Mood change as a function of stress of protagonist and degree of identification in a film-viewing situation. *Journal of Personality and Social Psychology, 2*, 612–616.

Taplin, P. S., & Reid, J. B. (1973). Effects of instructional set and experimenter influence on observer reliability. *Child Development, 44*, 547–554.

Tavormina, J. B. (1975). Relative effectiveness of behavioral and reflective group counseling with parents of mentally retarded children. *Journal of Consulting and Clinical Psychology, 43*, 22–31.

Thelen, M. H., Dollinger, S. J., & Roberts, M. C. (1975). On being imitated: Its effects on attraction and reciprocal imitation. *Journal of Personality and Social Psychology, 31*, 467–472.

Trachtman, J. (1971). Socio-economic class bias in Rorschach diagnosis: Contributing psychological attributes of clinicians. *Journal of Projective Techniques and Personality Assessment, 35*, 229–240.

Trombetta, D. (1982). Custody evaluation and custody mediation: A comparison of two dispute interventions. *Journal of Divorce, 6*, 65–76.

Trunnell, T. L. (1976). Johnnie and Suzie, dont cry: Mommy and daddy aren't that way. *Bulletin of the American Academy of Psychiatry and the Law, 4*, 120–126.

Tuma, J. M., & McCraw, R. K. (1975). Influences of examiner differences on

Rorschach productivity in children. *Journal of Personality Assessment, 39*, 362–368.

Twaites, T. N. (1974). The relationship of confidence to accuracy in clinical prediction. *Dissertation Abstracts International, 35 (6-B)*, 3041.

U.S. Bureau of the Census. (1977). Washington, DC: U.S. Department of Commerce.

Vanderkooi, L. & Pearson, J. (1983). Mediating divorce disputes: Mediator behaviors, styles and roles. *Family Relations, 32*, 557–566.

Vernon, P. E. (1964). *Personality assessment: A critical survey.* New York: Wiley.

Voelz, M. (1970). Effects of cognitive complexity and training on clinical judgment ability and confidence. *Dissertation Abstracts International, 30(10-B)*, 4801.

Vogler, R. E., Weissback, T. A., & Compton, J. V. (1977). Learning techniques for alcohol abuse. *Behavior Research and Therapy, 15*, 31–38.

Wade, T. C., Baker, T. B., & Hartmann, D. P. (1979). Behavior therapists' self-reported views and practices. *The Behavior Therapist, 2*, 3–6.

Wahler, R. G., & Nordquist, K. M. (1973). Adult discipline as a factor in childhood imitation. *Journal of Abnormal Child Psychology, 1*, 40–56.

Wahler, R. G., House, A. F., & Stambaugh, E. F. (1976). *Ecological assessment of child problem behavior: A clinical package for home, school, and institutional settings.* New York: Pergamon.

Walker, T. (1967). Measuring the child's best interests—A study of incomplete considerations. *Denver Law Journal, 44*, 137–146.

Wallace, J. (1966). An abilities conception of personality: Some implications for personality measurement. *American Psychologist, 21*, 132–138.

Wallace, J. (1967). What units shall we employ? Allport's question revisited. *Journal of Consulting Psychology, 31*, 56–64.

Wallace, J. & Sechrest, L. (1963). Frequency hypothesis and content analysis of projective techniques. *Journal of Consulting Psychology, 27*, 387–393.

Wallerstein, J. S., & Kelly, J. B. (1974). The effects of parental divorce: The adolescent experience. In E. J. Anthony & C. Koupernik (Eds.), *The child in his family: Children at psychiatric risk.* New York: Wiley.

Wallerstein, J. S., & Kelly, J. B. (1975). The effects of parental divorce: Experience of the preschool child. *Journal of the American Academy of Child Psychiatry, 14*, 600–616.

Wallerstein, J. S., & Kelly, J. B. (1976). The effects of parental divorce: Experience of the child in later latency. *American Journal of Orthopsychiatry, 46*, 256–269.

Wallerstein, J. S., & Kelly, J. B. (1980a). *Surviving the breakup.* New York: Basic Books.

Wallerstein, J. S., & Kelly, J. B. (1980b). Effects of divorce on the visiting father–child relationship. *American Journal of Psychiatry, 137*, 1534–1539.

Walsh, W. B. (1967). Validity of self-report. *Journal of Counseling Psychology, 14*, 18–23.

Walsh, W. B. (1968). Validity of self-report: Another look. *Journal of Counseling Psychology, 15*, 180–186.

Walters, R. H., & Parke, R. D. (1964). Influence of responses consequences to a social model on resistance to deviation. *Journal of Experimental Child Psychology, 1,* 269–280.

Walters, R. H., Leat, M., & Mezei, L. (1963). Inhibition and disinhibition of responses through empathic learning. *Canadian Journal of Psychology, 17,* 235–243.

Walters, R. H., Parke, R. D., & Cane, V. A. (1965). Timing of punishment and the observation of consequences to others as determinants of response inhibition. *Journal of Experimental Child Psychology, 2,* 10–30.

Wasik, B. H., & Loven, M. D. (1980). Classroom observational data: Sources of inaccuracy and proposed solutions. *Behavioral Assessment, 2,* 211–227.

Watson, C. G. (1967). Interjudge agreement of DAP diagnostic impressions. *Journal of Projective Techniques and Personality Assessment, 31,* 42–45.

Weick, K. E. (1968). Systematic observational methods. In G. Lindzey & F. Aronson (Eds.), *Handbook of social psychology.* (2nd ed., Vol. 2). Reading, MA: Addison-Wesley.

Weinrott, M. R., Garrett, B., & Todd, N. (1978). The influence of observer presence on classroom behavior. *Behavior Therapy, 9,* 900–911.

Weiss, D. J., & Davis, R. V. (1960). An objective validation of factual interview data. *Journal of Applied Psychology, 44,* 381–385.

Weller, L., & Luchterhand, E. (1969). Comparing interviews and observations on family functioning. *Journal of Marriage and the Family, 31,* 115–121.

Wells, K. C., McMahon, R. J., Forehand, R., & Griest, D. L. (1980). The effect of a reliability observer on the frequency of positive parent behavior recorded during naturalistic parent–child interactions. Unpublished manuscript, University of Georgia.

Wenar, C., & Coulter, J. B. (1962). A reliability study of developmental histories. *Child Development, 33,* 453–462.

Werry, J. S., & Quay, H. C. (1969). Observing the classroom behavior of elementary school children. *Exceptional Children, 35,* 461–476.

Westman, J. C., & Lord, G. R. (1980). Model for a child psychiatry custody study. *Journal of Psychiatry and Law, 8,* 253–269.

Westman, J. D., Cline, D. W., Swift, W. J., & Kramer, D. A. (1970). The role of child psychiatry in divorce. *Archives of General Psychiatry, 23,* 416–420.

White, G. D. (1972). The effects of observer presence on family behaviors. Unpublished doctoral dissertation, University of Oregon. Cited by G. R. Patterson, J. B. Reid, & S. L. Maerov. (1978). The observation system: Methodological issues and psychometric properties. In J. B. Reid (Ed.), *A social learning approach to family intervention. Vol. 2. Observation in home settings.* Eugene, OR: Castalia.

White, G. D. (1973). Effects of observer presence on family interaction. Paper presented at the meeting of the Western Psychological Association, Anaheim, CA. Cited by R. N. Kent & S. L. Foster. (1977). Direct observational procedures: Methodological issues in naturalistic settings. In A. Ciminero, K. S. Calhoun & H. E. Adams (Eds.), *Handbook of behavioral assessment.* New York: Wiley.

Widiger, T. A., & Schilling, K. M. (1980). Toward a construct validation of the Rorschach. *Journal of Personality Assessment, 44,* 450–459.

Wiesenthal, D. L., Endler, N. S., & Geller, S. H. (1973). Effects of prior group agreement and task correctness on relative competence mediating conformity. *European Journal of Social Psychology, 3,* 193–203.

Wiggins, J. S. (1966). Social desirability estimation and "faking good" well. *Educational and Psychological Measurement, 26,* 329–341.

Wiggins, J. S. (1973). *Personality and prediction: Principles of personality assessment.* Reading, MA: Addison-Wesley.

Wildman, B. G., & Erickson, M. T. (1977). Methodological problems in behavioral observation. In J. Cone & R. Hawkins (Eds.), *Behavioral assessment: New directions in clinical psychology.* New York: Brunner/Mazel.

Wildman, B. G., Erickson, M. T., & Kent, R. N. (1975). The effect of tw o training procedures on observer agreement and variability of behavior ratings. *Child Development, 46,* 520–524.

Wildman, R. W., & Wildman, R. W., II. (1975). An investigation into the comparative validity of several diagnostic tests and test batteries. *Journal of Clinical Psychology, 31,* 455–458.

Wincze, J. P., Hoon, E. F., & Hoon, P. W. (1978). Multiple measure analysis of women experiencing low sexual arousal. *Behavior Research and Therapy., 16,* 43–49.

Wing, C. W., Jr. (1968). Measurement of personality. In D. K. Whitla (Ed.), *Handbook of measurement and assessment in behavioral sciences.* Reading, MA: Addison-Wesley.

Wolf, R. (1966). The measurement of environments. In A. Anastasi (Ed.), *Testing problems in perspective.* Washington, DC: American Council on Education.

Woody, R. H. (1978). *Getting Custody: Winning the last battle of the marital war.* New York: Macmillan.

Wright, H. F. (1960). Observational child study. In P. H. Mussen (Ed.), *Handbook of research methods in child development.* New York: Wiley.

Wrightsman, L. S., Jr., & Baumeister, A. A. (1961). A comparison of actual and paper-and-pencil versions of the Water Jar Test of Rigidity. *Journal of Abnormal and Social Psychology, 63,* 191–193.

Yarrow, M. R. (1963). Problems of methods in parent–child research. *Child Development, 34,* 215–226.

Yarrow, M. R., Campbell, J. D., & Burton, R. V. (1970). Recollections of childhood: A study of the retrospective method. *Monographs of the Society for Research in Child Development, 35,* (5, Serial No. 1380).

Young, R. A., & Higginbotham, S. A. (1942). Behavior checks on the Rorschach method. *American Journal of Orthopsychiatry, 12,* 87–95.

Zegiob, L. E., & Forehand, R. (1975). Maternal interactive behavior as a function of race, socioeconomic status, and sex of the child. *Child Development, 46,* 564–568.

Zegiob, L. E., & Forehand, R. (1978). Parent–child interactions: Observer effects and social class differences. *Behavior Therapy, 9,* 118–123.

Zegiob, L. E., Arnold, S., & Forehand, R. (1975). An examination of observer effects in parent–child interactions. *Child Development, 46,* 509–512.

Zegiob, L. E., Forehand, R., & Resick, P. A. (1979). Parent-child interactions: Habituation and resensitization effects. *Journal of Clinical Child Psychology, 7,* 69–71.

Zigler, E., & Phillips, L. (1961a). Case history data and psychiatric diagnosis. *Journal of Consulting Psychology, 25,* 458.

Zigler, E., & Phillips, L. (1961b). Psychiatric diagnosis: A critique. *Journal of Abnormal and Social Psychology, 63,* 607–618.

Zigler, E., & Phillips, L. (1962). Social competence and the process-reactive distinction in psychopathology. *Journal of Abnormal and Social Psychology, 65,* 215–222.

Ziskin, J. (1975). *Coping with psychiatric and psychological testimony.* (2nd ed.). Marina Del Rey, CA: Law and Psychology Press.

Ziskin, J. (1977). *Coping with psychiatric and psychological testimony.* (2nd ed.), *1977 Pocket Part Supplement.* Marina Del Rey, CA: Law and Psychology Press.

Zubin, J., Eron, L. D., & Schumer, F. (1965). *An experimental approach to projective techniques.* New York: Wiley.

Zuckerman, M. (1979). Traits, states, situations and uncertainty. *Journal of Behavioral Assessment, 1,* 43–54.

Author Index

Subject Index